a Holiday Rivals series

ROAD TO
Gingerbread
GROVE

KIMBERLY HANSON

Cover by: Pages and Pines

Edited by: Daley Author Services

For my husband and children.
I can't thank you enough.
Love you to the moon and back.

Avery's Jingle Bell Jams

Would you like to listen to Avery's elf-approved playlist while you read? Scan the QR code below for Avery's Jingle Bell Jams.

Chapter One

MATTHEW

This blinking cursor is going to be the death of me.

I let out a heavy sigh as I stare blankly at my computer screen, wishing the code would write itself. I've been working on this software update for over an hour, but I can't keep my focus. I'm hypnotized by the flashing line in front of me. It's taunting me. Mocking me. Waiting for me to input a code that it knows I can't grasp.

Rude.

Frustrated with my lack of progress, I take off my glasses and throw them onto my desk, rubbing my eyes with enough pressure that I start seeing colourful dots, reminding me of the blinking cursor.

I can't get away from my failures today.

The last few weeks have been like walking through a brightly-coloured fog. It's December, which means the streets are full of twinkling lights, hanging garlands, and painted windows. People rush in and out of stores trying to buy the perfect presents for their loved ones. Seemingly cheery music streams through every speaker and plays on every station.

It makes me so frustrated. All I want to do is open my window and shout 'Bah Humbug!'

And then I feel like every Christmas movie villain that ever existed.

This is all thanks to my hometown of Woodland Springs—sorry, now Gingerbread Grove. Even though I made my escape before the name change and the adoption of some Christmas festival rivalry, it still plays a big part in my overall avoidance of the area and everyone in it.

Again, Bah Humbug.

I much prefer the tradition that my friend and business partner, Mitch, and I have started, consisting of takeout food and movie marathons. *Non*-Christmas movie marathons. Endless Marvel and DC binge sessions with pizza and sushi make me forget that there's even a holiday to be celebrated. Just the way I like it.

"Hey, man. What are you still doing here?" Mitch asks as he fills the doorway of my office, crossing his arms over his chest and leaning against the frame. His dark blond hair is sticking up, making it look like he's being running his hands through it all day. "I thought I was the one that pulls all-nighters, not you."

"I'm beginning to wonder that myself." I push my rolling chair back, giving me room to stretch out my legs. "I'm not getting much done on the most recent update."

I take a good look at my friend and realize how worn down he's looking. He has dark circles under his eyes and his shoulders are slouched. How have I not noticed how run down he was getting? Maybe I'm too caught up in my own yuletide sadness to pay attention to anyone else's problems.

"Then go home and try again tomorrow. You still have a while before the deadline." He walks into my office and takes a seat in the chair across from me, placing his ankle on his opposite knee.

"Same could be said for you."

He waves a hand at me, disregarding my comment.

"What's really going on with you? You've been off for weeks now."

I let out an exasperated breath. "I don't know."

I swivel in my chair to face the window overlooking the skyline, and steeple my fingers in front of my lips as I look out at the city below. The twinkling lights and soft falling snow give the otherwise dreary concrete buildings a festive glow, but I can't seem to make my heart grow to enjoy it. Instead, I'm filled with a sense of—dread? Foreboding? Possibly even of looming disaster?

It was sheer luck we were able to find this office on Vancouver's waterfront all those years ago. The first office space we leased when Mitch and I first came to the city fell through the night before we were to move in. We had to frantically call all the companies that were to be delivering our office furniture the next day, stalling them while we tried to find a new space. The week before Christmas. We ended up running our business out of our shared apartment for three miserable months.

Just another Christmas disaster in a long list of many.

Some say miracles happen at Christmas. I think that's only reserved for the lucky, or maybe for those that look for anything that might be a sign or a gift during the season. What do I see it as? An excuse for people to see what they want to believe.

While the office we ended up with might not be as trendy as our original one, it has its merits. Located in the industrial side of the city with a less than picturesque view, it still gives me a sense of pride knowing that we were able to do it. We found space and opened our company in Vancouver, just like Mitch and I had been talking about since high school. It's given us both a feeling that we've made it from our little nowhere town. We had a lot of doubt and ridicule thrown at us as we left Woodland Springs and moved to Vancouver, but both Mitch and I were willing to grin and bear it to make our dream come true. Which we have.

So why am I so unhappy?

"Do you miss Emily?" Mitch asks, pulling me out of my growing feeling of nostalgia.

"No. She hasn't even crossed my mind," I answer truthfully with a chuckle as I turn back around to face him.

Emily is beautiful and fun, but I knew what we had wasn't going to be long term. We both did, even if neither one of us wanted to admit it. We were both tired of being alone and enjoyed each other's company. I didn't mind all the restaurants she wanted to try or the movies she wanted to see. She was genuinely interested in my work and liked going for walks along the seawall or strolling through the downtown core on a Sunday afternoon. She didn't ask for more than I was willing to give her, which was basically just glorified friendship. She was comfortable to be around. Easy to talk to. There just wasn't a spark there, and we both knew it early on, even if neither one of us wanted to admit it. Thankfully, she pulled the plug a few weeks ago, asking me to be her plus one to her company Christmas party to avoid any unnecessary questions and we could part ways while remaining friends, which we've been able to do.

"Then, what is it? Don't tell me you're homesick." Genuine concern crosses Mitch's face.

"Definitely not. There is nothing about Woodland Creek that I miss."

"Gingerbread Grove," he corrects with a smirk.

I groan. "Don't remind me." I rub my hands over my eyes again before picking up my glasses and placing them back on my face. "I don't know what it is. I feel... unsettled."

"Unsettled? How?"

I turn my chair to the side, looking back out the window. I don't know how to explain it. This off feeling I've had, but it's there, burning in the pit of my stomach. "I don't know. Just that something's missing."

"Again, is that Emily?"

"You know we were only ever friends. In fact, if I remember correctly, you were the one that constantly pointed out how much we were more like brother and sister than boyfriend and girlfriend."

"Yes, but that doesn't mean her absence hasn't left a hole in your life. Maybe you need to get back out there. Date. Find someone who you genuinely connect with."

I groan, not wanting to have this discussion. Not now. Not ever, really.

As if saved by the Christmas miracle that everyone speaks of, my phone rings, halting the conversation. It's only when I look at the caller on my screen that I sigh, realizing that there is no miracle to be had here. "It's like she knows we're talking about the town and my love life."

Mitch chuckles, looking down at my screen. "Are you going to answer it?"

He leans back in his chair, resting his hands behind his head as he dons a smirk on his face. I know he only wears that expression because his only relative back in our hometown hasn't contacted him since the day we left.

I, on the other hand, have a family that calls to try to lure me back as often as they can. Which I'm sure is what is about to happen right now.

"Hi, Mom," I say as I put my phone to my ear, bracing myself for the guilt trip that's about to occur.

"Oh, honey, I'm so glad I caught you!" Her voice sounds a little more frantic than usual, but still has the same pleading tone she uses when she wants me to come back home.

I love my mom, I really do, but I can't go back. Especially since it's currently being turned into Santa's Village, or some cookie-themed variation of it. I know that I'll be able to get her off the phone quickly with my usual promise of not 'falling to the dark side of the big city.' It's the same song and dance we do every time. It's almost as if she works herself up into a tizzy and needs reminding that I'm just fine.

That's right, she's got me using words like 'tizzy.'

"What's going on?" I ask, waving Mitch back into his seat as he moves to leave.

"It's your dad. He's taken a fall."

I sit up straighter, locking eyes with Mitch as my assured demeanour falls. He responds with a raised eyebrow, leaning closer in his chair.

"What happened?"

"He was up on a ladder fixing a strand of Christmas lights that had fallen off its hook when he missed a rung and fell from halfway up." Mom's voice shakes as if she's fighting off tears. "He's in the hospital, Matty."

"Is he okay?" Right now, my concern for my dad outweighs my irritation at the use of my childhood nickname, which I have never been able to stand.

"He will be. He broke his leg and bruised some ribs."

"Why didn't Todd do it? Isn't he supposed to be home for Christmas?" Unlike my aversion to Gingerbread Grove, my brother Todd has never had an issue with returning. A fact I hear about every Easter, Thanksgiving, and Christmas.

"He left a day early. He had to get back to Sun Peaks. Something about a conference or major booking."

Ah, yes. The important hotel manager that couldn't be spared at all from his job for more than a few days.

"Anyway," she continues, "it was something, and it's beside the point. I need you to come home as soon as possible."

"What?" Panic courses through my veins as I sit up straighter. "Mom, you know I can't do that."

Mitch mimics my movements, sitting up and leaning into the desk, his questioning looks turning to concern.

"Of course you can, Matty. We need you here. Your dad will be coming home from the hospital today, but he's going to be on bed rest for weeks, and I can't run the store and look after him."

The store. Of course. Part of the reason I left town and never looked back.

"Can't Todd help? He's closer."

"No, he can't come back until the new year. He only stopped by this weekend because he was going to miss Christmas with us because of their bookings, you know. It's a very busy and important hotel in the city…" Mom's voice goes quiet, leading way to a soft sniffle on the other end of the line. I know it's been a shock with dad's fall, but even she has to admit she's laying it on thick. "Please? I know I ask you to come home a lot, and that's because I miss you. Seeing you in the city isn't the same. But this time we need you here, and it is Christmas and all. Please?"

I close my eyes and pinch the bridge of my nose with my free hand. As much as I don't want to admit it, I know I have to go. If the shop has to close for the holiday season, my parents will take a financial hit I'm not sure they'll be able to recover from.

Even at the sake of my own sanity.

I let out a breath and close my eyes. "Let me talk to Mitch. I'll call you back tonight."

"Oh, thank you, Matty!" Mom replies excitedly. "You have no idea how much this means to me!"

"I haven't promised anything, Mom. I don't know if I can get away, especially with it being the end of the year…"

"I knew you'd help. You may have moved away but you're always a Gingerbreadian at heart."

I cringe. "Mom, I'm not a…"

"Love you!" she yells before ending the call, not letting me finish.

I look down at my screen, wondering what had just

happened. "She just called me a 'Gingerbreadian?' Is that really a thing?"

"Yes," Mitch answers without batting an eye, now sitting on the edge of his seat. I'm beginning to worry that I'm missing more than just how tired he is if he knows words like 'Gingerbreadian.' "Now, what was all that about?"

I drop my shoulders and meet his gaze, not even bothering to hide my defeat. "Looks like I'm going back to Gingerbread Grove."

Chapter Two

AVERY

"Are there any updates on flight 276?" I ask, leaning on the desk at the gate. It's the third time I've asked since my plane was supposed to depart, and I have yet to get more than a 'we'll let you know.'

"Sorry, not since the last time you asked," the airline employee says with a tight-lipped smile, barely looking up from her computer screen. "Don't worry, we'll get you back to the North Pole in time for Christmas."

I smile at her through gritted teeth. Good, I'm getting on her nerves. At least she can feel my pain.

Spending ten hours in the Vancouver International Airport wasn't how I'd planned on spending my night, but here I am. I'm running out of my Christmas patience, and this woman is about to be on the receiving end of my less-than-jolly-elfness. Sure, it wasn't *entirely* her fault. I can admit now that coming to the city had been a colossal mistake. I should never have left Kamloops. I love my city with the amazing lakes and rivers. I have my friends and my dream job. I even have the coffee shop on the corner of Landsdowne and Third, where the baristas know how to perfectly make my ginger-bread oat latte with eggnog sprinkles. They even keep it fully stocked year-round for me when other cafes are quick to take it off the menu as soon as Boxing Day hits, (Who wants to get rid of Christmas the day after anyway?). It might not be the biggest city, but it's my city, and that's all that matters.

I know that now.

Instead of being in said amazing city, I'm stuck in Vancouver, wearing an elf costume, and acting anything but cheery with the gate agent.

"Surely someone must know if the plane is on its way here, or at least when it'll arrive. It's not like it just disappeared. Heck, they have better tracking than Santa's sleigh."

The gate agent sighs and doesn't even bother looking up from her screen this time. "We will let you know of any updates as soon as we can. In the meantime, please take a seat."

"Thanks." *For nothing.*

Walking back to my seat, I slump down, pulling out my third candy cane out of my purse and ripping the plastic wrapping open more aggressively than necessary. Shoving the minty treat in my mouth, I let the calming coolness lower my less-than-festive anger.

"I take it there are no updates," a deep voice says from the seat beside me.

In all of my frustration, I hadn't noticed the seat beside mine had become occupied while I was at the desk.

"No. You'd think they would have something to tell us since our flight was supposed to leave hours ago. But nope." I slump back in my seat, narrowing my eyes at the gate agent as she currently laughs with her coworker. I guess there's a lot to laugh about when you don't have to worry about how you're getting home.

"Too bad," the deep voice says next to me in a tone that makes it sound like he's anything but sad the flight hasn't left. I look over to find a flop of dark blond hair curtaining his features as he stares down at a book.

"You don't sound bothered by the fact that we've been stuck here for hours."

"Because I'm not," he says, not looking up.

I'm not usually one to get flustered at many things, but I'm getting tired of people talking at me without actually paying attention to me. Lifting my candy-free hand, I place it on his book, forcing it down on his lap. Is it a little bold to interrupt a stranger like this? Absolutely, but I've lost my patience with people ignoring me.

I'm rewarded with him raising his face to mine, but then I find myself momentarily dazed by a pair of stunning hazel eyes behind black-framed glasses.

"Is there something I can help you with?" That voice. That voice that had seemed like some form of disembodied grump now has a very real—and very handsome—face.

I shake my head slightly, breaking the momentary hold he has over me. "No. Sorry. I guess I'm just anxious to get out of here."

I snap my hand back from his book as if it burned me, placing it on one of my heated cheeks, hoping to cool it down as I put the candy cane back in my mouth. I look away from him, running my gaze over the growing number of frustrated people at the gate, but not really seeing them.

"Right." I feel his eyes on me for a breath longer before movement out of the corner of my eye tells me he's picked up his book once again.

Dropping my hands, I run them along my thighs, wiping off the thin coat of sweat as I rock slightly in my seat. My heart beats so fast I'm surprised he doesn't hear it. My body heat rises, the polyester of my outfit becoming stifling as the anxious feeling in my chest grows rapidly like the Grinch's heart—but not in a good way.

I need to get out of here. Not just the airport, but Vancouver in general. I need to get back home. Where it's not so crowded. I'm not stranded with no way out.

Where I'm not reminded of the complete embarrassment I suffered before heading to the airport.

"Are you all right?" The stranger beside me asks.

"Yup, why wouldn't I be?" I ask a little too happily. I offer him an overly-wide smile, trying to exude the calm and peace I don't have—even if it feels like I've had about ten cups of coffee.

"Well, you're dressed as an elf, for starters," he says, looking up at my hat before gazing down at my outfit.

I totally forgot what I was wearing amidst all that has happened today. If only I knew when I donned the green and red outfit that I would end up stuck at an airport gate, devastated, desperate to get home.

"Occupational hazard," I say, avoiding his eyes. I will *not* be hypnotized by them again.

"Occupational...you're an elf?" He closes his book, holding his page with his finger while he shifts slightly, giving me all of his attention.

That attention I wanted earlier? Yeah, I'm not sure I'm prepared for that now. Not when his hazel eyes are watching me intently, but with a curiousness and cautiousness.

"Well, obviously not a *real* elf, but yes. I flew into Vancouver for an elf convention."

"An elf convention..." he repeats slowly.

"Yes. We get training and updates on all the latest things relating to Christmas."

"Riiight." His eyebrow raises.

It's then I realize just what this looks like. A jittery woman dressed like a fictional character, talking about Christmas and conventions. My eyes widen. "Okay, I know how that sounds now." I take my hat off and try to straighten the frizzy mop on top of my head with my free hand, candy cane in the other. "Yes, technically I'm an elf, but let me explain. I'm more of a...logistics manager. I work for an international company that brings Christmas to underprivileged children. We arrange presents to be delivered, turkey dinners, clothing, etcetera. We also respond to letters that are written by children every year."

"Wow, that's…that's really great."

I lift my shoulder briefly. "I've always wanted to make sure that kids have a good Christmas, you know? I mean, it is the best time of the year. Everyone deserves to feel a bit of the magic."

His demeanour changes, a sadness now crosses his face that wasn't there before as he opens his book once more. "If you say so."

I open my mouth to find out more about what could have made him so sad during such a happy time when a voice comes over the loudspeaker. "Attention everyone at Gate C30 with Flight 276 to Kamloops. We regret to inform you that the flight has been cancelled."

Everyone at the gate groans collectively, some standing and yelling, making it impossible to hear what the agent continues to say about collecting baggage.

Slumping back into my seat, I stare in shock at the screen above the desk as 'cancelled' appears in big red lettering.

So much for getting a Christmas miracle.

"Well, I wasn't expecting that," the man says, placing his book in his bag.

"Really?" I turn to him, crossing my arms over my chest.

"No. I can't say this is how I pictured my day going, but it is what it is." He looks down at the phone in his hand as it lights up, showing an incoming call with 'Mom,' listed. He doesn't hesitate before answering. "Hi, Mom. Yes, we just found out our flight was cancelled. How did you…? Right, of course you did."

He looks over at me, catching me staring and eavesdropping on his conversation.

Embarrassed, I feel my face flush as I turn in my seat and look away.

"I mean, I can see if I can get another flight. No, of course. Mom, you know that's not...I can't control flights, Mom. No, I understand. Fine. Yes, love you, too."

He sighs and I see him rubbing his face with his hands. Well, I assume that's what he's doing, because I'm absolutely not watching him. Nor am I intrigued about why he's clearly reluctant about heading to Kamloops right before Christmas to what I'm assuming is his family. But it's none of my business. None at all.

"Well, good luck, I guess," he says, giving me a nod before flinging his bag over his shoulder and walking off, instantly disappearing into the crowd as people push their way toward the gate.

I have no idea why I'm so intrigued by this man. Sure, he's handsome with his glasses, hazel eyes, and hair that's slightly too long and styled in a way that reminds me of a 90s heartthrob. But there's something else about him that I can't quite put my finger on. Something that made me hesitant to tell him what I was doing in Vancouver in addition to the conference. The thing that now makes me cringe for being so naïve to think it was ever a good idea.

I'm knocked out of my thoughts as people start stampeding to the front, knocking into me and my bag. I know if I don't leave now and try to find another way home, I'm going to be stuck here until tomorrow at least, and that's just *not* going to happen.

With no other choice, I place my elf hat back on my head, pick up my bag, and head for the exit.

It might take a real miracle, but by Santa, I will make it to Kamloops tonight.

Chapter Three

MATTHEW

I 've never been so happy I didn't check in a bag.

Between all the yelling at ticketing agents, overfilled baggage carousels, and people pushing their way through the crowd, I can't imagine the headache it would be to try to get my bags back. In the walk from the gate, I overheard at least three other flights being cancelled. From what I could hear, some are because of weather, and others from staffing issues. While it's horrible so many people are stranded here, all I'm concerned with is getting out of this airport as fast as possible.

I can't deny that I was excited when I first heard my flight had been cancelled. I would have done pretty much anything to delay my trip back to Gingerbread Grove, but my mom squandered any plans I might have had when she tracked my flight and looked up alternative routes.

Now, here I am, standing in the lineup for rental cars, taking deep breaths to drive away the building feeling of panic that sits in my chest. Not only does the thought of returning home sit like a pit in my stomach, but so does the thought of driving five and a half hours in the dark while it's snowing. I might have grown up in the country, but it's been years since I've driven, well, anywhere. I haven't had much use for a car in the city, so I sold my truck once I got settled in my apartment. It was too big for the narrow downtown streets, and it meant that I could make a little extra money by renting out my parking space.

Tapping my fingers along the strap of my bag that sits on my shoulder, I peer over the person in front of me, hoping they both do—and don't—have a car for me. If they don't, it's one less method to get me to Gingerbread Grove, although I'm sure my mom would stop at nothing less than a flying reindeer to get me back home tonight.

After what feels like a small eternity, the person in front of me steps aside and I'm greeted with the exhausted face of a man about my age behind the desk, looking like he'd rather be anywhere than where he is right now. His eyes have dark circles under them, his hair is dishevelled as if he's run his fingers through it frequently, and his shoulders are slumped.

"How can I help you?" The corner of his mouth lifts in an attempted smile. I'll give him credit for his effort.

"I'd like to rent a car, please. Anything you have is fine," I state as I reach into my jeans pocket for my wallet.

"You're in luck. We have one car left." The agent types frantically, not taking his eyes off the screen. "Driver's licence, please. I'll get this started for you."

I slide my licence across the counter, finding myself shifting from foot to foot. Now that I know I'll be getting a car, the anxious feeling is growing. All while I'm answering questions, filling out paperwork, and handing over my credit card—while not paying attention to how much this is going to cost me because I know it'll hurt—I can't help but draw my attention to the doors. The snow is starting to pick up, with the flakes getting bigger and bigger the longer I'm standing here.

"All right, that's it. The attendant will bring the car out to you at the curb marked with our company logo. He'll give you the keys and then you're on your way."

"Thank you." I breathe a sigh of relief that this portion is over.

"Merry Christmas," the agent says again with that sad smile of his. I look down to see 'Dave' on his name tag. I feel for the guy, and the backlash he's about to get from the crowd of agitated travellers behind me after they find out I'm taking the last car.

"Merry Christmas to you, too, Dave." I give him a nod as I walk away, holding the strap of my bag tighter on my shoulder. While I may not like the holiday, I can appreciate the man's attempt to find anything joyous in this headache.

I can tell the moment he puts up the sign there are no more rental cars when there is a large uproar of groans and yelling behind me. I block it out once I step outside, feeling for Dave, but knowing that I have my own challenge ahead of me I need to focus on.

My eyes scan the curb side of the airport as I search for the rental company's name. Bus charters, taxi companies, and shuttle service logos light up in front of me as I pass by. Wrapping my jacket tighter around me against the bitter cold, a shiver wracks through my body as my eyes continue searching. Finally, as if a beacon against this miserable night, I see the company's bright green logo at the end of the line. Because, of course, it would be the farthest from their counter inside the airport. Where it was nice and warm. Where they would make you walk through the arctic tundra that is the wind tunnel of the airport's arrival terminal.

"Hey!" I hear the shout behind me, but considering I don't know anyone here, I don't bother turning around. Instead, I put my head down to keep it from the blast of cold air that comes with a passing bus and pick up my speed. I can only pray my car will be waiting for me when I finally make it through this marathon of angry people.

"Hey, gate guy!"

That gets my attention. I turn to find the frustrated elf from the gate running up to me, her laptop bag falling off her shoulder as she struggles to pull a rolling bag behind her while not losing the ridiculous green and red hat on her head.

"Gate guy? I have a name, you know."

"Well, obviously," she says with a huff and an eye roll as she comes to a rolling stop in front of me. "But I don't know what it is."

"It's Matthew." I turn back around the corridor of cars coming and going, hoping mine is one of them.

"Well, Matt, I'm Avery," she says as she struggles to keep up with me.

"Matthew," I correct, trying to suppress the irritation at the nickname.

"Not one for nicknames?"

"No." I come to a stop at the rental car sign, seeing no car in sight. It only adds to my irritation, but I take a breath to hide it. It's not Avery's fault I'm stuck in this mess and hate nicknames. At the same time, who uses a nickname with a stranger?

"Right. Well, it's nice to meet you, *Matthew*." Now I want to roll my eyes at how she emphasizes my full name. "So… you got the last rental car."

"Looks like it," I answer, looking down the line of arriving cars, searching like I know which one is mine, which I don't.

"And we were both on our way to Kamloops…"

"Yup." I shove my hands in the pockets of my jacket, trying to warm them up. I didn't bring gloves with me because I didn't expect to be standing in the bitter cold.

"So really, the only logical explanation would be for us to share the car."

"Sorry, what?" I turn to her, my brain not comprehending her train of thought.

"Think about it. You're going to Kamloops. I'm going to Kamloops. You have a car. I don't." She looks at me like that answers it all.

"You can't be serious." I close my eyes and pinch the bridge of my nose.

"Of course I am. I don't just walk around asking strangers for rides all the time."

"I sure hope not," I mutter under my breath, although I'm not at all convinced that isn't exactly what she does.

"Please? I wouldn't be asking if this wasn't important. I need to get home. To Kamloops. Tonight."

"Then talk to the airline. Get on the next flight." I rock on the balls to the heels of my feet, feeling a little bad for how I'm treating her. It's not my problem that I beat her to the last rental car. At the same time, a tiny spark of my long-forgotten Christmas spirit is ignited, hating the feeling of leaving this elf stranded until who-knows-when, especially when she sounds so sad about needing to get out of the city.

This car needs to hurry up. Now.

"They aren't rebooking anyone right now. They told us we're on our own until next week and I am *not* staying in this horrible city that long *and* over Christmas. Please?"

The desperation in her voice made me look down at her. *Really* look at her for the first time. She's a good foot shorter than me, maybe more with the ridiculous red and green hat on her head. The blonde hair sticking out of her cap curls at her shoulders and her big blue eyes look up at me, pleading with me to take pity on her.

"How do you know I'm not some serial killer?"

"Well, are you?" She tilts her head to the side, narrowing her eyes at me.

"No, but you don't know that."

"Let's just say you were for fun. I highly doubt you'd be

taking a plane from the largest airport in the province to another city within the same province. That wouldn't be a great place to run from the authorities. Now, maybe if you were leaving the country, that would be a different story."

"Should I be worried about how quickly you came up with that answer? Maybe I need be asking if you're the serial killer."

"Don't be silly. Only eight-point-six percent of serial killers are women, so statistically speaking, the chances of you running into one at the Vancouver International Airport at any given time are ridiculously low."

"You knowing that stat off the top of your head is not helping your case."

Avery shrugs. "My sister listens to a lot of true crime podcasts. I guess some of it has rubbed off on me."

"It's still not safe for you to just ask some random man to take you on a five-hour car ride. At night. In the snow. It might be the norm in the North Pole, but not in Vancouver."

She rolls her eyes. "I'm hardly from the North Pole—and if I wasn't desperate to get out of the city, I wouldn't. Plus, we aren't strangers now. We've exchanged names. You know about my family and my job. We're practically friends." She hesitates for a moment but then slumps her shoulders when I don't respond. "Please? I'm only asking because I can't stay here. I need to get home."

I don't know what's come over me, but I have the biggest urge to help this woman out. I don't know if it's pity, the small town chivalry that's been instilled in me since I was born, or the Christmas spirit that for some reason decided to make a return after years of being absent, but I know I can't leave this woman stranded.

Exhaling loudly, I watch as it forms a cloud in front of me in the cold. "Fine. But there are rules."

"Yay! Thank you so much!" Avery jumps on the spot,

leaning in as if she is going to give me a hug, but then pulls back at the last moment, thinking better of it.

Just as she's about to speak again, my sedan pulls up in front of us. It's smaller than my tall frame would comfortably fit in, but if it means I'm getting out of this airport, I'll take it.

For the first time in a long time, I pray. Not for safety, but rather, that I'm not going to regret my decision.

Chapter Four

AVERY

A parade of lights pass us on the highway, lighting up the otherwise blackened road. Cars rush by us as we make our way out of the city and into the valley. Matthew hasn't said a word to me since we loaded the car with our luggage, and I'm not sure what to make of that. I mean, who drives for an hour without saying *anything* to their passenger? Not that he owes me anything. I'm well aware that I owe him every-thing. That I imposed on his road trip, but it would be nice not to spend the next four hours in complete silence.

I mean, he hasn't even turned on the radio. Who drives without listening to anything?

Have I been too pushy? Maybe. Well—the answer is yes, most definitely. But I needed to get out of Vancouver and fast.

When I learned that I was being sent to the city for the convention, I thought it would be the perfect excuse to surprise Maxwell, the man I thought was the love of my life. The conference itself had been magical. I connected with so many other elves across the country as we learned how to reach more families and bless more children with the best Christmas they've ever had. Some people question why we do it so close to Christmas when most of the planning has

22

been done, but really, it also doubles as our Christmas party. Even elves need to celebrate every once in a while.

But unfortunately, the party ended in a nightmare when I showed up at Maxwell's apartment.

Looking down at my red and white striped leggings and red-trimmed green skirt, I think I should have at least changed when I got to the airport. In my frazzled, heart-broken state, I didn't think about it.

At least I wasn't wearing my matching green booties.

Unable to stand the silence any longer, I reach over and push the radio button, bringing the speakers to life. A catchy holiday pop song blasts through the speakers. While not my usual choice in holiday entertainment, it's better than the deafening silence we did have.

"No. Absolutely not," Matthew says as he clicks off the radio.

"You have to give me something." I turn in my seat as I cross my arms over my chest. "We can't spend the rest of the time in silence."

He glances over at me for a moment, lifting his eyebrow before turning back to the road. If ever there was a 'watch me' look, it was that.

"Fine, but if you won't turn on the music, you have to tell me about you."

"There's not much to tell." His tone lets me know he wants to talk about himself less than he wants to listen to Ariana Grande.

"Why are you on your way to Kamloops?" I ask, settling in for what I'm sure is going to be a thrilling conversation.

"I'm not," he replies flatly.

"But you were about to get on a plane going there. "

Matthew sighs and sneaks another glance at me. "I'm heading to Gingerbread Grove. Kamloops is the closest airport."

"Gingerbread Grove?" I sit up, fascinated with where the

conversation is going. "I've wanted to visit there since they changed their name. I've heard about the hotel that's opening that looks like an actual gingerbread house. It's fascinating." To say I was thrilled when I heard about Woodland Springs officially changing their name a few years ago and completely overhauling everything to be a Christmas tourist destination similar to Candy Cane Creek is an understatement. I didn't think anything could beat their rival holiday town with the festivals and events, but from what I've heard, they are doing their best to be *the* Christmas hot spot.

Unfortunately with Christmas being my busiest time of the year since becoming Head Elf of the Interior BC region (yes, that's my official title), I haven't had a chance to go during the height of the holiday season.

"Yup. Fascinating," he replies flatly, as if finding it anything but.

"You don't sound like you want to go there." I can't help but prod him. Every answer from him is like another piece of a Christmas jigsaw puzzle. A handsome city guy going to a small town that not many people know of. Especially a holiday-themed town when he doesn't seem interested at all in Christmas.

"And you sound like someone that asks a lot of questions."

"If I'm going to be in a car with someone for a long period of time, it would be nice to get to know them." I can't help but get my defences up, seeing that maybe it wasn't such a great idea to get into a car with a complete stranger.

"Maybe I should install a 'no talking' rule," he says under his breath.

I huff, leaning back in my seat and looking out at the road in front of us. The road is cloaked in complete darkness except for our headlights reflecting off the rapidly falling snow. As we pass through what I'm assuming is nothing but farmland, there's nothing but us, the road, and the snowy night sky.

This isn't how I saw my day going. Or my week.

"I'm sorry," Matthew says, not taking his eyes off the road. "It's just been a really long day."

"I'm sorry, too. I shouldn't have asked you all those questions. I shouldn't have even asked you for a ride, but I didn't have any other choice. I just…" I take a deep breath, fighting off the tears welling in my eyes. "I just couldn't stay there."

"You're not in trouble, are you?" He shifts uncomfortably in his seat, wiggling around like he can't get comfortable.

"Define trouble." I play with him.

"Is someone after you? Were you hurt?"

"No, nothing like that," I say. Not physically, anyway. Emotionally? I'm more damaged than I care to talk about right now.

"And legally? I mean, you have knowledge of those true crime things. I'm not going to be your next victim, am I?" he asks, sneaking a glance my way with a smirk as he stops squirming.

That smirk makes my stomach fill with butterflies. Butterflies I have no business in feeling, especially after my fiasco of a weekend. Even more so for a man I won't see again by morning.

"No, I'm not in that kind of trouble. As for the serial killer part, I haven't decided yet. It depends on how the next hour goes." I tilt my head and study him, trying to give him my best 'I'm-still-deciding' face, but I know it comes off as nothing but hysterical as Matthew laughs, filling the car with his rich tone.

It's a sound that I could get used to, or even find myself craving. I get the impression he doesn't give laughs freely, which makes me feel a sense of pride at earning one.

"Well, I guess I'll be on my best behaviour, then. But, seriously, are you in trouble? You seemed like you're in a hurry to leave the city."

I sigh. I don't know how much to tell him. Or maybe it's good that I won't see him after tonight. I can spill everything to him and not have the embarrassment of having to face him ever again.

It would be nice to tell *someone*. I haven't even told my sister, and I tell her *everything*. But I know her feelings on my now-ex, and I'm not ready to face all the 'I-told-you-so's' that will be coming my way.

"Do you promise not to laugh?" I ask, still not entirely convinced I'm making the right decision.

"I promise," he answers, and for whatever reason, I believe him. I don't know why. He's a stranger, but there's something about him that makes me feel like I'm safe with him.

"I had a boyfriend in Kamloops. He moved to Vancouver in the fall for work. I couldn't leave right away because of my job and the ramp up to Christmas, so we agreed to stay long distance until I could figure out a way to transfer to the city. We never planned on it being for a long time. Heck, we even talked about getting married once I moved."

"So, what happened?" He keeps his eyes on the road, but I notice how his hands tighten on the steering wheel, like he's bracing for the impact of what I'm about to tell him.

"I was really busy with work, with it being the holidays and all. I didn't think that I was going to be able to get down to Vancouver to see him for Christmas, and he said he couldn't get the time off from his new job to fly back home. The conference at work came up, and I thought it would be a perfect time to get some training and surprise him. And it was a surprise, all right."

"What did he do?" he asks, gripping the wheel even harder, making his knuckles turn white in the soft light from the dash.

26

"He's dating someone else." I can't stop the hurt from filling my voice. I'm so embarrassed to think of what Maxwell did to me—that I believed we could make it long-distance. That he loved me. I believed him when he said I was the only one forever. How could someone tell one person they wanted to marry them while spending time with another?

Most importantly, how could I be so much of a fool to believe that he would love only me. The elf from Kamloops compared to all the beautiful city women he's surrounded by.

"I'm sorry." Matthew's words are soft, but I can hear the anger behind them.

"Thank you." I nod, swallowing the lump forming in my throat. "I thought it would be fun to surprise Maxwell since I was going to be in town for work anyway. We haven't seen each other since the end of September. We mostly text, not really finding the time for calls or video chats. But when I showed up at his door—hoping for a warm welcome—I was met with him having dinner with his new girlfriend."

I angrily wipe at the tears falling down my face, thankful for the darkened car around me. I hate that Maxwell made me cry, and I hate it even more that I'm doing it next to Matthew.

I take a deep breath and sneak a glance at the stoic and silent man next to me. His hands continue to grip the steering wheel tightly. The reflection off his glasses make it hard to see the expression hidden behind them, but I can tell by his clenched jaw that he has an opinion on it.

"Why aren't you saying anything?" I ask, nervous about what his response might be.

The silence filling the car makes me regret saying anything in the first place. I was so naïve to think that Maxwell would wait for me while he was in the city. Looking back, I can see that I had always been more invested in the relationship than he was. He had been the one to put the distance between us when he moved. He was too busy for the calls. He had excuses as to why we couldn't video call. I just didn't want to see it, and that leaves me feeling heartbroken and embarrassed.

"I'm trying to think of something to say that would be appropriate." He sucks in a breath, not taking his eyes off the road. "Mostly, I want to say I'm sorry that he put you through that."

"Thank you, but you don't need to apologize for him," I whisper.

"I know, but..." He takes another deep breath before continuing. "I know what it's like, and no one should be put in that position. So for that, I'm sorry. I'm also sorry that he wasn't man enough to tell you how he felt instead of leading you on."

For the first time in a long time, I feel like I'm truly being heard and understood. As I sag back into my seat, I feel as if an enormous weight has been lifted off of my chest. Maybe telling this stranger the most embarrassing story of my life might not have been the worst thing to do.

Chapter Five

MATTHEW

Hearing the downturn of Avery's trip has put me on edge. It's too much like my own story with McKenzie. It pains me to know this beautiful, annoyingly happy elf knows the pain of the long, dragged-out process of thinking we had our happily ever afters, only to find out that our relationship was completely one-sided.

Now that McKenzie has crossed my mind, it gives me more stress about this trip back home. My heart rate picks up and I grip the steering wheel tighter, pushing the thoughts of my ex-girlfriend away and focus on the road. The snow falls harder and is building on the roads quite quickly. It's getting hard to see in the whiteout conditions, making the choking feeling of dread crawl deeper into my chest.

"You've gone through this, too?" Avery's unsure voice drifts across the console, sniffs hidden under the sleeve of her jacket.

"Similar, yes. It's actually why I've been avoiding going back to Woodland Creek."

"You mean Gingerbread Grove?' she asks. I don't need to look over to know she's got a sneaky smile on her face.

"Yes. Gingerbread Grove," I sigh. "I don't think I'll ever forgive the city for changing the name."

She chuckles and takes a moment before she speaks again. "What happened?"

"My girlfriend in high school and for most of college. We both left our hometown for school. She went to school in Kelowna while I went to Vancouver. It was fine for the first couple of years until we both came home for Christmas one year and I find out she's engaged to someone else." It may have been almost ten years since it happened, but it doesn't make it any easier to talk about. Especially since McKenzie has since moved back to Gingerbread Grove and my mother keeps insisting on updating me on her.

"Engaged? Wow! She never mentioned anything to you?" Avery shifts in her seat, her voice stronger.

"No. She said she didn't think we were 'exclusive' since we lived so far away from each other and assumed that I was also moving on as well. Apparently, we had different definitions of what a 'long-distance relationship' looked like."

"That's horrible. I'm so sorry." Avery places her hand on my arm, sending a rush of nervous energy of what I could only assume is what people call butterflies in their stomach.

It shocks me how much my body responds to her touch, even through my jacket. I haven't felt anything like that since McKenzie. Even my time with Emily when we first started dating didn't provoke this gut reaction at a simple touch.

"Uh, yeah. So, I haven't been back to town in a while." I clear my throat and straighten in my seat as her hand falls away. I immediately miss the connection, but I can't dwell on that. Not when she's a stranger I won't ever see again after we hit Kamloops, and I'm trying to focus on not driving the rental car off the road.

"So, why now?" Avery asks, placing her hands back in her lap.

"My dad fell and there's no one else to help run the family store," I mutter.

While my relationship with my dad has always been strained, I don't wish him any ill will. Just because I don't have any desire to run the family store, or have any interest in selling hardware at all, doesn't mean I don't care about my family or the business in general. I just prefer to support it from the city. I would probably visit home more if I didn't have to hear about my 'poor life choices' every time I visited.

My dad started the store when he and Mom first married. I grew up in the store, and while I appreciate everything that my dad has done building it up and supporting the family with it, it doesn't mean that I have any desire to take over from him. I wish he understood that his love for hardware is like my love for computers. And that it wasn't a source of an argument every time we spoke.

"Wow, that's nice of you to drop everything and come back home."

Avery's soft voice draws me out of my thoughts. Some might see this as an honourable act of a son, but really, it's motivated by guilt.

"Well, I didn't have much of a choice," I mutter.

"What do you mean?"

"My mom." I feel the anxiety rising in my chest as I think back to the phone call that started it all. It takes everything in me not to take my hand and rub at the gnawing ache in my sternum. I need to focus and have two hands firmly gripping the wheel as the snow starts to fall unbelievably harder.

"Ah," Avery muses, turning to face me again. "Is that who you were talking to on the phone back at the gate?"

"When you eavesdropped?" I joke, sneaking a glance at her.

"I did not!" Avery gasps as she playfully swats my arm. "You were right beside me!"

"Sure," I laugh, finding myself feeling freer for the first

time in ages. The tightness in my chest starts to ease and I notice my grip lessen on the wheel. "But, yes, I was talking to my mom. She saw that our flight had been cancelled and was making sure I wasn't just going to turn around and go back to my apartment."

"It sounds like she really misses you."

I want to believe Avery's words, and I know that she does miss me, but I also know it's more than just a mom missing her son. It's the loss of a life my parents thought they had planned out for me. They never understood the draw of the city, or my love for computers and programming. Instead, they skirt around it, acting as if it's a short stint to get it out of my system until I come home and take over the store.

"I'm sure she does, but they mostly just need someone to run the store. That's why she's in a hurry to get me home."

"You don't have any brothers or sisters to help?"

"One brother, but he works in Sun Peaks and had to rush back."

"I see," Avery says, her gaze straying to the road.

I can tell that she wants me to elaborate, but I can't. My voice won't form the words that since he's the younger son, he's not expected to take over the store like I am. Or how because he works in the hospitality industry that it's like working in the store and seen as better than 'hiding behind a computer.'

So instead, silence falls over the car, and only when I find it more distracting than Avery's questions do I let her turn on the radio. A classic Christmas song comes through the speakers, and I can't help but smile as Avery hums along with the crooner singing about a White Christmas. How fitting. I even find myself starting to tap my fingers to the beat as we let the music surround us.

I like that even with her million questions, she can find peace in the silence and doesn't *have* to talk to avoid it like most of the other women I've dated. What astonishes me is that the more we are silent, the more I find that *I* have questions for *her*. I want to know more about her. Mostly, I want to know why she was with that jerk for so long.

I don't know the guy, but I can't picture this elf with someone named Maxwell. No matter his name, she didn't deserve what happened to her earlier tonight.

"So, uh, I know you were in town for a conference but…" I look over at her, taking in her green and red elf dress with matching hat, with her blonde hair running down over her shoulders. "Do you normally dress like an elf?"

I relish in the moment as she throws her head back and laughs. "No, definitely not. Let's just say I thought it would be fun as part of the surprise for Maxwell and a 'Christmas surprise.'" The joy drops from her words at his name, and I find myself with a renewed sense of anger on her behalf. It seems short-lived as the smirk returns as she continues. "And being from Gingerbread Grove, I thought you'd be more of a Christmas guy."

I think about her statement. I used to love Christmas. As a kid, it was my favourite time of the year. We would always go to the events in our neighbouring town, Candy Cane Creek, to take part in all the festivities. I guess somewhere in growing up and the strife with my family, I lost that magic.

Plus, my town is going overboard with the 'rebranding.'

"I don't *hate* Christmas. I guess I've just grown out of it."

Avery gasps. "What? How do you just grow out of Christmas?"

"I dunno," I stammer, shifting in my seat. "Life happened, I guess. The magic was gone. It just sort of…happened."

"That's so sad." And I believe her. She sounds genuinely sad for me. She takes a moment, and the crushing weight on my chest starts to come back.

I don't know when it actually happened, when I stopped feeling the holiday spirit. It was well before I moved to Vancouver, that I know. It was probably somewhere around me graduating from university and my parents realizing my passion for computers wasn't just a hobby.

"So," she continues, "did you forget your sleigh at home?"

I risk a glance at her, raising my eyebrow. "Sleigh?"

"Car? Truck? Snowmobile? Why rent a car if you're from the city? I can't imagine fighting for the last of the cars in that nightmare was ideal."

I chuckle. "No, I don't have a vehicle—sleigh or otherwise. Well, not anymore. I had a truck, but I sold it once I got settled into the city."

"Why?" she asks.

"No need for it there. I live and work downtown. I rarely leave and if I do, I can take transit or get a cab. It didn't make sense for me to keep it. So instead, I rent out the parking space in my condo building and make some extra money."

"That's smart, actually."

Silence falls over the car again. I find myself needing to concentrate harder and harder on the road as the snow begins to cover the road lines. The pitch-black sky isn't helping with the visibility as my headlights only reflect off the fast falling snow, making it a virtual whiteout. I try my best to remember the curve of a road I haven't driven in years, praying we don't end up in a ditch.

Another reason why I never return home. The road conditions can be so unpredictable, especially in the winter.

I can feel my breath return back to normal when there's a small break in the snow, or more accurately, the intensity of it. I look over to find Avery slumped against the passenger window, hands curled under her head as she sleeps. I don't dare risk taking my eyes off the road for more than a second with these conditions, but I'm completely enthralled by how peaceful she looks. She no longer appears to be the stressed out, frustrated woman that she was at the gate. Nor is she my inquisitive, unexpected passenger. Now she's a beautiful blonde elf, finding her peace for the first time in what might be a long time.

I don't know why but looking at her sleeping makes me feel a fraction of the stillness that I used to feel. A peace that I thought I had found in McKenzie. I've never put much stock in finding someone that could give me that sense of security again, thinking nothing short of a Christmas miracle could do that. But spending time with Avery makes me think that maybe anything could be possible.

Chapter Six

AVERY

"**A**very."

A distant voice calls my name, luring me out of the most wonderful dream I was having. I can feel the warm summer sun on my face as I run through a snow-covered field. I laugh as I run playfully from the man behind me, dodging half-heartedly thrown snowballs as I zig-zag out of the way. The man catches up with me, pulling me into his arms as we laugh hysterically and fall into a snowbank. A pair of familiar hazel eyes looking down at me behind black rimmed glasses. Eyes that I know I have no business dreaming about, but I can't help it.

"Avery."

There's the voice again, this time followed by a gentle shake of my arm.

I nestle in further against the car window, stuck in the warm place between dreaming and awake, where I don't want to leave. But the cold car, and reality, are winning as I lose the battle with sleep.

"I fell asleep." I don't expect an answer as I sit up, stretching out my aching muscles.

"Yeah, around Chilliwack. We're stopped in Merritt. I'm going to get gas if you need to go in and grab anything."

I blink my eyes awake and start to take in my surroundings as Matthew gets out of the car. Looking down at my phone screen, I see that I've been asleep for nearly two hours. What I wouldn't give to be back in that dream where he laughed freely and escaped whatever heartaches he's currently hiding.

Pulling off my elf hat, I do the best I can to make my hair less of a chaotic mess in the tiny vanity mirror. I choose to ignore the red line at the top of my forehead where the material dug in during my nap, or the matching lines on my cheek from where my hands doubled as pillows.

A hot elf mess. That's what I am right now.

The gas station attendant has seen worse as people pass through. Right? At least that's what I tell myself as I slip on my black jacket and pull it tight around my body, bracing to brave the blustery December air.

After running to the bathroom and looking at myself under the bright lights, I fully realize the car's small vanity mirror didn't truly convey the extent of the disarray of my appearance. Knowing there isn't anything I can do about it now, I decide that it's the ideal time to act like my life is perfectly normal and fill up on road trip snacks.

Making my way out of the back hallway, I hold my head high as I peruse the aisles and fill my arms with whatever looks appealing. Chips, chocolate bars, jerky, and pop bust from my torso before I see the coffee machine. I don't have high hopes for it tasting anything but bitter, but we both need caffeine, and it should do the trick to get us through the rest of the drive.

Dumping my array of junk food onto the counter, the clerk starts to ring everything in as I pour us two cups, putting in more cream and sugar than necessary in hopes of hiding whatever over roasted bitterness awaits us.

I smile as I place the paper cups down, scanning the front counter to see if there's anything I want to add to our food choices. The clerk doesn't say anything as he continues to scan, but I can't help but notice the not-so-subtle glances he sends my way as he reaches for the next snack.

"I don't usually dress like this," I blurt out, feeling the need to justify my awkward appearance.

He remains silent but raises his eyebrow at me as he scans my All Dressed chips.

"I'm an elf." That earns me both eyebrows raised and a glare over his glasses. "I mean, not a *real* elf. I'm not from the North Pole or anything. Just Kamloops. But I help kids with Christmas, organize toy drives, write letters. That sort of thing."

I don't know why I'm rambling, or why I feel the need to tell this stranger I'm never going to see again my life story. I guess it's the theme of the night.

"The costume is for a conference. It's sort of a uniform. I mean, we don't wear it all the time, just when we deliver gifts and things..." He glances at me again. "We thought it would be fun to get a group picture before heading home." Another raised eyebrow. "All right, I'll stop talking now."

I look around, seeing that a tiny red garland hanging off the screen facing me is the only decoration in the store. It makes me a little sad to think that it's the only bit of holiday joy. Maybe if he had a little more decor, he would be in the holiday spirit.

The clerk gives his head a shake. "Thirty-five, eighty," he says in a gruff voice.

Maybe not.

Or maybe a rambling, dishevelled elf *is* the craziest thing he's seen.

I pay and grab my items, rushing out of the gas station as fast as I can, making a mental note to never come back here ever again. I might never even stop in Merritt again at this rate.

Rushing out of the door, I nearly crash into Matthew.

"I came to see what was taking you so long." He looks down at the bags and cups in my hands. "What's all this?"

"I bought us snacks."

He brings his eyes up to meet mine with a smirk on his face. "I see that."

"And coffee," I say, lifting my hands slightly, showing off the cups. "I can't promise it's good coffee, but it's hot and caffeinated."

"My favourite kind," he laughs. "You know there's only about an hour left on the drive, right?"

I pass him a cup as we head back to the car. "Yes." I take a long sip and can't hide the wince on my face as the bitter, over-roasted liquid hits my tongue. My nose scrunches and my eyes close as I wait for the horrid taste to pass off my tongue.

Yup, called it. The coffee is disgusting.

What I was wrong about, however, is that no amount of cream and sugar was covering how horrible this coffee is. As I open my eyes, I find Matthew staring at me, his own cup halfway to his mouth. "What? Did I spill on me?"

That would be the icing on the cake of the night. Possibly staining my elf costume with horrible coffee in front of Matthew.

He gives his head a slight shake before answering. "It looks like you bought half the store."

Oh. That. At least it's just my impulse for buying too many snacks.

"Well, I didn't know what you'd like," I answer as we climb into the rental. "I mean, I don't know if you're a sweet or salty guy, so I just bought a little of everything." I stop and look up at him, panic rising in my chest. "Oh my gosh, you aren't diabetic, are you? Food allergies? Am I going to kill you with one of my snacks? Please tell me it's not a severe peanut allergy."

Placing my coffee in the cup holder, I start rifling through the goodies. the first thing I grab being a chocolate-covered peanut butter cup. My eyes frantically search the rest of the bag as Matthew places his hand on mine, stilling my actions.

"No, no medical concerns here. I guess," he stalls for a moment, searching my eyes. "I guess I'm just not used to anyone being that concerned about what I like, or don't like, or even buying snacks for me at all."

"Really? No one?"

"Well, I have my friend and business partner back in the city that picks me up the occasional coffee or lunch, but no, I can't say that I've had anyone that's done that in a very long time."

My heart sinks. While Maxwell wasn't the best boyfriend —especially with recent events—when it was good, he'd always brought me flowers, coffee, or treats. He would surprise me with things that he knew I liked, just because. Even my friends would load up on my favourite snacks for a day out on a road trip or a movie marathon. I find it incredibly sad to think that someone as seemingly wonderful as Matthew hasn't had the same experience.

Placing my hand on top of his that is still resting on my arm, I give it a gentle squeeze. Looking deep into his hazel eyes reminds me of my dream, I know that I want that to change for him.

"I'm so sorry, Matthew." I don't know what else to say that won't sound trite or impersonal.

"It's all right."

The sadness in his voice kills me. No one should be this sad, especially during the holidays. As we sit here, locked in each other's eyes, I can't help but pray that a Christmas miracle will fill this car and show him that the world *can* be a wonderful place. There *are* people who can care for him, buy him snacks, and respect that he loves working with computers. I want to be the one that helps him find that happiness. I can't deny that we're starting to make a connection. A connection of what? I don't know, but I know I'm feeling something. Certainly it wouldn't be in a romantic situation; I literally got out of a relationship today. But I know that I want to be there when Matthew discovers it.

"Anyways," Matthew says, clearing his throat and turning in his seat, taking a sip of his coffee without even a wince at the bitter taste. Maybe he is a psycho or serial killer. "We should get going if we want to make it to Kamloops before we get snowed in here."

"Right, we wouldn't want that." I look away, buckling my seatbelt and reaching into the bag to pull out a bag of chips. The lack of holiday treats leaves me to stick with my go-to non-holiday snack—All Dressed chips. "Help yourself to whatever I bought. I don't know about you, but I couldn't eat before the plane was supposed to take off and I'm starving now."

Matthew laughs and once again I'm relaxed at the sound.

"Now that you mention it, I am." He places his coffee next to mine in the cup holders and grabs the chocolate peanut butter cups I had been holding, tearing into them as the car warms up once again. A wide smile crosses his face as he takes a bite. "I rarely have these, but whenever I do, I love them. I don't know why I don't have them more often."

"Maybe you should indulge yourself a little more often," I add, enjoying how much he's letting himself relax.

"You know, maybe I should."

"So, Big City Man, what do you do for fun?" I take another bite of my chip and watch him as he ponders, chewing his own treat.

"Oh, I don't know. I like to stay home a lot when I'm not working, so I guess reading and watching movies?"

"I'll accept that," I joke. "Let me guess, you like reading thrillers? Maybe action movies with spies and superheroes?"

He laughs. "Actually, yes. How did you guess that?"

"I'm Santa's helper, remember? But seriously, tell me one movie that is so out of left field for you, but you totally love." He narrows his eyes at me. "We all have them. A movie that doesn't fit our typical genre, but we love it anyway." My eyes widen as he clenches his jaw. "It's a Christmas one, isn't it?"

He pops the last peanut butter cup into his mouth, looking out the window to avoid my gaze.

"It is! Oh, let me guess. *The Grinch? Elf? Home Alone? Santa Clause?*" When he doesn't answer or look my way, I groan. "Don't say *Die Hard*. That doesn't count."

That earns a laugh from him. "No, but that is an awesome movie."

"Agreed, but not for the holidays. Come on, tell me. I know it is one."

He lets out a sigh as he turns in his seat and faces me. "I've had this tradition ever since I was a kid. I don't think it started with my family because I don't ever remember watching it with them, but every night on Christmas Day I need to watch *Miracle on 34th Street*." He blows out a breath and runs his hands through his hair. "I can't believe I'm even telling you this. I've never even told Mitch, and we make a point to watch everything *but* Christmas movies together during the holidays. Especially on the big day."

"Why would you hide something like that? Who's Mitch?"

"My business partner and best friend. As to why I would hide it, I don't know. We both aren't fans of the holidays so we do everything we can to try to make it just a regular day. We order in food that doesn't resemble turkey and have movie marathons with all the genres you rightly guessed I would watch." He chuckles sadly, but the laughter doesn't meet his eyes.

"Except when you watch *Miracle on 34th Street*."

"Except when I watch *Miracle on 34th Street*," he echoes, this time with a light in his eyes. "I wait until he goes home or at least falls asleep on the couch and then I put it on."

"I hope you find someone to watch it with, Matthew. Even if you do it in secret."

With a smile, he finishes the last of the chocolate cups. "Thank you, Avery."

We sit there for a moment, just staring at each other with shy smiles on our faces, letting Michael Bublé and Dolly Parton's voices fill the air around us. It isn't until he buckles up and pulls out of the parking lot that I realize there's so much more to Matthew than I first thought.

When the night first started, I couldn't wait to get back to Kamloops. Now that I'm getting closer to being home, getting to know this mysterious stranger from the airport, I realize I don't want the night to end.

Chapter Seven

MATTHEW

"So, tell me about McKenzie."

Avery's question startles me. Not because I find it completely unexpected after our conversation earlier, but mainly because it's been a while since anyone other than my mom has brought her name up with me. After finding out we had very different opinions of where our relationship stood, Mitch stood by my side as I grieved the loss of what I thought my future would look like and helped me move on. Since then, her name has never been brought up. We don't discuss her in any form and haven't in years. Hearing her name so casually mentioned by Avery makes me think that maybe I didn't deal with the hurt, but rather just pushed it aside. Buried it deep down so that I didn't have to feel because if I didn't hear her name, I couldn't be reminded of the pain that was now associated with it.

The funny thing is, hearing it from Avery doesn't bring that same pain.

"What do you want to know?' I try to keep my voice level as I focus on the road ahead of me. The snow is starting to lighten up, which I'm relieved about because that means so is the pressing weight on my chest as I try to get us to where we're going.

I don't want to admit it to Avery, but there have been a few times on the drive so far, most while she had been sleeping, where the roads were a little more dicey than I would have liked. The Coquihalla Highway is fantastic in the summer, but the steep climbs and windy curves make it treacherous in the winter.

"Why are you letting her stop you from going back home more often?"

"Wow, right to the point, huh?" I ask, taking one hand off the steering wheel to rub at my sternum. It's a habit that I developed when I was younger; almost as if the physical act would help with the building pressure of anxiety in my chest.

"Sorry, I can be blunt. I just...I mean, I guess I get it. I wouldn't be thrilled if Maxwell decided to move back to Kamloops with his girlfriend."

"Yes, but imagine Kamloops being a fraction of the size and everyone in town knows everyone's business." I can't help but let my bitterness leak through with that statement. McKenzie is only one of the reasons why I haven't gone back to Gingerbread Grove. Everyone knows everything. They all know I don't want to run my dad's store. They all know McKenzie left me for Cal. They especially all know that I ran away to the city because I didn't want to deal with any of it.

"Okay, I see it now."

"Plus, ugh, her husband is now the mayor."

"He's *what?*" Avery exclaims from her seat, nearly dropping her cup of coffee.

"Yeah, elected a couple of years ago. From what my mom tells me, after they moved back to Gingerbread Grove, he set up a real estate office that did surprisingly well for a small town. He focused on the vacation properties and also got into rental management or something. Built up a real name for himself in the town and was a big factor in them becoming a 'destination Christmas town.'"

"So, he just came into the town and…"

"Took it over? Pretty much." The gnawing ache in my chest burns again as I think back to the few times I did return to Gingerbread Grove over the years. Cal and McKenzie act like they own the city and I was just a visitor. Sure, I technically was since I no longer live there anymore, but it didn't feel like my hometown. If anything, I felt as if I had never lived there with all the changes they had made to it.

"That must be incredibly frustrating."

"Yes and no," I answer honestly. "I never saw myself living in Woodland Springs my whole life, especially once I knew for sure my parents weren't going to accept my career as a Software Engineer. And don't get me wrong, I've made a decent name for myself in the tech world in Vancouver. Mitch and I are doing the best we can to build our small company and we're growing every year. But it's…" I let my voice trail off, not knowing how to finish my sentence. How do I sum up ten years' worth of emotions and baggage surrounding my family, my career, and my small town?

"Frustrating?" she finishes for me with a sympathetic smile.

"Yeah, that." I give her a smirk without taking my eyes off of the road. I know if I even glance her way, I'm going to be lost. I don't know how this stranger dressed like an elf muscled her way into my life, digging up things I haven't thought about or felt in a long time, but here we are.

"But you could avoid them the best you could, can't you? You don't have a reason to hide or anything. But maybe you could just sort of feign indifference?"

"I would, but it's also the time for the Christmas Festival."

"The what?" Avery asks, sitting up straighter in her seat.

"It's something Cal started when he became mayor. He said it would 'help the morale of the town' and 'boost the

Christmas economy.' So, he started a festival in the lead up to Christmas. If you ask me, it's because he wanted to directly compete with Candy Cane Creek, and they already had their events established for decades."

"The rivalry between your two towns is real, isn't it?" She reaches into her bag from the gas station and pulls out a stick of jerky.

"That's putting it lightly."

"I've heard of the Candy Cane Creek Festival, but what's so different about yours?"

Mine. The thought that I have anything to do with Gingerbread Grove or its ridiculous festival is comical. "I haven't been since they started, but from what I hear there is a mix of baking, holiday events, and some sort of epic snowball fight."

"Epic Snowball fight?"

"From what I hear, it's quite popular, like laser tag, but with snowballs. People train for it all year."

Avery is quiet for a moment. I'm not sure if I've stunned her with how ridiculous my town has become, or what, but it's making me antsy.

"I think you should go."

"What" I ask, nearly swerving the car while I look over at her.

"I think you should go. Even better, I think you should enter the competition."

That's it. I've officially gone on a road trip with someone who's completely lost her mind. "No."

"Come on! You should go and show them that you aren't intimidated—or frustrated—by them and show just how great you are!"

Just how great I am, huh? The idea is laughable.

"There's one problem. The competition is for *couples*." The thought of showing up alone in town is bad enough, but to try to even watch the competition without a significant other? No thank you. I'm already showing up to work at my dad's store, just like I vowed I never would. Now the fact I'm doing it alone is just icing on the cake.

"Hmm, being single could be a problem," she ponders out loud.

That felt like a shot in the gut hearing her say that out loud. Being single had never bothered me. I didn't stay with Emily as long as I did because I was scared of being alone; it was just more comfortable than anything else. But now hearing Avery talk about it feels—odd.

"I mean, I'm just assuming you're single. You could have a girlfriend back in the city." She begins to ramble, wringing her hands in her lap. "Of course you do. I mean, it only makes sense you're holding back because she's not here with you rather than not exist."

I bite my lip, trying not to laugh at her antics.

"I'm sorry. I'm going to stop talking, and assuming," she continues, before slamming her palm to her forehead. "Why do I do this?"

I can't hold back a chuckle. "Don't worry, you're right. I'm single. But what do you mean by 'of course you aren't?'" Glancing over at her as headlights flash from an oncoming car, I see her pink cheeks as she lowers her hand.

"I just mean—uh—well, you're a good looking man, obviously smart, and successful. I just assumed…"

I can feel myself blush at her words. I know I'm not the *worst* looking guy, usually, but I've always been placed in the 'computer geek' category with women. Only talking to them if they need help with technology or being flirted with if there is some way I could help them. My favourite is when they assume I am rich because I co-own a tech company but aren't interested any longer when they find out it's very far from the truth.

"Um, thanks, but I'm single, so it doesn't help me when it comes to the competition. If anything, it was also part of the reason why I didn't want to make a big deal about coming back to town."

"What if I came with you?" she shoots back.

"As what? The elf that begged me to give her a ride?" I joke.

"No, silly. I could pretend to be your girlfriend."

I had to stop myself from slamming on the brakes at her words. "Pretend to be my girlfriend," I repeat.

"I did it again, didn't I? I spoke without thinking. I do that sometimes. And ramble. Oh gosh, I'm doing it again. I'm sorry." Both hands cover her face now, more muffled words as she mutters them.

Without thinking, I reach over and place my hand on hers, lowering them back down to her lap. Without risking taking my eyes off the road, I link my fingers with hers. I hate the turmoil in her voice.

"Tell me how it would work."

She squeezes my hand and part of me is worried she'll let go, but she doesn't.

"I don't know. I didn't think that far ahead." We both chuckle, still holding hands. "Is that something you'd be interested in? Would it make you more comfortable going home?"

I pause, truly not knowing how to answer that. My mom would have a million questions about why I would have kept a relationship secret. I never told her about Emily, so hiding a real girlfriend from her wouldn't be far from the truth. I never saw a reason to bring it up unless I knew it was serious, which Emily never was. One thing I do know is that if I do this, I'm going to have to learn everything there is to know about Avery, and fast.

But the alternative is showing up to Gingerbread Grove in the height of the holiday season alone. I would need to face McKenzie and Cal—and my parents—and romantic relationship or not, it would be nice to have someone that would be on my side through it all.

"I think I would." I answer, and she immediately lets out a breath.

"That's great. But I think the real question is, would I even be someone you would want to date—fictionally, of course. I mean, am I your type?" She closes her eyes and scrunches up her nose. "I'm doing it again. What I mean to say is, will everyone buy that you're dating someone like me?"

"What do you mean by that? You mean, do I normally date elves?" I joke. I'm genuinely intrigued why she would think that someone as beautiful, seemingly smart and thoughtful wouldn't be my type. If anything, it would be the other way around. Sure, I might not date women who look like they escaped Santa's workshop, but I can't say my dating history leaves me in a position to comment on someone that may or may not have experience in a toy workshop.

"I mean, I can be—abrupt. I don't always have a filter when I talk. I ramble when I'm nervous. I ask more questions than I should." She looks down. "I dress like an elf."

"I can't say I've ever dated someone with your current attire, but honestly, I'd say all of that makes you perfect. You can take some of the heat off of me," I laugh, letting her know that I'm not serious. Not completely, anyway. It dies off when I see she doesn't share the sentiment. "Hey, I'm serious. I don't see why anyone would have a problem dating you, fake or not."

"Well, my experience today would suggest otherwise," she mumbles.

I hate how small her voice sounds, and how I can see she's folding herself into the seat next to me. I may not know her well—or at all—but I know that she deserves more than this.

"What would you get out of it?" I ask, pretending like I don't see how small she's trying to make herself.

Movement catches my eye as she sits up sharply. "What do you mean?"

"I mean, I get to put on a face and greet the town with you on my arm. You're saving me from having to show up to do a job I don't want to do, with people I don't want to see, and in a town I don't want to be in. What do you gain? Why do you want to help me?"

The car is quiet again, with only the soft, soulful voice of Bing Crosby sitting between us. For a quick moment, I worry I said the wrong thing, but I genuinely want to know why she would be willing to help me out like this.

"I don't know. I guess as a thank you for driving me up here when you really didn't have to? Or maybe it's just a way to distract myself from Maxwell and his harsh rejection."

My heart sinks when I think of the way Avery was treated. I know the pain she's going through. I know the embarrassment and devastation that comes along with it. While I may be selfish in using what she's gone through to make my life a little easier, I wonder if maybe it's what she needs, too. But it won't be easy. My family—and the town—will have questions.

"Please, Matthew. I want to help you." The softness in her voice is the deciding factor for me. I may be selfish for letting her do this, but I also feel like deep down, it would be helping her, too. Plus, it would be nice to have someone do things for me, like picking up coffee and candy. I never thought in a million years I would be in this situation. In a car with a Christmas-loving stranger I met at the airport discussing a fake relationship. What's even crazier are the words coming out of my mouth.

"Okay, let's do it."

Chapter Eight

AVERY

"What do you mean, you just asked him for a ride?" Meg asks me as she stops her coffee mug mid-air while going to take a sip. "You can't just do that to people, Avery! Have you learned nothing from those podcasts I sent you?"

"It wasn't like that. Matthew isn't a serial killer." I roll my eyes as I place my elbows on the kitchen island in front of me, holding my mug in both hands. The steam from the coffee and the warm spices of the gingerbread creamer wrap around me like a warm hug, deflecting the criticism from my well-meaning sister.

After hearing I was back in town, Meg invited herself over with sugar cookies from my favourite bakery to get the full story of what happened in Vancouver and provide support. I purposely waited until she was good and mad at Maxwell before telling her about my adventures home. Since her anger was focused on my ex in the city, I thought that I could slide in my late-night hero into the narrative, but I was wrong.

Thinking of Matthew now gives me the feeling of a thousand tiny butterflies flitting through my stomach. Since he dropped me off at my apartment in the early hours of the morning, we have been texting about what to do with our fake relationship. What started out as us getting to know each other with basic things a couple would know, quickly turned into him needing support once he made it to his parents' place and his mom started fussing over him.

One thing I learned was Matthew does *not* like being fussed over. Especially the way his mom currently was.

But then my thoughts drift back to the surprise on his face when I brought him the coffee and treats. Maybe it's the little things that he appreciates the most. The subtle acts of kindness, not the overwhelming, smothering kind.

But as we were both drifting off to sleep, he started to fill me in about the competition. The 'Yuletide Games,' as they call it. I couldn't help but enter into a fit of giggles when he started to describe events like pairs speed skating and downhill sledding that the town had done in the past. He was more than mildly relieved to learn the pairs speed skating had been removed from the docket this year after a particularly over-competitive run last year where multiple couples ended up in the hospital with minor injuries after there was some behaviour that was not fitting for the season, including pushing and tripping. He told me there were even rumours of tampering with the icing for the gingerbread house competition. Something about running icing and collapsing structures. It's why they ultimately had to scale back the allowed sizes of their entries.

"There's something you aren't telling me." Meg raises an eyebrow as she lowers her mug to the countertop.

Bringing my gaze back to my sister, I realize the goofy grin on my face that appeared while thinking about Matthew and the games.

"Matthew and I sort of, uh, agreed to fake date," I say, looking down, talking more to the coffee in my hands than Meg.

"Sorry, repeat that again," she demands, using her older sister voice on me.

"Well, he has it rough going home to Gingerbread Grove. He has an ex like Maxwell, but actually much worse because now her and her husband pretty much run the town. Then he has a mother that hasn't accepted he doesn't want to live in his hometown anymore, a dad that doesn't like his career choice. Then there's the whole Yuletide Games…" I know I'm rambling, but I can't help but feel like I'm ten years old again getting interrogated about breaking mom's expensive vase. Meg would always back me up with my parents, but then take it upon herself to find out the truth when we were alone.

"And you fit into this because…?"

"Because he saved me, Meg. I would still be stuck in Vancouver if it wasn't for his help, stranded like a sad elf with no way to the North Pole."

"You could have changed out of your costume."

I roll my eyes. "That's not the point."

"Plus, you're acting like Vancouver is some sort of war zone."

"An emotional war zone," I mutter, taking a sip of my latte.

Meg continues, ignoring me. "He gave you a ride—a risky ride, if you ask me. He didn't save your life. In fact, you put your life in danger not only with stranger danger but also driving that highway at night in a near-blizzard."

I remain silent and avoid eye contact while she speaks, finding my cooling coffee very interesting. I know what she's saying is true. It goes against everything our parents taught us while growing up. Don't get into cars with strangers. Don't drive the highway at night in the winter if you can avoid it. Did I listen? No, but thankfully it worked out for me in my hour of desperation.

"He's good looking, isn't he?" Meg exclaims, more of a statement than a question.

"What? No! I mean, yes, but that has nothing to do with it." I can feel my cheeks warm under Meg's gaze, but I try to convince myself it's from the wafting steam off my coffee. It's certainly not me being attracted to Matthew. Not with his dark blond hair, piercing hazel eyes, and dark-rimmed glasses. I've never fallen for the 'intellectual looking' guys before, but Matthew is changing what I thought I knew about myself and what I want.

I don't know what I'm thinking anyway. I just met him. Not to mention Maxwell and I just broke up. Or maybe we broke up a while ago and I just didn't know.

Is that even possible? Can someone break up with you and just forget to tell you?

"Okay, walk me through how this happened. I thought you were just going into Vancouver for a conference."

"I was." I place my mug down on the counter and rub my hands over my face. "I thought it would be a good idea to surprise Maxwell while I was there." I fill her in on every embarrassing, horrific detail of my time in Vancouver. Including how it all happened while dressed like an elf.

"That jerk! I always knew you were too good for him," she spat, starting to pace. "He's lucky he's in Vancouver. He'd better not think to even show his face in Kamloops again."

"Meg, it's bad, but it's not *that* bad." I pick up my coffee again and take a sip, trying not to wince at how cold it is.

She stops and looks at me, placing her hands on her hips. "Avery…"

"Meg…" I lower my voice to meet her level of seriousness while trying to lighten the mood. When I see it's not going to have its desired effect, I sigh. "Look, am I upset about it? Yes. You know how I felt about him and where I thought our relationship was going. Heck, I was planning on moving down there. Even quitting my dream job to make that happen."

"You were going to quit being Head Elf? Avery! You've worked so hard to get there!"

"I know." Pain stabs my gut for even *thinking* of leaving my job, but at the time, I was willing to do it if it meant that I would have a life with Maxwell. Now, I can't believe that I was so silly.

Meg rounds the island and pulls me into a hug, resting her chin on the top of my head. "Love makes us do silly things sometimes."

I close my eyes and wrap my arms around her. Just like that, I'm transported to being a kid again, comforted by hugs from my big sister. I fight back the tears as emotions that I don't want to feel bubble up—especially emotions linked to Maxwell Gladwin.

Bah Humbug to him.

"So tell me how this turns into you being a fake girlfriend for some Christmas contest," she says with a final squeeze before letting go and taking a seat on the stool beside me.

"We got to talking and he's been through something similar. Except now he has to go home to his hometown and be face-to-face with his ex and her husband, who is now mayor."

"No," she gasps.

"Yes, and they're the ones that started the whole change to Gingerbread Grove and the Yuletide Games." Meg sits beside me, riveted by the whole ordeal, like she is watching a soap opera. "So, I couldn't just leave him to face all of that by himself in a place he doesn't even want to be. Not to mention, I looked him up and he's successful in his own right, but he just doesn't see it. For whatever reason, he thinks this Cal guy is better than him, and I don't know why."

"I heard they changed their name. Something about a rivalry with Candy Cane Creek?"

"Yes! I looked more into it last night, but it seems like some townspeople thought that Candy Cane Creek was 'hogging the Christmas limelight' and wanted to one up them. Then there's something about rival inns...I'm going to have to investigate it further when I get there because I find it all fascinating. But the most interesting part is that Cal isn't even from Gingerbread Grove."

"How did you find this all out?" Meg has a look on her face that's a mix of awe and terrified, causing me to chuckle.

"The internet, silly. Social media is really resourceful. It looks like they met at university in Vancouver and moved back to Woodland Springs shortly after they graduated."

"I'm a little shocked—and scared—at your sleuthing skills."

"I blame you and your true crime podcasts. Don't tell me you've never done some internet research after listening to one of those." I give her a pointed look, knowing that's exactly what she does. "Plus, they posted it on their own socials; it's not like I'm being a total creeper."

"Not a *total* creeper, no," she jokes, playfully bumping her side into mine. "I guess I can see why you would want to help this Matthew guy out."

"I thought you were against me helping him."

"I still am, but I can see why you would want to. Especially now that I'm pretty sure you're not going to end up on one of those podcasts. Plus, I haven't seen you this smitten with a guy in a long time. Not even with Maxwell." Meg shrugs her shoulders and grabs an oversized cranberry orange muffin from the box she brought with her this morning.

"I'm not smitten. It's too early for me to be smitten. Maxwell and I just—well, I don't know when we actually broke up now that I think about it. But I was just heartbroken, and Matthew and I just met. There's nothing to be *smitten* about."

"Whatever you say," she replies with a smirk before taking a bite of her muffin.

I open my mouth to respond when my phone chimes, letting me know I have an incoming text. I try to keep my nerves at bay as I see Matthew's name on my screen.

MATTHEW

All set for tomorrow. See you at the town square at 5?

"You're blushing! It's from him, isn't it?" Meg exclaims, trying to peer over my shoulder at my phone.

Even though there's nothing in our texts that would be considered scandalous, I hold my phone to my chest, not letting her see. Something in me wants to keep my conversations with him private. If Meg wasn't my big sister and my best friend, I wouldn't even be sharing this with her.

"Yes, it's from him and no, I'm not blushing." I bring my free hand to my cheek, immediately feeling the heat.

"Liar," she jokes.

Ignoring her, I turn my back and look back down at my phone, typing out my reply.

Yup. See you then! 😄

"Wow, exclamation mark *and* a smiley face? You've got it bad," Meg jokes as she walks past me and places her mug in the sink.

"Oh, stop." I place my phone—screen down—on the counter and narrow my eyes at my sister. "This is nothing. It's not even real, remember? I'm just pretending to be his girlfriend so that he doesn't have to face his family and the town alone. If anything, I'm just saving him, like how he saved me from being stranded in Vancouver. Think of it as…" My brain struggles for the right word. Payment makes it sound like it's something nefarious, when it's anything but. Squaring Up? Reimbursement?

"Calling it even?" Meg states with a smile.

"Yes! We'll be even. He helped me and I helped him. Once he's back in the city after Christmas, we'll just go our separate ways. No harm, no foul."

"Right…" She sounds as unconvinced as I feel. Which is ridiculous; it's just an arrangement. Two people helping each other get out of uncomfortable situations. That's it.

My phone dings again and I rush to flip it over, momentarily forgetting my nosy sister is right next to me.

MATTHEW

Great, I can't wait. Be sure to dress warm and, uh, maybe not like an elf 😜

"He sent a winky face?" Meg practically yells in my ear as she laughs. "Avery, you're in so much trouble."

Looking down at the message in my hand with a wide, goofy smile on my face, I think she might be right.

Chapter Nine

AVERY

I don't know what I was expecting when it came to Gingerbread Grove's town square, but this wasn't it.

The snow from last night blankets the streets and rooftops, reflecting the twinkling lights off the fresh powder. The light posts are all shaped like candy canes, painted in bold red and greens that spiral up the poles, decorated with red glittery ribbons at the top. All the trees are evergreen, adorned with multicoloured lights and ornaments, all topped in mismatched stars. Then there's the tree in the middle of the square. It's unlike anything I've ever seen.

The height could rival any town's central tree. The lights and decorations are a mix of whimsical and nostalgic that should clash, but somehow don't.

The square itself is bustling with the holiday market. Booths set up into aisles along the shovelled out pathways, carving frozen roads, allowing people to stop table-to-table to buy trinkets and baked goods. Each booth has fairy lights that zig zag from one another, adding to the magical ambiance as the sun sets behind the gazebo in the middle of the square.

It looks like most other small town outdoor markets that I have been to. Well, except for the decor. The one time I visited

Candy Cane Creek, I thought they had gone overboard. Gingerbread Grove makes me feel like I stepped into the North Pole itself, or at least a baked goods version of it. While not a bad thing—especially given my occasional elf attire—it's not what I was expecting.

But now that I think of it, I wonder if I could use something like this to bring joy to the families at work. It would take some planning, but I would love to coordinate something for them to experience this.

Glancing down at my watch, it strikes five exactly, and I feel my nerves start to grow. Even though meeting here at this time was his idea, what if he doesn't show? What if he changed his mind, deciding that fake dating a stranger he met at an airport was as ridiculous as it sounds?

The smell of apple and cinnamon wafts from a nearby table, making my stomach rumble, reminding me that I haven't eaten today. My nerves wouldn't allow it. I barely drank any of my gingerbread oat latte, which I made sure to grab before starting the drive over here. Would the caffeine this late in the day make me a jittery mess? Probably, but I needed the comfort of my drink, and the decaf version just doesn't hit the same way. Not that it mattered in the end. Every time I took my hand off the wheel to take a sip, a wave of nauseous nerves rose in my stomach, making me put my cup right back down into the holder.

In other words, I'm a Christmas mess.

Now that I'm standing here at five-o-two, what do I do if he does show? Can we pull off being a couple? I'm sure that anything we don't know about each other that couples would, could be explained by not being together long. Matthew and I had agreed that we would say it's new and that can explain away a lot. But what about making people truly believe we have chemistry? Do we hold hands? Do I link my arm with his?

I still. What if we have to kiss?

"You made it," a familiar deep voice says from behind me, making me turn.

I'm met with a pair of glasses-framed hazel eyes and a smile that reaches them. A smile on the lips I was just thinking about kissing.

"Avery? Are you okay?"

Realizing I was staring at the lips I should *not* be thinking about kissing, I dart my gaze back to his eyes. Eyes are neutral territory. You don't kiss eyes. But as I find myself getting lost in his, I think that maybe I won't have to fake chemistry. Not on my end, anyway.

"Uh, yeah. I'm fine." Plastering on a fake smile, I act like I wasn't just daydreaming about him. And his lips.

My eyes dart down before I drag them back up.

Nope. Not falling for that again.

Standing here awkwardly looking at each other, I'm sure we look like anything but a fresh couple. I find myself not knowing what to do or say next. Do I give him a hug? Slide up next to him? I'm suddenly forgetting what we had discussed about the specifics of who we needed to fake this for. Instead, I can only recite what his favourite food is (sushi), his favourite colour (green), and dream vacation spot (Scottish Highlands). Anything else is a blur.

"I, uh, brought you coffee." Matthew hands me a red, white, and green striped paper cup with 'GingerBrew Cafe' stamped on the side. The smell of apple and cinnamon is quickly replaced by warm ginger and strong coffee.

"There's a theme in the town, huh?" I say, taking a sip. I won't say anything against the coffee shop back in Kamloops, but this has to be the best gingerbread latte I've ever had in my life. If there was a way to take the cookie, make it liquid and add coffee, that's what I'm holding right now.

"They go a little overboard," he mumbles, taking a sip from his own mug. His cup is brown with cartoon gingerbread men in various dance poses. "I didn't know how you felt about having it this late in the day, so I had Rachel make it half-caf. I hope that's okay."

"More than okay. Thank you. It's sweet that you brought me coffee." Half-caf; why didn't I think of that?

"It's the least I can do, considering I made you drive out here to do this."

"You didn't *make* me do anything, Matthew. I want to help you."

We stand at the edge of the town square, smiling at each other as people pass by. Maybe we are close to looking like the love-sick fools we are supposed to be. In my mind, I know it's just for show. There's no way the coy smile on his face right now is really for me. He must be a better actor than I thought.

"I'm sorry that it couldn't be your gingerbread latte with eggnog sprinkles. Rebecca didn't have any but was so inspired she was going to look at ordering some for her cafe."

"You remembered my favourite drink?" Those butterflies are back. They're shooting around my stomach like snowflakes in a snowstorm and if I'm not careful, I'll be thinking this is anything but fake.

"You might start a trend here if you're not careful," he jokes, taking a sip of his drink. "Oh, and I brought you these." With his free hand, he reaches into his pocket and pulls out a pack of chocolate-covered peanut butter cups and another of gummy bears. "I hope you still consider this as part of your road trip, as you'll be travelling back to Kamloops."

The smile on his face cracks every iron-enforced part of my heart that I put up in the hopes of surviving this fake relationship. The slight dimple on his cheek and the light in his eyes have me falling even more and more for him.

Meg's right…I'm in so much trouble.

"You brought me road trip snacks?" I can barely get the words out as I hold out my hand and accept the treats.

"Of course." His smile drops. "Did I get the wrong ones? I

remembered the cups, but do you not like gummy bears? I can go back to the store and get you something else."

"No, they're perfect. Thank you. I have to say, I'm a little surprised they sell something here that isn't cookie themed," I joke, looking down at them longingly before slipping them into my purse. As corny as it sounds, I don't know if I'll ever be able to have peanut butter cups or gummy bears without thinking of Matthew ever again.

"Shocking, I know, but there are a few odd items that sneak through," he smirks.

Relief washes over his face and we are once more standing looking at each other with smiles on our faces as people mill about around us. Once again, I'm not sure what to do. We're in this limbo of not knowing how to act like a couple. We didn't talk about PDA. My heart rate races and I can feel a cold sweat breaking across my shoulder as my mind races with a mix of what I want to do—hold his hand? Hug him? Kiss him on the cheek?—and what he expects me to do.

"Thank you again for helping me out, Avery. I know it's a long way to come…"

"Gingerbread Grove isn't that far. Plus, I've been meaning to come and see what you guys do for the holidays here, remember? Think of it as helping me with a research assignment. Maybe I'll get some ideas on how to improve things at C.O.C.O.A."

"Cocoa?" I want to laugh at the puzzled look he gives me, because it's the same one I get every time I describe my work.

"Yes, the company I work for. Christmas Offerings for Children and Outstanding Adults. C.O.C.O.A."

"And you are the head elf at this C.O.C.O.A.?"

"Yup! I've worked there for eight years, and I can honestly say I love my job. From October to December, we are living our best life while blessing children and families that would normally go without during the holidays. I love the look on their faces when we bring them toys and traditional Christmas dinners with a roasted turkey and all the fixings. I would do it for free if I didn't need to pay bills and you know, adult."

A smirk returns to his face. "Yeah, I know the feeling. Most days I feel the same way about my work, too."

"I would love to hear more about that; can you tell me about your company as we walk? There's a tent over there with bath bombs that caught my eye when I got here."

"Of course." He holds his arm out to me, and I naturally slip my hand in, holding on to his elbow as we begin to stroll.

Like a real couple.

But we aren't. I have to remind myself of that.

"Mitch and I grew up together, always messing around with computers. When we were old enough, we learned to code, and eventually went to school and got our degrees as software engineers. After we graduated, we started writing software for 3D printers."

"Wow, that's fascinating."

"It's okay, I know it's pretty nerdy…"

"No," I say, stopping him from walking any further. I wait until he turns to look at me. *Really* look at me. "You literally create software so people can express themselves by creating something out of nothing. I think that's incredible."

A light blush hits his cheeks and it warms my heart, knowing I put it there.

"Thank you, Avery. I don't think anyone's ever put it that way." He reaches up and rubs the corner of my mouth with his thumb before gently grazing his hand up my cheek and tucking a stray piece of hair behind my ear. "You, uh, had some whipped cream."

"Uh, huh." I don't have words. My brain is a melted puddle of snow as his hand stays at the nape of my neck and he's looking at me with those hazel eyes.

"Matty? Is that you?" A high-pitched sound comes from behind me, ripping us out of our little cozy bubble.

I don't want to know who that voice belongs to. I no longer even want to be standing in the town square at sunset, drinking my half-caf gingerbread latte, and on my way to look at bath bombs. No, I want to be back in the bubble where just Matthew and I exist and he's looking at me like maybe this isn't all just a dream—or a joke—that my heartbroken mind has made up.

"Matty, that is you! I didn't know you were back in town. Why didn't your mom tell me?"

There's that voice again.

And Matty? I thought he hated nicknames.

I turn to find a tall, blonde woman with curled hair and heavy makeup walking towards us.

"Here we go," Matthew mutters beside me as he takes a massive swig from his cup and grabs my hand. If we didn't just share a moment, I would think he's trying to crush me with how he's gripping me right now. But I also know the panicked look on his face as he watches the woman approach us has more to do with her.

"McKenzie?" I whisper, not taking my eyes off the approaching woman with the fake smile, tight fitting ski jacket and boots with fake fur trims. She looks like she belongs on the slopes, not a small town Christmas market.

"McKenzie," Matthew whispers back, not bothering to put on a fake smile of his own.

The closer she gets, the harder he grips my hand. When she's ten feet away, he ditches my hand and throws his arm around my shoulders, pinning me tight to his side. I keep the smile on my face, even though it pains me to do so. Not because I don't welcome his touch. The exact opposite, actually. It's because I want nothing more than to close my eyes and take in his outdoorsy scent of sandalwood and smoke, but it's not the time. I need to pretend like I'm used to being tucked into his side and surrounded by his scent of woods and campfires. I need to pretend like his touch is familiar and isn't sending my heart racing like it's on a reindeer dash. Most of all, I need to pretend like Matthew is my everything.

It's then I know there's no way I'm going to be able to fake anything with him. Because with Matthew? I want it all.

Chapter Ten

MATTHEW

My body comes alive as I have Avery tucked under my arm. Not only am I warring with the rushing anxiety of having McKenzie walking toward us, but am now overcome with a different set of emotions, having Avery's body pressed against mine. I want to rub my sternum to find some relief from the building anxiety, but I can't. McKenzie knows it's my telltale sign of being uncomfortable, and I have a sneaky suspicion that Avery picked up on it during our drive last night. I can't let either of them know they affect me the way they do, even if it's for very different reasons.

Even though my body is alive with conflicting feelings, there's an undercurrent of calm. Like a stillness in the eye of a storm. With every breath, Avery's scent of warm gingerbread spices takes a little of the stress away. Leaning into her, the squeeze of her hand on my waist and the gentle weight of her head on my shoulder, brings more of a calm. By the time McKenzie stands in front of us, I start to feel my heartbeat calm, returning to near normal.

Interesting.

"Hi, McKenzie," I manage to make out, gently squeezing Avery's shoulder in a silent thank you.

"My goodness, it's been a long time," McKenzie says as she loops her hand through the arm of the man next to her, a fake smile plastered on her face.

I remember that smile. It was reserved for two types of people. Those she wants to impress but doesn't actually want to spend time with, and those that she's forced to spend time with out of politeness. I think we fall somewhere in the middle of those two.

"Yup, it's been a while." Diverting my eyes to the man next to her, I tip my chin with a mumbled, "Cal."

"Matthew," he responds, thankfully not using the same nickname McKenzie apparently refuses to give up.

Shifting my attention to look down at Avery, the last of the tension in my chest dissipates at the sight of her smile. There's nothing fake about it. In fact, there's nothing fake about Avery at all. The more I get to know her, the more I see that she's exactly what she seems. Maybe it's my history with McKenzie or being in the city all these years, but it's like a breath of fresh air being with her.

"Who's this?"

McKenzie's inquisitive voice draws me out of the hold that Avery's gaze has on me. Reluctantly, I break away from Avery's blue eyes that now remind me of the Christmas ornaments my mom used to put on our tree, especially in the glittering lights from the tents.

Fitting for my little elf.

"I'd like you to meet my girlfriend, Avery Geller."

"Girlfriend?" McKenzie squawks, rolling her eyes over Avery from top to bottom. "Your mom didn't mention anything about you having a girlfriend."

The reminder that Mom keeps McKenzie, and the town, updated about me, irks me, but at the same time, knowing that it's about me being with Avery makes it more—tolerable.

"We were keeping it quiet for a while. You know how my mom is. I tell her Avery and I are dating and the next thing I know, she's sending wedding invites," I joke. I was hoping to diffuse the situation, but now I see I made it even more awkward.

It brings up the memories of my mom telling the whole town that McKenzie and I were going to get married after university, only to have her engaged to Cal. I couldn't handle the level of pity and sadness on everyone's face whenever they tried to talk to me. It's one thing that pushed me to move to Vancouver sooner than I had planned.

Then there's the way Avery is holding on to my waist so tightly I can feel her nails bite into me through my clothes. I feel bad knowing she didn't sign up for things to move this quickly. I *may* have downplayed how intense my mom can be. While she won't be sending out actual invites, knowing my mom, the town will know every detail we give her about the relationship before the end of the night.

"Right," McKenzie says unconvincingly before turning to Avery. "It's nice to meet you, Ava."

"Avery," she corrects with a beaming smile.

"Sure." McKenzie's tone is flat before she turns to Cal, patting him on the chest, the large ring on her left hand shining in the winter sun. The size of the diamond is something that I never would have been able to afford during our time together. Even now, I can't help but think that the price would be equivalent to the down payment of a home, possibly even the outright purchase of one in a town like Gingerbread Grove.

"Matty, you remember this stunning man here from all those years ago." She blinks her eyes up at me as she gives his chest another pat. "Angela, this is Cal."

"It's Avery," she grits through her now forced smile. "And as you probably remember, *Matthew* doesn't like to be called any nicknames."

A sense of pride surges through me as Avery corrects her about my nickname. Like my mom, it's always been pointless to correct McKenzie as she never listened, even when we were dating.

"Oh, Matty. What's a nickname between friends, right?" McKenzie insists, her fake smile getting wider.

"It's Matthew," I correct firmly, with more confidence than I've had in a long time.

"It's nice to meet you, Avery," Cal says, shooting a sideways look at his wife. "Welcome to Gingerbread Grove. You're just in time for the kickoff to the Yuletide Games. I hope you and Matthew are going to sign up and compete."

"We were thinking about it," Avery say, smiling up at me.

She takes my breath away when her smile shifts to one that is genuine. True. One that I know is for me because now that she's met McKenzie and seen Gingerbread Grove, I think she gets it. She understands why I was hesitant to come back alone and face all of this without someone by my side.

"So…what about Mitch? He didn't come back here with you?" McKenzie asks, her voice getting higher the longer we are talking.

I know it's her sign that she's getting frustrated with the conversation. Likely, because I'm not showing up like the heartbroken fool I was years ago.

Another reason I will be forever in Avery's debt. Even though I haven't wished to be with my ex-girlfriend for years, I no doubt would have tried to avoid her at all costs rather than be reminded that I'm alone.

Except now, I don't have to be.

"He's still in Vancouver." Even though I don't want to, I draw my gaze away from Avery, scanning the crowd to see if there's any way of getting us out of his conversation. "He's running the office while I'm here."

"You two were always inseparable," McKenzie muses.

"And you still are, aren't you, babe?" Avery says. "You should hear all the things these two get up to in the city; isn't that right, Matthew? But I guess you don't have much time to get into too much trouble anymore now that your company has taken off the way it has. These two work harder than anyone I know!"

"Uh, yeah." I cover my mouth with my hands to hide my laugh listening to Avery's antics. I don't know where Avery is going with this as she's never even met Mitch, but I'm letting her roll with it and enjoying the entertainment while she's doing it.

"I'm not sure 'Matthew' and 'trouble' have ever been uttered in the same sentence before," McKenzie utters under her breath.

Avery hugs me tighter as her smile becomes more strained, and she glares at McKenzie in a way that's almost terrifying. "I guess that's what happens when you lose touch with people. They change. Grow. *Move on.*"

I wonder just how many of those true crime podcasts she's listened to.

"Anyway…" Cal says, clearing his throat. "Happy to have you back, Matthew. You'll be a last minute entry as a couple, but I'll be sure to add both of your names to the games and get a schedule sent off to you."

Avery continues her stare off with McKenzie as she speaks. "Thank you, Cal. Babe, do you mind showing me that tent with the apple cider you were telling me about? I can smell it from here and it smells amazing."

"Of course," I answer blankly as I try to decipher the silent war the two women seem to be having. "I guess we'd better get going, then."

"Nice seeing you two." With another nod, Cal leads his wife off in the opposite direction, whispering frantically to her as they walk through the snow-lined path.

"So that was McKenzie…"

"Yup." I turn and lead her toward the tents, needing space from whatever just happened.

Amidst the tension in that conversation, there's something

else that I'm feeling. I can only hope that she's feeling the same thing, too. I don't know if I'll be able to put myself out there just to be hurt—to find out that she was only faking this whole time. Whatever this is feels real—like, *really* real—and I don't know if I like it.

Needing to break the spell she has over me at the moment, I take my arm from around her shoulders and grab her hand, linking her fingers with mine. We both walk in silence as we toss our now-empty coffee cups in the trash before making our way towards the cider tent.

"That was…" I start, not knowing how to address the terror that just happened.

"Interesting." Avery finishes, squeezing my hand. "I don't get it."

"Get what?"

"You and McKenzie."

"I know." And there it is. It's what most people thought when we were together. The popular girl and the geek. Most thought she was with me to help her study or there were rumours that I was secretly rich from selling a computer game—neither were true. What happened was that we were just two people who felt lost in high school and somehow found each other. When she wasn't putting on a front of being the popular cheerleader, she was quiet and unsure of herself. She was smarter than she ever let anyone believe she was, and funny. So funny. We would spend hours laughing as we drove the back roads of town, talking about everything we wanted to do with our lives that didn't involve Woodland Springs.

But on the outside? She was so far out of my reach that I didn't deserve to be in the same realm.

"I mean, sure, she's pretty, but I don't get it. She's so… mean."

"Wait, what?" I stop us, facing her, but still keeping our hands linked.

"I don't want to say anything negative but, that's not who I pictured you with."

"Because she's out of my league? I know."

"No! Matthew!" With her free hand, she reaches up and cups my cheek, making sure that my attention is solely on her —which it is.

Now that we're holding hands *and* she's brushing her thumb along my skin, I barely register there's anything outside of the two of us. Nothing except for the light snow that's starting to fall. I only even notice that because flakes land on her eyelashes, making her look like a snow princess.

"That's the exact opposite of what I mean."

I'm about to open my mouth and ask her to explain when I hear my name being called behind me.

"Matthew? Matthew Roberts? Is that you?" Agnes Miller's eyes open wide in shock as she calls us over to her tent. "I didn't know you were back in town!"

"Really? My mom didn't broadcast it across the town square?" I joke, but knowing my mom, she was likely one step away from doing just that the moment I walked through the door last night. I know she was messaging on a group chat she has with some of the other women in town.

I swear my mom with a cell phone should be considered a weapon.

"She mentioned you were heading home to help with the store after your dad took the fall, but I didn't know it would be this quickly. Welcome back!" She turns her attention to Avery. "And who is this you have with you?"

"This is my girlfriend, Avery." Referring to anyone as 'my girlfriend' feels odd, but I find the more I use it to describe Avery, the more I like the sound of it. "Avery, I'd like you to meet Agnes Miller. She makes the best caramel apple cider that you've ever tasted."

"Oh, you." Agnes waves her hand at me as a blush rises in her face. The woman may be older than my mom, but she still blushes like a teenager when it comes to her apple cider. "It's a pleasure to meet you, Avery. And girlfriend? Another thing your mom didn't mention to me on our knitting nights. I'm going to have to have a word with that woman. Keeping us up to date on everything but this!"

"It's not her fault, Mrs. Miller. I kept it from her too because it's so new. She only just found out herself this morning. She hasn't even met Avery yet."

I try not to cringe when I think back to the conversation. There were a lot of raised voices and a few tears from my mom over the breakfast table.

"Well, how wonderful is it that you're back, and with your girlfriend, just in time for Christmas? And you're able to make it for the kickoff of the games tonight."

"We wouldn't miss it," Avery adds with a smile—a genuine one.

"How wonderful. And your mom will be in for a lovely surprise." Mrs. Miller grabs two cups and passes them to us. "Here, take these and enjoy a bit of the market before your mom gets here. I bet once she gets ahold of the two of you, you won't have a moment to yourselves."

"Thank you," I say honestly, taking the cup from her, immediately wrapped in the scent of apples, cinnamon, and caramel.

It's like a scent from my childhood. Mrs. Miller has been making and selling cider during the holiday for as long as I remember. Even before Woodland Springs became Christmas-crazy, it was a tradition that everyone looked forward to, no matter what they were doing to celebrate. As owner of the town cafe, she would create seasonal drinks that would instantly spark a connection for me that lasted until today. The smell of lemonade is summer, pumpkins are fall, and apple is winter.

I found out at my stop at what is now called the Ginger-Brew Cafe that Mrs. Miller retired when the town changed everything to Gingerbread and it's now being run by her daughter, Rebecca. I see that Mrs. Miller still comes out for the holidays to make her famous apple cider.

"Yes, thank you," Avery adds, accepting her own cup. "I've only heard amazing things about your cider. I can't wait to try it for myself."

I couldn't help but watch as Mrs. Miller holds on to Avery's mug for just a little longer as she lowers her voice and says, "Thank you for bringing Matthew back to us."

There it is, the stab of guilt to the gut that I had been expecting.

While I had been doing my best to avoid anything to do with the holidays, my family, and the town, I realized that everything wasn't all bad. I have fond memories of playing with my friends in this town square. Of growing up in a small town that was safe and happy. While having everyone know everything about you was annoying, it could also be comforting. If you needed help, someone was there. Lost? Someone would point the way. Hungry? There was a town full of people that would feed you off their own plate.

And some had many times while growing up for one reason or another.

That was something the city would never be able to compete with.

"Oh, I didn't have much to do with that," Avery adds.

That's not true. She had a lot to do with it.

"I'm not just talking about him being in town, dear. He seems like his old self, before that whole mishap with the mayor's wife. He hasn't been here for so long, but he's back here with you."

"Oh, I'm just here to help my dad..." I add, but I am waved off.

"Thank you," Mrs. Miller adds again to Avery before giving her a pat on her hands and moving on to the next person in line.

Have I changed? What did the town see in me, or think of me, that makes the mere fact that I'm in town helping my dad such an amazing feat that it needs to be pointed out?

Am I really as heartless as that sounds?

"Hey, are you all right?" Avery asks, placing her hand on my arm and giving me a squeeze.

"Yeah. I—I guess I just never thought much about how me leaving might have affected the people in town. I didn't think anyone other than my parents even noticed."

"I'd say they noticed." Avery stops and takes a sip of her drink. "Oh my goodness, this *is* the best apple cider I've ever tasted."

"I told you." I grin as I take a sip of my own. "Hey, there's something else I want to show you."

Grabbing Avery's free hand, I lead her off to the corner of the town square, checking to make sure no one is watching us.

There may have been a lot that has changed since I left Woodland Springs, but there's one thing that I know will always stay the same.

Chapter Eleven

AVERY

My palms are sweaty as I let Matthew lead me through the busy square. He doesn't stop as people say 'hello' and try to start a conversation with him. By the time we reach the edge of the market, the booths, products, and townspeople are just as much of a blur as the quickly falling snow.

Upbeat Christmas carols play from speakers, singing of finding love at Christmas.

How ironic.

"This place is wonderful, Matthew," I say as I try to keep up with his pace. "Can we check out more of the booths after…wherever we're going?"

"It has its perks," he says as he slows down to a stroll. "And of course, I'm sorry. You wanted to look at those bath bombs."

He looks over my shoulder back at the market, only seeming to have half of his attention on our conversation.

"Are you okay?" I ask, looking behind me to try to see what he's looking at. "Are we being followed? Is McKenzie coming?" I stop in shock as I look back at him. "Oh my goodness, you *are* a serial killer, aren't you? I can't believe I didn't listen to my sister and her warnings…"

"What? No, I'm not a serial killer. It's..." he trails off before his eyes shoot behind me. "We have to go. *Now*."

The next thing I know, Matthew tugs on my hand and I'm being pulled through cedar bushes. I wasn't prepared for the jarring realization we were going through the bushes. Unlike everything else in the square, there weren't any lights or decorations on them. In fact, if Matthew hadn't pulled me this way, I wouldn't have even realized they were right in front of me. But boy am I aware of them now.

The pointed branches slap my face and snow slides over my eyes and through my hair. I want to bat it away but between Matthew and my apple cider, I have no hands to defend myself.

"Matthew, pulling me through bushes out of the eyesight of the town is *not* the way to convince me you aren't a serial killer."

I hear a huff before he stops abruptly, causing me to knock into him, splashing a bit of my apple cider out of the lid of my cup. I frown as I stare at it. If this is going to be my last drink before becoming his next victim, I want to be able to enjoy every last drop of it.

"I want to show you something." His voice is soft and filled with an emotion I can't place.

Once my eyes readjust from being battered with branches, I stand in wonder at the vision in front of me. I'm greeted by a beautiful moonlit garden filled with snow-dusted holly bushes and pots filled with different winter plants that seem to thrive in the cold. We're surrounded by evergreen trees and the hedges that I had just sworn as my arch nemesis—but I see now they have a purpose. They hide the people enclosed within these walls from prying eyes while looking like regular ol' greenery from the outside.

"What is this place?" I can't hide the awe and wonder in my voice as I grip his hand and take it all in.

"No longer thinking I'm luring you here to by my next victim?" he jokes.

"I never said that," I say as I bump my hip into his and roll my eyes.

"It's a little garden the locals like to keep to themselves," he continues, leading me toward the middle. "The hedges and trees are used to keep tourists out. We like to keep it just for ourselves. "

I smile, hearing how he includes himself as one of the townspeople.

The snow crunches under our boots as we approach a bench. Matthew lets go of my hand to brush off the built-up snow, and I already miss his warmth. It's funny how small things like that make you realize how close you've gotten to someone in a short amount of time.

Even if I thought he was going to murder me.

"Are you starting to get many tourists here in Gingerbread Grove?"

He motions with his hand to the space he just cleared, and I sit, enjoying the return of his warmth as he sits next to me. I lean back, take a sip of my apple cider and try to appear calm as he rests his free arm long the back of the bench, brushing along my shoulders.

"I hear that it's picking up, especially as the Inn is getting closer to being opened. I know they were hoping for it to be opened in time for Christmas, but my mom said there was something about delays, and as she put it 'sabotage from those Candy Cane Creekers.'"

"There's a real feud going on, huh?" I take another sip of my apple cider. Even though it's significantly cooled off, the warm spices of cinnamon and cloves filled my body with warmth.

It's either that or having Matthew so close to my side.

"I know far too much about it, if you ask me." He takes a

sip of his own cider as he stares off at the flowers in front of us. "When I left, there wasn't a feud or any issues that I know of. But then Cal became mayor and started telling everyone that we could be just as much of a destination town as Candy Cane Creek and there was no reason that they need to 'hog the holiday thunder.'"

"There's a campaign slogan for ya," I joke.

He chuckles. "Exactly. Next thing I know, I hear that the town has changed its name and most of the people are on board to make it seem as if the town is literally made out of gingerbread. Businesses changed their names. Street names were swapped for festive ones. I heard they even lobbied the province to have all government buildings play along, but they wouldn't have it."

"I would think not. What about those that didn't like the change?"

A heavy sigh erupts from Matthew. "They left. Pushed out with anything remaining of Woodland Springs."

"That's sad." As much as I love the idea of a Christmas-themed town, I wouldn't wish anyone losing their home or friends because of it. "But what does Candy Cane Creek have to do with the Inn being held up?"

"Well, they can't prove that it was anyone from Candy Cane Creek, but blueprints would go missing right before a decision was made by the city council, contractors would refuse to work with the town after committing to the job, things like that."

"Why would they want to do that? Wouldn't tourists to Gingerbread Grove be good for Candy Cane Creek, too?"

"That's what I think, but what do I know. I don't live here anymore."

Sadness returns to his voice, and it physically hurts my heart. Even though I know he was gone before the town started to change, I can't help but wonder if he feels like one of the townspeople that was pushed out, too. I know there was the rift with his parents and the store, but it seems deeper than that. But I don't think now is the time.

"So, why the hidden garden?"

"I don't know the full reasoning. It's been this way my whole life. I can ask my mom, she's more up to date on every-thing that goes on in the town, but I think that as it started to grow, the original members wanted something just for them. They're happy to share everything else, but this place is special. I think it has to do with the original founders."

"I wonder what they would think about all the changes," I muse. Letting my gaze drift over to the corner, I tilt my head and gasp. "Is that a well?"

"Oh that," Matthew says, acting as if it were the most natural thing in the world to have a well in the middle of a modern town. "That's the original water source for Woodland Springs. Other than the springs themselves, of course. Before everything was developed into what it is now, the people would come here and get their water. It's why the square was built next to it. But the more people moved to town and the number of tourists grew, the more trash and destruction we would see with it. The town wanted to do something to protect it, even if it's not where the water comes from anymore."

The grey-bricked well is topped with wooden posts, an old-fashioned wooden rope pulley and a hinged roof. The only lights inside the garden are the faint warm-white string that lines the edge of the roof. It reminds me of something out of a fairy tale. In what I'm learning is typical Gingerbread Grove fashion; it's currently adorned with red ribbons and solar red and green decorative lights.

"Why do you talk like you aren't part of the town anymore? The people here seem to think you clearly still are."

"I haven't been a part of the town for a long time, Avery." He answers, looking down at the cup in his hand.

I know there's more to the story, but it's not my place to push. Well, no more than I already have. I have to remind myself that I'm not here for a long time. There's no reason for me to try to jump in and fix things—if I even could—because I won't be in Matthew's life long enough to really make a difference.

Plus, for the sake of my own heart, there's no reason to get any more involved than I already am.

"Well, if you ever decide that you want to be again, even just for the time you're here, I'm sure they would welcome you with open arms."

"I'm sure they would," he answers coolly, still looking down at his drink as if it has the answers to all of his problems.

I feel a stab in my own heart with the sadness laced through his words. I don't want him to be sad. I want him to feel like he belongs, wherever it is that he wants to be. With whoever he chooses to be with.

"Hey," I say, shifting in my seat so that I'm facing him, but can still feel the warmth of his arm along my back. I may be selfish in wanting to feel his touch when I really have no right to, but I'll take whatever I can get. "Forget about them for right now. What do *you* want to do?"

"Other than go back home to Vancouver?" The corner of his mouth ticks up in a coy smile, calming a little of the pain in my heart.

"Is that what you really want? To run again?"

"Ouch, right to the point." Matthew places his hand over his chest and clutches it dramatically.

"Only to those that don't want to face the truth and answer the hard questions they are trying to avoid."

So much for not getting involved.

Matthew sits quietly for a moment, staring at the well. I wonder if I've pushed him too hard. Just a moment ago I didn't want to get involved and now here I am, sticking my nose right in it. I can't help it. There's something about Matthew Roberts that makes me want to get to know him. I want to ease his pain and right any wrong that's been done to him. Even if I thought he was a serial killer leading me to my last moments in this hidden garden, I know deep down he's a good guy.

"Maybe I was running," he answers after a long pause, still not bringing his gaze from the well.

"Why? You didn't do anything wrong." I reach over, placing my hand on his arm.

"Maybe not, but I was embarrassed. Who doesn't know their girlfriend is dating someone else? Engaged to someone else?"

"More people than you think," I whisper, trying not to think of my own situation.

Even though it's entirely too similar to his, I can't help but think how easy it is to lose someone you thought was your everything. Someone who you were convinced thought the same of you, only to find out it had all been a lie.

Closing my eyes, I will the tears not to come. I feel them threatening to spill as my own hurt and guilt at not seeing the warning signs with Maxwell rush through me. *I'm* one of those people. *I* didn't see it coming. *I* was completely shocked when he opened that door to find him having a romantic dinner with someone that wasn't me.

"I'm so sorry, Avery."

Warm hands cup my cheeks and brush away my tears. I lean into them, letting him wipe away the hurt that comes with thinking of my selfish ex-boyfriend. Especially when right in front of me is someone who would never treat another person like that. Someone that gets how I feel.

"It was thoughtless of me to say that," he continues, still brushing his thumbs over my skin even though I think the tears have stopped. "Of course you know what it's like."

Opening my eyes, I find myself lost in his. For the first time, they remind me a little of gingerbread themselves decorated with green and gold glitter, which I find ironic and hilarious at the same time.

"Something funny?'" he asks with a smile of his own.

"Nothing, I…" I lose my train of thought as I watch the snow fall around us, dusting Matthew's hair and wetting his glasses. The only light is from the moon in the cloudless sky and the faint lights from the well. The sounds from the market are more distant now, like the soft hum of a song in the background. If anything, it's as if there's only the two of us in the whole square.

"Avery…" His voice trails off as we keep staring into each other's eyes.

"Yes, Matthew?" My voice is breathless as I try to figure out what he's thinking. What he is almost saying.

I want to know why he brought me here to the secret garden. Why he's cupping my cheeks and looking at me like he wants to kiss me. No one is around. There's no one to impress or convince we are a couple. Anything we are experiencing now is just for us. That's both exhilarating and terrifying at the same time.

Without a word, he leans in and brushes his lips softly against mine. My breath hitches as his fingers curl into my hair, holding me close. I can't think, can't breathe. My hands move on their own as I grasp on to his forearms, as we pull apart slowly, our foreheads touching as we catch our breath.

Keeping my eyes closed, I let the lingering rush of our kiss remain on my lips. I feel as heated as if I were warming by the fire. I'm sure my cheeks are flushed, as the white puff of our breaths mix together between us.

"Matthew! There you are!"

A loud feminine voice pulls me out of my post-kiss bliss. Eyes wide, my gaze darts to the small older woman with her hands on her hips, the expression on her face that is levelled at Matthew, a mixture of frustration and love.

Matthew sighs before sitting straight and taking my hand. He stands, pulling me up with him.

"Hi, Mom. I'd like you to meet my girlfriend."

Chapter Twelve

MATTHEW

Of all the ways I expected my mom to meet Avery, this isn't one of them.

My palms are sweaty as I hold on tightly to her hand, grasping for any amount of strength Avery is willing to give me at the moment.

When I told Mom about Avery this morning, it had gone worse than expected. Well, I didn't really know what to expect, exactly, but what happened wasn't it. In hindsight, I should have waited until after breakfast when there weren't breakables around. Possibly after I'd finished my cup of coffee to prepare for the full wrath of my mother, but I just wanted to get it over with.

"What do you mean you have a girlfriend, Matty? Why didn't you tell me? Why are you just telling me now? You've been back home for a full eight hours!" Mom exclaims after dropping her butter knife, letting it clatter against her plate.

And I attempted to sleep for at least five of those hours…

Dad winces and glances over—likely making sure the plate didn't break—before picking up his coffee and taking a sip.

"It's still new, Mom. We didn't want to say anything until we were sure it was going anywhere."

"*And is it? Are you going to marry this girl? Richard, are you hearing this?*"

"*I heard him,*" Dad replies flatly, his attention back on his newspaper.

"*I'm telling you now.*" I try to keep the frustration out of my voice, needing to smooth the news over. "*And she's coming to the square this morning. You'll meet her there.*"

Which is exactly where I intended for my mom to meet Avery.

But now, here she is.

Did I think she would follow us into the well and interrupt our first kiss?

"Mrs. Roberts!" Avery says, jumping up. "It's so nice to meet you."

I'm stunned for a second, saddened at the loss of connection with her before I come to my senses and stand as well.

"I assume you're Avery. You'll have to forgive me, Matty here didn't even tell me you existed until a few hours ago. I knew when I saw you two sneak in here from across the square, I had to come and introduce myself."

Of course she did.

"We weren't sneaking, Mom. I wanted to show her the garden." I don't even bother trying to hide how exasperated I am.

"Whatever you say, dear," Mom replies in a tone that lets me know she's anything other than sorry.

"Please don't blame Matthew, Mrs. Roberts, it's all my fault we didn't tell anyone about us right away." My mom opens her mouth to answer, but Avery continues. "See, I just got out of a not-so-great relationship. I was worried that if we said anything too quickly, we would jinx it. My family was a little too attached to my ex-boyfriend, you see. They didn't understand that there was no way we were getting back together."

I grab Avery's hand, lacing her fingers with mine, giving it a light squeeze. I know she's doing that thing where she rambles when she's nervous. I feel the need to rub my chest, feeling the uncomfortable pressure that I know all too well, wondering if she feels the same when she does this. And then I realize that there's a lot about her that I don't know but want to. Like, is what she's saying true? She hasn't talked much about her family, and she certainly hasn't discussed what they thought of Maxwell.

Why didn't I ask? Am I that selfish that I didn't see past my own family problems to not even think about asking how all of this would affect hers?

"Is that true, Matty?"

I snap out of my thoughts to find both women looking at me. Lost in my selfish thoughts—again.

I must look as bewildered as I feel because Avery repeats herself.

Coming to my rescue.

Again.

"You were so sweet, making sure you gave me the time I needed. But you insisted on bringing me to meet your family for Christmas. Isn't that right?"

"Yes. Christmas."

Two words. She's here saving me from the wrath of my mother, and I give her two words.

"He's told me such wonderful things about Gingerbread Grove; I just couldn't wait to see it for myself. It's everything I hoped it would be," Avery continues excitedly.

Mom's face lights up at the mention of the town. "Yes, we Gingerbreadians have worked hard to create the utmost authenticity for the town. Santa himself would be proud."

"I would say so," Avery agrees.

"On that note, we should get going if we are going." There. I found words.

Yay me.

"Of course. You wouldn't want to miss the lantern lighting," Mom says, eyeing me suspiciously. "Speaking of, I ran into Cal and McKenzie on the way in here. They mentioned that you two were joining the games. Yet another thing you neglected to tell me."

I know I'll be interrogated when I get back to the house tonight.

"The lantern lighting?" Avery asks, giving me a questioning look while keeping the smile on her face.

"Oh, yes. All the couples that are taking part in the games have a lantern with their names written on it. They will be lit tonight and as each couple gets eliminated from the games, their lantern gets blown out."

"This is starting to sound less like a Christmas event and more like some type of winter *Survivor*," Avery mutters to me.

"You're telling me. This is the first I've heard of this," I whisper back, not taking my eyes off my mom, who's looking at us with an odd expression on her face. I don't know if she's about to jump for joy or burst into an angry tirade. With her, either is likely.

"Avery, you must join us for dinner tomorrow," she says suddenly, her smile shifting from a little sinister to something resembling a genuine smile.

"No, Mom," I say at the same time Avery says, "I'd love to."

Avery shoots me a side gaze that I know very well is telling me to keep quiet. So I do.

"Perfect. Matty will close the store at six, so how about six-thirty?"

"We have the sledding competition, remember?" I add, thankful that we have a way to get out of the dinner. I'm not ready for Avery to be inundated with my parents. Not yet. If there's anything I can do to save her from this, I will.

"Oh, well, another night, then." She shoots me a glare that lets me know that I'll be hearing about this later, too. "Let's get off to the lantern lighting, shall we? I'll see you two out there." Mom gives me another appraising look before disappearing through the cedar hedges.

"So that was your mom," Avery says, still looking at where Mom disappeared from.

"That's my mom..." I say, still struggling to find words. When my brain manages to catch up with what happened, I turn to Avery and cup her cheek, bringing her attention to me. "Thank you."

"That's what I'm here for. Thwarting parental conflicts. Saving the Christmas spirit. I'm a regular ol' holiday superhero."

"You are to me," I whisper.

I hold her gaze for a moment longer, reliving the moment before we were interrupted. I hadn't planned on kissing her when I brought her to the garden. I'd only wanted to show it to her, and give us a moment after the run in with McKenzie and Cal.

"I mean it, Avery. Thank you. I don't know what's wrong with me. I didn't mean to freeze like that."

"You're overwhelmed. You're back in your hometown, which doesn't feel like home, and you're forced to deal with the things you left behind. At Christmas. Which you don't like."

"I don't *not* like Christmas..." I try to protest, but she rolls her eyes.

"Fine, forced to face all of this during a holiday that isn't your favourite," she jokes.

I look over her shoulder, envisioning the scene that's going to welcome us on the other side of the hedges. The crowd of people as the whole town descends on the square to watch the lanterns being lit.

"Hey," she whispers, covering my hand on her cheek with her own while still clasping mine in the other. "You're doing great. Everyone believes us so far."

Yeah, maybe because I'm not entirely pretending.

Clearing my throat, I break away, dropping my hands and physical contact with her. The more I touch her, the more real this feels, and I can't have it become any more real than it already has.

"We should get going. The lantern ceremony is going to happen any minute."

"Of course, wouldn't want to miss that."

I don't know if I'm imagining it, but there's a sadness to her tone that guts me, knowing I put it there.

Turning to the hedges, I see her back straighten and shoulders drop, as if putting on a brave face for whatever we are about to encounter.

"So, do you need a magic password to get through these? Do I have to hold hands with a Gingerbreadian? Or does the old-fashioned 'just believe' work?"

I chuckle, in awe at how quickly she can recover from the moment we just had while still being able to crack a joke.

"I think it's just the 'I believe.' Although if that was the case, I'm not sure how it still lets me in here."

Facing me with her hands on her hips, she tilts her head and narrows her eyes. "I think you believe more than you let on, Mr. Roberts. Now come on and show me this Gingerbread Grove ceremony. If we make it through, you also still have bath bombs to show me, and my payment now includes a gingerbread cookie. Whatever it is the town has planned with lanterns sounds ominous, and I'm not sure we're actually going to make it through the evening. There's hope to land on a true crime podcast yet," she chuckles.

"This town may be quirky, but I don't think there's anything to fear from what they have planned," I chuckle. "And I will, of course, still take you for bath bombs and a cookie."

Three bags of Christmas-scented bath bombs, two cookies, and one reindeer knitted hat later; we are standing with the crowd in front of the tree.

"The tree is…"

"Ridiculous? Over-the-top?" I finish for her.

"Wonderful," she says as she turns to me, her face lit up brighter than the tree in the centre of the square.

Looking at it again, I try to see what she sees. To me, it's a sixty-foot fir splattered in red, white, and green with wooden gingerbread people and mismatched lights scattered throughout. It's nothing but a chaotic North Pole explosion.

There has to be more to it than that.

Quizzically, I glance back at her, seeing she still has the look of Christmas morning. The tree is creating a sense of magic that I don't understand, but for the first time, I want to.

Taking a deep breath, I face it again, trying to push aside any Scrooge-like bah humbugs that apparently fill my Christmas cheer.

Tilting my head, I look at it—really look at it. The decorations don't look as chaotic as I first thought. A mix of gingerbread men, women, and houses are evenly spaced across the towering branches. Red bows are accentuated by green and white curled ribbons, and a burlap garland. The strands of lights are wound around the tree in even spaces, and they blink in a cheery pattern that matches in time with the music if I look hard enough.

It's still more cartoon than classic, but it fits with the town.

"The topper is my favourite," Avery says in awe, looking up. The knitted cap with antlers mixed with her nose reddened from the cold makes her look even more adorable. "I never thought about using a gingerbread man as the topper, but it's so fitting."

The decoration in question has to be at least five feet tall and is surrounded by an eruption of even more red and green curled ribbon that seems to stick outright, defying gravity.

"Oh look, there they are!" she exclaims, pointing just past the tree to the gazebo. A dozen red and dark green lanterns hang from the beams of the structure, all unlit.

"Ladies and gentlemen, thank you so much for joining us for the kickoff of the annual Gingerbread Grove Yuletide Games!" Cal exclaims from the platform that is constructed in front of the tree, microphone in hand.

My hands move on their own, clapping slowly while the rest of the town cheers and hollers. Cal continues on—something about the 'revitalization of the town' and the history of the games—all with McKenzie glued to his side with an overly-enthusiastic smile on her face.

I should be paying attention, or at least pretending to be, but seeing the tree through a Christmas lens has me interested in looking at the rest of the town, seeing if maybe there's something I've been missing. I haven't been back since they had made the full change to Gingerbread Grove. The last time I was here, there were still normal street signs and regular storefronts.

Now, the red-bricked stores on Main Street that I grew up on are adorned with white gingerbread trim along their awnings; their windows painted with colourful holiday reindeer, snowmen, and elves, much like the stores back home in Vancouver. The street lights are wrapped in red and green ribbons—not to be confused with the red and white ones from Candy Cane Creek. I still cringe thinking of the phone call from my mom months ago, letting me know every detail from the town hall meeting when there was a concern brought up that the particular decoration was too close to their rival town.

"Now, without further ado, let's get the couples up here and get these lanterns lit!"

Cal's voice and the excited energy bring my attention back. With everything that's happened in the last few days, I hadn't thought through just how public these games are going to be. I didn't realize that the lantern lighting meant Avery and I literally getting up in front of the town and lighting our lantern with the other couples.

The pressing weight returns to my chest as I see everyone start to make their way to the front. Cold sweat breaks out across my forehead, and I swear I start to see black dots in front of my eyes.

"Hey, we've got this," Avery whispers as she grabs my hand and gives it a squeeze.

Inhaling deeply, I let her scent of warm spices of apple cider and gingerbread soothe me. My shoulders drop and my muscles relax. I don't know what it is, but there's something about her that makes me feel like maybe I do, in fact, have this.

She waits for a moment to make sure I'm okay—the black dots are retreating—and I nod, letting her lead me through the cheering crowd. I avoid all eye contact as I walk the few steps up the gazebo, scanning the lanterns which have glittery ornaments hanging from the bottoms that match the lanterns themselves, each couple's name written in an elegant gold cursive.

It didn't take long to find ours. The bright red paint on the metal mixed with the shiny writing may as well have been a blinking beacon of 'Matthew Roberts and Avery Geller' the way that it glitters in light. A single unlit candle sits inside the glass walls, waiting to be lit. But knowing my luck, it won't stay lit for very long.

And we're right in front. For everyone to see.

Looking down at the crowd, I see McKenzie with her fake beaming smile. She had to have planned this. She knows how much I hate being in front of crowds and especially being the centre of attention.

"Hey, you okay?" Avery whispers, holding on to my hand even tighter.

"Just great," I reply dryly, looking away from McKenzie's smug look.

Yup, she definitely planned this.

"Let's countdown the lighting of the lanterns!" It's Trevor

that announces it this time as Cal and McKenzie make their way up to the gazebo, standing on the other side of the stairs from us. Cal nods as they take their spot, and McKenzie has her smile frozen on her face.

"Is her face always like that?" Avery asks through her own polite—and less creepy—smile, never taking her eyes off the other woman.

"Pretty much," I whisper back, needing to look away.

But I don't have anywhere else *to* look. There are too many people in the crowd. I swear the whole town is here. I can turn my back and look behind us. So, I do the only thing I can —I look down at Avery.

She's smiling up at me and all of a sudden, I don't notice the crowd anymore. Well, not as much anyway. Even though we're up on this gazebo, in full display of the town, it's just us.

It's just us as someone passes us a lighter.

Still just us, as Trevor starts to count down.

Something is different.

It's the woman smiling up at me while counting down from ten.

By the time we hit five, I'm counting down with her, never taking my eyes from hers.

By three, I'm smiling.

By one, my heart wants to explode with a rush of emotions I'm feeling about Avery Geller.

Cheers erupt around us as everyone lights their lantern. I open the glass door and let Avery light the candle, but I still focus my attention on her.

I should be panicking. There should be a tightening feeling in my chest knowing that Avery and my names are on one of these ridiculous lanterns, even though we aren't really a couple. But there's no panic. No pressure building inside of me. Instead, all I can think about is Avery. My beautiful elf, clad in an absurd reindeer toque, who's looking up at me like maybe I'm not the only one feeling this way.

"Matthew?" she says, breathlessly.

"Yes, Avery?"

"I think I like it here."

Before I know what's happening, I say, "Me too."

Chapter Thirteen

MATTHEW

Standing behind the counter of Nutmeg & Nails, formerly Roberts & Sons Hardware, I watch as June Williamson bends down and inspects a tree stand, the clear rain bonnet that covers her white hair still slowly dripping snowflakes down the sides.

She's been looking at the same one for the last ten minutes, mumbling something before looking around, huffing, and going back to the stand.

I tilt my head to the side, wondering if she's lost in thought or genuinely confused about tree stands. "Can I help you?"

"Oh, yes, maybe," she says, placing her hand on her knee and pushing herself up. "I don't know what sort of tree stand to get. Ours broke last year and, well, there seems to be a lot more choices than there were the last time we had to buy one. What do you know about them?"

"They hold up your tree. There's not much more to know." I sigh, picking up the price tag gun and placing stickers on the latest shipment of wood glue.

"You would think, but your stock here suggests otherwise. Do I get the good old-fashioned one, or are any of these new fangled stands good? And why on earth would you need a spinning one?"

"Depends on if you want to decorate all the sides of your tree. But isn't the best part of having a back so you can hide the worst side?"

"Oh, good point." June taps her perfectly manicured finger against her chin as she turns back to the boxes in front of her.

I watch her briefly before going back to my task of pricing glue. This wasn't what I pictured when I thought I was coming back to help run the store. I had convinced myself that I would just help the odd customer that came in, take a shipment or two, and make sure the shelves were stocked. I thought that I would be able to spend most of my day doing my actual work behind the desk while taking a break to help with the store, but that hasn't been the case. I may have only been here a few days, but I already feel like I'm falling behind on everything I thought I would be able to do.

Which makes me think of Avery.

It's been three days since I got the life-changing call from my mom.

Two days since I packed up my life, left the city, and had Avery Geller blow her way in.

One day since our kiss in the garden changed everything I thought I wanted.

I'm not a romantic. I don't believe in soul mates or fate, but I know something bigger than me has been working at throwing Avery and me together. There's no way that she just so happens to need to get to the same place I do, suggests we fake date, and then have said dating be more real than I expected.

Looking around the store, I don't know what God's plan is bringing me back here—and to the shop—especially since it's something I swore I would never do.

But here I am.

The bell over the door rings, drawing my gaze up from my task. A burst of blustery air rushes into the store behind a bundle of red wool.

"Matty! There you are!" A booming voice beneath the wool sounds as the shop door shuts with a thud.

"Mom, where else would I be? You called me here to work the store, remember?" I roll my eyes, placing another price stamp on a bottle of wood glue.

"Oh, you! You're as bad as your father." She waves her hand at me as she turns to the other woman. "June, it's good to see you. We missed you at the quilting club this week. We finished up the gingerbread potholders that we're going to sneak over to Candy Cane Creek."

"You're going to do what?" I ask, placing the price tag gun down.

"Oh relax, Matty. It's just a little harmless fun. We're just going to hang them around the town. The worst we'll do is throw gingerbread house quilts over their bushes."

"And why would you do that?" I take off my glasses and pinch my nose, wondering just what parallel universe I walked into.

"Just so they know who the real heroes of Christmas are, of course," June answers.

"Of course," I sigh. Because of course the most natural thing to do would be to throw gingerbread items around town like you're rebels with toilet paper and too much time on their hands.

"I'm sorry I missed that," June continues. "I had to take Henry into town for an appointment. Now that you're here, I need your opinion. Which tree stand is best?"

"Just the traditional. No reason for all the fancy nonsense. Plus, you want to be able to hide the thin side of your tree."

I chuckle, which I then have to hide in a cough once both women snap their attention to me. Hearing her confirm what I had suggested already brings up memories of her making dad turn the tree endlessly so she could figure out which was best. I would sit on the couch with my brother and a bowl of popcorn as we watched Mom decorate the tree, only to have her change her mind and make Dad turn the tree again and again. Only then would she settle for having it the way she'd done it originally.

On second thought, maybe rotating stands would save husbands from afternoons of tedious tree turning.

"You're right, thank you, Sharon." June grabs the standard tree stand and brings it up to me at the counter. "I'll take this one, please."

"And be sure to give her the friends and family discount, dear," Mom says, giving me a pointed look. "She's been a loyal customer since your dad opened this shop. Her Henry has, too. We need to remember to reward such loyalty." Mom pats June's arm while giving her a warm smile.

"Of course," I say as I ring up her purchase, being sure to hit the discount button.

This is the first I've ever heard of a friends and family discount since all of Gingerbread Grove would fall under one of those two categories, but I'm not going to argue with her over a couple of dollars, especially since there's a large red button on the screen that is all but yelling at me to be tapped.

But now I'm wondering if I need to look closer into the books for the store. If Dad's giving everyone a discount, there's no way he's making a decent profit with these prices.

Mom and June continue chatting about whatever prank the town is plotting against Candy Cane Creek when my phone rings, lighting up Mitch's name on the screen. Moving quickly, I bag the tree stand and pass it to June before mumbling some half-hearted excuse about some inflatable gingerbread scenes that just arrived in our latest shipment that need sorting.

I wish that sentence was made up. It's not, but that's not the reason I'm escaping from the main part of the store.

"Mitch," I answer on what I'm sure was to be the last ring as I slip into my dad's office in the back, closing the door behind me. I don't bother hiding the annoyed—and slightly winded—tone to my voice.

"Going well in Gingerbread Grove, I see," he chuckles.

"How are things back there?" I don't want to talk about the last couple of days; I don't want to talk about the town, and I especially don't want to talk about Avery. Not to Mitch. There are a lot of people I can lie to and hide things from, but he's not one of them.

"Same old. Everything is under control." Mitch continues, filling me in on our clients and upcoming projects. I pace the small room as I listen, dodging piles of boxes and tacky Christmas decorations as I go. I've tried to work remotely the last couple of days when I haven't been at the store or with Avery, but I'm quickly starting to realize there aren't enough hours in the day to do everything.

"Don't worry about it. I'll be able to finish those files this weekend and get it back to you with plenty of time left." I grab a pen off the desk and start twirling it with my fingers.

The anxious feeling I've become so accustomed to begins spreading in my chest. I knew I was going to be spreading myself thin, working alone at the shop all day and then doing my actual job at night and weekends, but it's what I'm going to have to do while I'm here in Gingerbread Grove. What I hadn't expected was Avery and being entered into the Yule-tide Games.

"So, what happened with your trip up? I heard most of the flights out of Vancouver have been cancelled since the day you left."

"Uh, yeah" I slam the pen down on the desk harder than I mean to. Bringing my hand up to my chest, I start to rub the fiery burn that erupts over my sternum. "It was no big deal. I just rented a car and drove."

"That must have been fun," Mitch says sarcastically. "Driving alone at night on the Coquihalla? I'm surprised you didn't turn around and wait it out until the next flight."

"I was going to, but my mom called as soon as she saw my flight was cancelled and, well, you know her." I never realized you could track flights that aren't yours in real time, but my mom figured that one out. I wait a moment before admitting the next bit of information. The one that I was going to keep to myself, but the burning feeling in my chest increases the longer I hold it in. "And I wasn't alone."

"What do you mean you weren't alone? Who did you drive with?"

"I sorta met this elf who was also flying to Kamloops, and she talked me into giving her a ride when I took the last rental."

"An...elf..." he repeats.

"Well, obviously not a real elf. A woman."

Mitch is quiet for a moment. "And?"

"And..." I close my eyes and take a deep breath. I'm not sure how I'm going to explain this to my best friend. Everything about the entire trip home has been out of the ordinary for me. From driving at night to picking up a wayward elf that's not my fake girlfriend. "Well, we got to talking, and I told her about McKenzie and Cal, and the Yuletide Games..."

"I don't think I like where this is going." Mitch interrupts.

"She's...well, we are..." My pacing picks up. "She suggested that she be my fake girlfriend."

The silence on the other end of the phone is deafening.

I hold my breath and realize that for some reason, I need Mitch on my side. I don't know why, but I need to have someone that knows me to convince me that I didn't leave my sanity back in Vancouver.

"Why would she care about a small town festival? Is she from Gingerbread Grove?"

"No, she's from Kamloops, but she loves Christmas so much it's literally her job. Plus, she just got out of her own messy, long-distance relationship and wanted to help me out. She gets it." I suck in a breath, muttering the last part, hoping he doesn't hear.

"Help you out how? I'm not following any of this."

I picture my best friend and business partner pacing the floor of his office, which is what he likes to do anytime he's trying to solve a problem. Only now, I'm the problem that needs solving.

"She's...uh...I don't know how to say this."

My eyes dart around the small office as if one of the framed pictures of hammers and screwdrivers has the answer. I just need to spit it out. Get it over with. Let Mitch have his burst of whatever reaction may come from him and we can move on.

"Just tell me, Matthew. How did you become entangled with a literal elf?"

"She's pretending to be my girlfriend; everyone in town—including my mom—thinks we are in love. We ran into Cal and McKenzie and we're signed up for the Yuletide Games. There was a lantern lighting, and it had our names on it, and I kissed her at the well." I blurt out without taking a breath.

Avery must be rubbing off on me. That's the most panic rambling I've ever done.

The line goes quiet for so long I pull my phone away from my ear to make sure our call didn't get disconnected while I blurted out everything that happened in the last forty-eight hours.

"You there, Mitch?"

"Yeah, I'm just trying to process all of that. Did you hit your head somewhere during your trip? Are you hallu-cinating?"

"What? No—I didn't hit my head." I take my glasses off, using the back of my hand to rub my eyes before putting them back on. "Look, it just happened. It's fine."

"It's fine," he jokes. "This is the most un-Matthew like

thing you've ever done. Wasn't it just last year you were making jokes about the lanterns and they're *Survivor*-like games?"

"Well, yes…"

"So why are you now taking part in them? Why do you even care what your mom or the town thinks?"

"I don't…" I say, not really believing my own words. "I mean, I do, but not in the way you think." I wish I knew how to properly express how I felt, and how I got myself into this mess. "I don't know…I guess just the thought of seeing McKenzie with her mayor husband around town. The fact that I'm back home with no one during the holidays, working at the shop, I swore I'd never run. It sounded like a good idea when Avery suggested it."

"So, her name is Avery, huh?" I can hear the smile in Mitch's voice. I don't know which is worse, having Mitch rile me up about this whole fake dating nonsense, or having him encourage it.

"Ugh," I groan, sinking into my father's squeaky chair, letting my head fall back to rest on it. "This is why I don't tell you things."

"You tell me everything." Mitch laughs. "But seriously, are you sure it's just fake? I mean, this isn't something that you normally do."

"Yes, Mitch. This is fake." I think. "It's really not all that different from my relationship with Emily."

"That's not true. You never said what you two were doing was fake. You had feelings for each other; they just weren't romantic ones that lead to a 'happily ever after' sort of love."

"You're talking in fairy tales now?" I huff.

"Don't tell me you've never been roped into watching one of those sappy Christmas movies on TV and don't change the subject. You and Emily were comfortable. You were both happy just letting it be what it was until it had run its course. This is nothing like what you two shared."

"Well, what Avery and I have can't be anything but fake because she doesn't even live here. She lives in Kamloops. I mean, I don't even live here, so Kamloops to Vancouver would be even worse. I'm not going to start up another long-distance relationship when we've both been burned by them in the past."

"Are you trying to convince me or you?"

I don't answer him because I'm not sure what to say to that.

"Look, you can't let your experience with McKenzie dictate your dating status for the rest of your life."

"And you're one to talk?" I know I'm toeing the line of going too far, especially considering Mitch's dating history, but I can't help it; he hit a nerve. He's saying all the things back to me that I've said to myself, but it still feels raw, like an open wound that won't heal. I don't know how to let it heal, but now it's making me say hurtful things that just slip off my tongue that I can't take back. "I'm sorry, I shouldn't have said that."

I let out a deep breath, realizing that bringing up the past stirs up a lot of the same memories from Gingerbread Grove that Mitch has. He also has heartbreak within these city limits, and it's not something he needs to be reminded of just because mine came rushing back up to the surface.

"No, you're right. I'm not one to talk, but I'm your best friend. I want to make sure that you're doing what's best for you."

"Can we quit it with the emotional talk? Nothing is happening with Avery and me. We're not even friends. We are just two strangers helping each other out for a short time. I drove her to Kamloops. She's helping me save face around town; it's fine."

"Strangers who kiss in the town's secret well," Mitch chuckles.

I groan, instantly regretting telling him that.

I hear the bell above the door chime and excited female voices through the door. Opening it slightly, I peer out to see Avery laughing with my mom and June, looking beautiful in her grey parka with pink fur trim. Her dark jeans and high black boots make her look very different from the distraught elf I picked up at the airport.

I can't take my eyes off her. Even from here, hidden away in the office down the hallway, the way her bright blue eyes shine under her grey toque takes my breath away.

"Matthew, you still there?" Mitch's voice rings in my ear.

"Ugh, yeah. Look, I have to call you back," I say, opening the door and walking back into the store, never taking my eyes off her. At that moment, she turns and her smile lands on me. It changes slightly, becomes a little wider. It's then I know that it's almost like a secret she has just for me, and my heart warms knowing I can have that affect on her.

"She just walked in, didn't she?" Mitch laughs.

"Not now, Mitch. I'll call you later once I have the Tristar project completed."

"Uh, huh. Okay there, lover boy." He continues to laugh as he hangs up.

"Matthew! There you are. Avery here was just telling June and I about how you two met."

I freeze, drawing a blank on what we had agreed on saying. Now, with my mom and June looking at me with a mix of awe and suspicion, I'm wondering if this will all be over before it ever really starts.

Chapter Fourteen

AVERY

Matthew is looking at me with his panic eyes. The ones that tell me that he's frozen and can't remember what we agreed on for a plausible meeting story.

"Meeting at the airport is so romantic," June says, placing her hand on his arm.

"Yes, but I'm not sure why you didn't tell me about your trip to Kamloops. You could have stopped by and visited," Sharon adds, making Matthew's eye pop out even farther.

"It was just a quick trip for work, wasn't it?" I add, nodding my head toward the women and flaring my eyes, hoping that something will jumpstart his brain into joining the conversation.

"Right. A business trip."

Well, that's better than nothing, I guess.

"He's so funny. He saved me, really. With our flight being cancelled he offered to drive me home when he got the last rental car. Such a gentleman," I add, trying to subtly increase my nodding. I'm hoping he catches on before they start to notice.

"That's my Matty, always the gentleman. He gets that from his father, you know," Sharon beams.

"Right, well, I couldn't just leave her stranded," Matthew says, seeming to *finally* be shaken from whatever trance he was just in. "And I was only in town for the day, Mom. No way I could have made it work getting to Woodland Springs."

"Gingerbread Grove, dear," she corrects sternly. Any adoration she had for her son was gone with the slip of the wrong name. "Anyways, I must be going. I only stopped in to see how things were going while picking up your father's medication."

"I must get going, too," June adds, tapping her bag with the tree stand. "Thank you for your help, Matthew. It's good to have you home."

A look passes over his face at the kind words, but it's gone as quickly as it came. I don't know him well enough to be able to decipher it, but it looked like a mix of longing and surprise. He watches after them as the two older women leave the store, chatting about something to do with potholders and if I heard correctly, throwing yarn all over a tree.

I really do wonder if Matthew doesn't know how much he's genuinely appreciated in Gingerbread Grove. Just on my way from parking on the street to walking into the shop's doors, I was stopped by three people, all speaking highly of him and thrilled that he's back home.

I just wish he could see it that way.

"So," I clap my hands in front of me and look around, "this is the famous family store."

"This is it. If you need anything hardware or—Christmas," he says with a tinge of disbelief as he looks over at a display of light up gingerbread window displays, "we've got it."

"I'll have to keep that in mind."

A silence falls between us as we stand in the middle of the store, staring at each other. I want to find something witty to say, but at the moment nothing comes to mind. Standing here looking at him, seeing how handsome he is in his flannel shirt and jeans, his heartthrob hair flopped to one side, partially hiding his glasses, makes him look like some sort of lumberjack Clark Kent.

Which then makes me think of our kiss.

I love the way he pulled me into the beautiful garden and introduced me to a place that only true Gingerbreadians know about. How he tucked me under his arm and brushed my face, making me feel like the most beautiful woman in the world.

But it also makes me think of the way his mom walked in on us and saw everything. Not that we were doing anything wrong, but it's still not the impression I wanted to make.

It is also a reminder that this is all fake. Just a show for the town.

So why doesn't it feel fake?

"So, what's the event tonight?" I ask, trying to distract myself from falling down that heartbreaking rabbit hole.

"Oh, uh." Matthew rubs the back of his neck, finding his shoes very interesting. "I just got the email about it."

"And?" I ask excitedly, rocking up onto the balls of my feet.

"It's the toboggan race."

"Are you kidding me?"

"We don't have to say yes; we can always skip this. Or the whole Games. Or town. We don't even have to watch. But everyone meets at the big hill just at the edge of town and races down. One couple per toboggan."

"But if we don't go, won't we get eliminated?"

"Well, yes…"

"It doesn't sound very…Christmasy. It's not what I was expecting for something called the 'Yuletide Games.'"

Matthew pulls out his phone, and with a few taps, he's reading out the contents of his email. "Contestants will race down Gum Drop Hill in toboggans built to appear to be made from candy. With red and green runners and gingerbread-decorated footboards and handles, couples will fly down the hill and race to the bottom to avoid elimination to become the Gum Drop Champions."

"We are *so* doing that. I love tobogganing. I haven't done it since I was a kid. We can't miss this and get eliminated on our first event! How would we win?" I'm bouncing on the balls of my feet now, hands clasped in front of me, a rush of excited energy rushing through my body. I'm ready to race to the hill right now and kick some tobogganing butt.

"Are you sure? I mean, we don't have to. If it's not your thing. I didn't mean for us to actually try to win the Games or anything."

I stop my bouncing, frozen by the look on his face. "You don't want to do this, do you?"

"No. Well… I mean, I don't know." He looks out the window. "I guess I'm not really much of a sports person, which shocks a lot of people around here. I don't like skiing or skating. I've never been interested in playing hockey. I don't even really like walking in the snow, to be honest."

"I'm sorry. Do you want to just get some cider and sit on the sidelines? Or skip it all together and go get dinner somewhere? I ran into someone named Nancy outside and she was telling me about a new holiday menu at the diner." Now I feel bad. I got so caught up in the excitement of tobogganing that I forgot that I'm not here for me. I'm here for Matthew and helping him get through his time in town. I'm sure last night at the lantern lighting ceremony was almost too much for him; doing something even further out of his comfort zone would be nothing less than torture.

"Are you sure? I mean, I don't want to stop you from doing something that you really want."

"I'm here for you, silly. I'm not going to drag you into tobogganing if you don't want to. We can just make an appearance at another event for the Games or write it off all together." I take a step forward, placing my hand on his chest. "We can show off to what's-her-name and her mayor husband some other way."

"McKenzie," he adds, looking down at my hand.

"Right, McKenzie," I breathe. "We'll show them you've moved on and you're having fun. You know, with your girlfriend."

As he lifts his head and his hazel eyes meet mine, I realize that I want nothing more than to beat McKenzie and Cal at the toboggan race. I want to win the Yuletide Games, be the last standing lantern, and show the town that Matthew is the most incredible man that's ever lived in Gingerbread Grove.

Well, he lived here when it was Woodland Springs...but the point still stands.

He lifts his hand and covers mine, pressing it further into his chest. I feel the rapid beat of his heart, and I melt a little inside knowing I'm not the only one affected by this.

Which leads me to be even more surprised by the words that come out of his mouth.

"Let's do it."

My heart races at a rapid pace as I look down the slope.

It's been years since I stood on fresh powder, eagerly awaiting my turn down the side of a mountain in any form, whether it's skis, snowboard, or, in this case—a toboggan.

In this case, it's more of a glorified hill that has been transformed into a sort of ski slope, but it's cute and charming. Everything Gingerbread Grove stands for.

There are even wooden cutouts of the town's favourite treats holding flags to guide you down the different paths. They wave in the wind as the cold wind picks up. It whips across my face, leaving the hint of burn on my nose and cheeks.

I love it.

"Remind me why you think this is fun," Matthew says beside me, rubbing his gloved hands together.

"Because of the thrill. Flying down the slope with nothing to help you but a rope in your hands and a prayer."

"Exactly," Matthew scoffs, narrowing his eyes behind his glasses at the people laughing and racing their way to the bottom. "There's no control. Where are the brakes on these things?"

"Where's the fun in that?" I laugh.

"Are you guys ready?" A man with a black toque and dark green eyes comes up, clasping Matthew on the shoulder. "I have to admit, Matthew, I couldn't believe it when I saw your name signed up for this."

Matthew gives the man a forced smile and mumbles, "I couldn't believe it either."

He looks from the man to me, and I see the tension in his face start to melt. Taking a step toward me, he wraps his arm around my shoulder and pulls me close, tucking me under his arm. My mind doesn't have a chance to respond before I'm curling myself around him, my head on his chest and arm around his waist.

This is getting entirely too real. I'm too comfortable.

But as I'm curling up into him while he smells of mint and wood, I don't care.

"Trevor, I'd like you to meet my girlfriend, Avery."

Girlfriend. There's that word again. The one that makes me giddy and guilty at the same time. Deciding that's not something I need to deal with at the moment, I thrust my hand out and put a smile on my face. "It's nice to meet you."

"Nice to meet you, too," he places his hand in mine, giving me as much of a handshake as he can through gloves.

"I heard Matthew had a girlfriend. I'm happy to see he brought you home and didn't hide you in the city."

Matthew groans beside me as I laugh. "I had to see the Yuletide Games for myself. I've heard so much about it and Gingerbread Grove. Plus, I'm determined to get this guy to try more winter sports. It's a shame to live in British Columbia and not spend more time outside. Especially in the winter." I send a wink to Matthew, loving the way his cheeks turn pink, and I don't think it has anything to do with the cold.

"Well, welcome. I'm happy you brought him back here and got him out of his shell."

"Okay, I'm not *that* bad."

I can't help but smile and hold Matthew close as he gets caught up with Trevor. I learn they went to school together, but lost touch when Matthew moved to the city. Trevor owns the steakhouse in town, which was named *The Longhouse* when the town was Woodland Springs but has now been rebranded as *Cinnamon & Sear* to 'fit with the gingerbread theme' as Trevor explains. I don't miss the way Matthew grimaces when Trevor talks about the transition from the 'boring' small town to the 'exciting holiday version,' or the way Matthew pulls me tighter to him while Trevor asks him questions about his software company back in Vancouver.

While they talk, I take in just how perfectly I curl right up into him. I love how I'm short enough to fit right under his chin when we hug, or under his arm as we're standing like this. He holds me tighter as he speaks, and I start to see there's a difference in the way he holds me. When he's feeling anxious about something Trevor is talking about, he presses me into his side like we're sides of a gingerbread house needing to be glued with icing. But when he's excited, he squeezes my shoulder in a relaxed sort of understanding, as if he wants me to share his enthusiasm. I may not be adding to the conversation at the moment, but he uses it to keep me a part of the discussion. Letting me feel included, and not just an outsider looking in. But the best part? He allows me to be there for him when he feels he needs the support.

This realization is almost a little too overwhelming for me. Maxwell never did anything like that. He would have me on his arm, but he would never include me, especially when talking business. Being in a different city, I never even got the opportunity to be on his arm at corporate events, giving him silent encouragement and letting him know that no matter what it was, he wasn't doing it alone.

But that's not how it is with Matthew.

I've only known him for a few days and already he's included me more in his life than Maxwell ever did. Our relationship may be fake, but it's better than any real relationship I've ever had.

And that's just downright depressing.

"Welcome to the Yuletide Games! Thank you for coming out to the first event, the Gum Drop Toboggan Race!" A voice booms over the loudspeakers, drawing everyone's attention to the side of the hill. A platform has been created, and of course, it looks like it is from a gingerbread house. The wood is been painted a dark brown and white scalloped trim adorns the edges. Standing on top is Cal, with McKenzie at his side—of course—holding the microphone in his hand. "Please go to your marked toboggans and wait at the starting line!"

"That's us," I say excitedly, rocking back and forth from my heels to my toes. The excitement of the race is already building inside me, and mixed with the rush of emotions from being tucked in beside Matthew, I feel like I'm about to burst like a hot chocolate bomb.

Matthew rolls his eyes and takes his arm off my shoulder. I'm left with a sense of longing—and cold—but it's quickly replaced when he grabs my hand and laces our fingers together.

I don't know if Matthew notices, but Trevor looks at us with a broad smile as he tracks the movement. "I'll let you get to it, then. Good luck!" he says before walking off with a wave while laughing.

"Why do you have that smile on your face?" Matthew asks, drawing my attention back to him.

"I met your friend?"

This seemed to confuse him even more. "And?"

"You said you don't have any connections here past your family."

Matthew rolls his eyes. "I mean, I would hardly consider Trevor still a friend. I haven't talked to him since I left town."

"I don't think he sees it that way. Sometimes you lose touch with someone, but the friendship is never lost. You just need to pick it back up where you left it. "

"Or you just lose touch with someone, and the friendship ends there. Not everything needs to be some dramatic alternate ending."

"No..." My thoughts are interrupted by the announcer making another call for everyone to head to the start line.

I wish I could make him see that the town still cares for him, but it seems it will almost take a Christmas miracle.

My eyes scan the top of the hill, following where the crowd of couples is heading. Some are running and laughing while throwing snowballs at each other, others are casually walking. Then there are those, like Matthew and I, where one of the couples needs a little more convincing to start moving.

Like a distracted reindeer with a candy bar, my previous thoughts are forgotten as I'm reminded of the candy-decorated toboggans that are awaiting us.

"Come on! Let's go find ours! I want to see what they look like!"

"You're entirely too excited about this," Matthew grumbles as I start walking with the crowd, pulling him behind me.

I know he's talking about the race, but a little part of me—in the back of my mind—wonders if he's also talking about us. Did I lean into him too much? Did I act like it was too real? Get too involved with his friendship with Trevor?

I hide my disappointment with myself as I put on a happy face and keep walking. Just like I have a tendency to ramble when I shouldn't, I also get involved in people's lives when I shouldn't. I really have no right poking into Matthew's life and his connections—whether imagined or not—with Gingerbread Grove. After all, neither of us is going to be here after the holidays.

Slapping on a brighter smile, I put my elf-face on and push it out of my mind—and my heart. I need to focus on the race and making sure that we beat the 'it couple' of Gingerbread Grove.

Chapter Fifteen

AVERY

"How can you not be excited about this?" I come to a halt as I see the toboggans. It's everything I expected and more, based off the description from Matthew's email. "They weren't kidding about them. They're fantastic!"

I don't know what material the runners are made from, but they are painted in red, green, and white stripes to resemble a candy cane (the green to be separate from Candy Cane Creek, of course). The main body is made from a dark brown painted wood, and each is decorated in different designs to replicate white painted 'icing.' They're not really a traditional toboggan or sled. They're almost like a mixture of the two, sort of resembling the candy gifts we give children at the holidays with the seat filled with cookies and chocolate.

I guess in this instance we are the cookies and chocolate, and that makes me giggle.

Matthew sighs, scanning the different sleds. "I don't know what they were thinking."

"Oh, come on, there's a—charm to them."

"That's one word for it," he grunts. "This is us."

He leads me over to a toboggan right in the middle of all the others. The side is decorated with painted icing ginger-

118

bread man and woman holding hands in a heart. Our names are written on a large wooden ornament, similar to the one that is hanging from our lantern in the square, where the license plate would be. The frame is decorated with alternating trees and cookies.

"That's so cute! Romantic and festive." My eyes are immediately drawn to the oversized red glittery bows tied to the front. "My favourite part is the bows on the warbles. Those are a nice touch."

"The…what?"

"The warble. The curved part of the candy cane. Every stick is made up of that and the strabe." I tear my eyes away from the toboggan to find him looking at me with a confused look. "I guess that's not common knowledge?"

"I've never heard those words before in my life. How do you even know them?"

"They were in our elf training manual."

The blank stare he's giving me tells me he's going to need more context.

"When any elf is hired on at C.O.C.O.A., we are given a manual with everything Christmas. It has recipes, trending toy ideas, folklore from around the world. Did you know that in Gävle, Sweden they have a forty-nine foot straw goat statue they make for the whole season? And that there's a tradition for vandals to try to burn it down? Or in Germany, how they hide a pickle in the tree and whoever finds it gets a present?"

"No, I can't say I knew about either of those."

"We take Christmas very seriously at C.O.C.O.A. We want to make sure that no matter what family we are helping, we can bring a little joy to them. Maybe it's something that they would do from their home if they are new to Canada or an old family tradition that they've done for years. We just want to make sure all our elves are Christmas experts and are ready for any holiday-related situation that may come up."

"That's…really great," he says in awe. "What's another interesting tradition?"

"Hmm, let me see. In Iceland they have the Yule Cat. It's meant as a way to sort of encourage the workers on a farm to do their best. If they work hard, they are given new clothes."

"And if you didn't?"

"Then you were eaten by a large beast resembling a cat."

"That's horrifying and not very jolly."

"No," I laugh, shaking my head. "Not all Christmas traditions are happy, jolly, or what we would consider festive. Most have nothing to do with the real reason behind Christmas, but they are interesting, and I love learning about them."

He brushes the back of my hand with his thumb where we are joined, and the flutters in my stomach come back. His hazel eyes are focused solely only mine, and my breath hitches as we stand there lost in time.

"You're making me want to learn more about them, too," he whispers.

Forget butterflies; I have Rudolph flying in circles in my stomach.

"Racers, climb onto your gingerboggans!" an announcer says through the speaker. Muffled words and static booms through the start line, causing everyone to cover their ears. "Why can't I call it gingerboggans? Tobogobread? Ginger-sled?" There are a few more muffled words before he comes back, his voice depleted of its earlier enthusiasm. "Ugh, fine. Climb your toboggans."

I chuckle as we break eye contact, both seemingly embarrassed as we realize there is a hill filled with people around us.

I drop his hand and climb into the front of the toboggan, straightening my legs in front of me and grabbing onto the rope. I take a deep breath and try to regain some composure.

I take a deep breath in. *You're just here for the Games. That's it.*

Deep breath out. *You're leaving to go back to Kamloops.*

Deep breath in. *This is all fake. It doesn't mean anything.*

Deep breath out. *He lives in Vancouver and doesn't even like Christmas.*

Feeling like I have my thoughts—and nerves—somewhat back under control, I peer over my shoulder and see Matthew gazing down at me with a perplexed look on his face.

"What's wrong?"

He tilts his head as he looks down at me. "How are we going to make this work?"

"Just climb on behind me." I wave my hand at the space behind me as I tuck my legs into the curved wood in front of me.

With a final tentative look down the hill, Matthew drops his shoulders and takes his place behind me. His legs press on either side of mine and his arms wrap around my body as he grabs onto the rope with me. I don't think as I lean back into him, taking in more of his smell and the heat radiating off him. If I don't watch myself, I could lose myself again. It's already hard enough to remember this is fake the longer I'm around him. I don't need to get caught up in things like warmth and scents when it's only going to lead to me getting my heart broken.

And that makes me feel anything but jolly.

"Alright, racers. Start your toboggans!" The announcer exclaims.

"Relax, Matthew. It'll be over before you know it. Who knows, maybe you'll have fun and be the one begging me to take you down the hill again after this."

"Doubtful," Matthew grumbles.

"On your marks!" The announcer booms.

Matthew tightens his hold on me. While I enjoy the thrill, it's not helping me focus on the game—both the race and the fake relationship we're putting on for the town.

"Relax," I whisper as the adrenaline races through my

own body. I don't know if it's from the thrill of the race or from being with Matthew.

I also don't know if I'm talking to Matthew or myself.

"Get set…"

"Get ready to get us started." I get myself into position. Tightening the hold on the rope, I brace my legs and lean back into Matthew, never taking my eyes off the hill in front of me.

"What? How do I do that?" I don't miss the panic in his voice.

"Go!"

"Push off!" I yell with a laugh, leaning forward to gain momentum.

Matthew hesitates for a moment before using his arms and legs to push us off, sending us flying down the slope. I can't control the bellowing laugh that comes out of me as Matthew shoves his legs back into the toboggan, wrapping his arms around me. I steer the best I can, focusing on the landscape whizzing past me while battling the butterflies in my stomach as Matthew holds me tighter, burying his chin into my shoulder.

We're starting to rush past other couples, gaining momentum as I shift us both to gain speed. After we're halfway down the hill, I hear Matthew's laughter in my ear as he begins to loosen his hold on me, making me even more determined to win this for us. For him.

Looking to my left, I see McKenzie and Cal rushing down next to us. They're both laughing and hollering as they speed to catch up. For a moment, I think that maybe Matthew has gotten it wrong. Maybe there isn't a competition between them or any reason for him to feel the need to have a fake girlfriend in front of her.

But then I see the gloating smile McKenzie sends our way.

"Not today, Martha May," I grumble under my breath as I refocus my attention on the path before us.

Bending my knees, I shift my weight even further toward the front of the toboggan, praying gravity makes us go faster. Matthew's grip on me tightens the faster we go, but I won't let myself focus on anything other than getting to the finish line.

"Avery, we're going too fast," Matthew says in my ear; the panic from earlier returns.

The toboggan starts to shake, and I admit, we may be going a little too fast. I don't know how well this flying candy ride is made, but there's nothing I can do about it now. We're getting close to the point where it would be easy to lose control. One little bump could send us tumbling and become gingerbread pancakes, but I can't think about that. All that matters right now is Matthew and I crossing the finish line. Preferably before Cal and McKenzie.

I hold my breath for the remainder of the distance between us and the finish line. From out of the corner of my eye, I can see we are neck and neck with the Whovier's—or whatever their actual last name is.

It's going to come down the wire.

A Santa's sleigh photo finish.

I send a last minute Christmas wish to the big man himself and hope that he can hear me.

I don't dare look over at the duo as we cross the line, unsure if we came out as the holiday victors. I know there's more to this than just winning the race. It's for Matthew and making sure he feels like he still belongs here, even if he lives in the city and everything about his hometown has changed. It's about showing McKenzie that just because she moved on and is now the mayor's wife, that doesn't mean it makes Matthew less than.

More importantly, it shows him that Christmas can be fun and doesn't need to be overshadowed by his town's overly enthusiastic love for it.

"We did it! We won!" Matthew cheers behind me as I lean

back, getting the toboggan to slow. The pure excitement in his voice drowns out any worry he had just a moment earlier.

After bringing our ride to a complete stop, Matthew jumps out and pulls me with him, enveloping me in a massive hug.

The cheering from the crowd is drowned out by the thumping in my ears. My heart's beating so fast, both equally from winning the race and being in Matthew's arms. My eyes are closed as I lay my cheek on his chest, feeling the excited rhythm of his own heartbeat that races in time with mine. I want to stay locked in this moment, just like this forever, but I know we can't.

I have to remind myself that this is fake. It's just to show that he's moved on from McKenzie. Not to mention he's going back to Vancouver soon.

But I want it to be real. I want that so badly.

Opening my eyes while still tucked into Matthew, I see Cal helping McKenzie out of their toboggan, narrowing his eyes at us before catching himself and putting on a fake politician grin.

I'm going to have to keep an eye on that one. He's not as easygoing as he likes to appear.

"Can you believe it, Avery?" Matthew asks, tipping my chin up to meet his gaze.

"I told ya we could." I stir up as much enthusiasm as I can while being sucked back into the moment where my brain thinks this is real.

His hand cups my cheek as he slowly lowers his lips to mine, never breaking his gaze. My breath gets lost in my throat as the gap between us closes.

The second his lips touch mine all thoughts and fears leave my mind. All that matters is right here. Right now. And right now, this doesn't feel like we're faking.

Chapter Sixteen

MATTHEW

I'm kissing Avery. Right now.

   She's in my arms and I'm kissing her.

Again.

Since getting to the hill, my only thoughts have been on not falling off the toboggan and seriously injuring myself—or worse. Standing at the top of the hill, I thought of the headlines that would read, '*Fatal Toboggan Race on Gum Drop Hill*' or '*Two Seriously Injured in Gingerbread Grove Not-So-Yuletide Games.*'

But instead…I had fun.

And now I'm kissing Avery Geller at the bottom of Gum Drop Hill.

And we won. Without crashing into a tree. And instead of dwelling on the scathing look Cal sent our way that normally would have made my chest burn, I focus on the feel of Avery in my arms instead. I normally wouldn't be this forward, but I just reacted. My gut instinct was to take Avery into my arms and kiss her, and that's when I noticed everything else start to fade away. The roar of the crowd is nothing but a whisper now; even the heated glare from McKenzie and Cal no longer feel like laser beams on my back.

The only thing that exists is Avery.

"Matthew! Avery! Congratulations!" Trevor gives me a hard pat on the back, making me break my kiss from Avery. "Matthew, I never thought I'd see the day you moved down a hill so fast!"

"Yeah, well, things change, I guess." I'm speaking to Trevor, but my eyes are only for Avery.

I take in the way her short breaths make little white puff clouds in front of her mouth and the way her cheeks are an adorable pink colour.

"Come on, let's get you over to the table and claim your prize. It's an edible replica of the toboggan. They're writing your names in icing on it as we speak!" he exclaims excitedly before running off toward the crowd.

"You did it!" Avery says with the brightest smile I've ever seen on her, gripping onto my arms.

"*We* did it," I correct, unable to get the dumbfounded smile off my face.

"Maybe, but you got on that toboggan and rode it like a real elf! You got out of your comfort zone, and if I heard you correctly, you were even having fun while you were doing it!"

"I don't know if I'd go so far as to say that I had *fun*, but it was…an adventure."

"I heard you laughing, Matthew. Don't you dare try to pretend that didn't happen," she laughs, giving my arm a squeeze.

Her smiling face draws me in again, making me almost forget that we're expected at the winner's table to accept whatever gingerbread monstrosity they have waiting for us.

"I admit nothing." The corner of my mouth ticks up into a smile.

Movement out of the corner of my eye catches my attention, only to find Trevor staring at us with a knowing grin on his face, which only looks more ridiculous with the green and red toque on his head with a big fluffy pompom stuck on the top.

Moving Avery's hand to the crook of my elbow, I start to lead her toward the crowd when a loud—and unwelcome—voice stops me in my tracks.

"Matty! I didn't know you liked to toboggan! Is that some new skill you picked up in the big city?" McKenzie asks as she walks up to us on Cal's arm. His sneer is gone, and in its place is the fake politician's smile.

"No, definitely not a skill or anything I've picked up from the city," I grumble, trying to suppress the cringe over the use of my childhood nickname. Again.

"Maybe not, but he sure did amazing! Didn't you, *Matthew*?" Avery asks, emphasizing my full name. "I mean, it was such a surprise when you practically begged me to sign up. That Christmas resolution list of yours is sure making us do a bunch of new things, isn't it?" To anyone else, the look on her face would be pure excitement, but I know that it's really a plea to play along.

"Uh, yeah." Once again with the two word answers when she's saving me.

"Christmas resolutions?" McKenzie asks, her eyebrow raised.

"Oh yes, Matthew here couldn't wait for New Year's, so he decided to make some Christmas resolutions. New things to try over the holiday season," Avery answers, patting me on the chest.

"Right," she answers, drawing out her syllables in disbelief.

"That's actually a good idea," Cal chimes in. "We could market that for the town. I bet those people over at Candy Cane Creek don't have anything like that. It could be unique just for Gingerbread Grove." Cal's eyes grow wide as he sucks in a breath. "We could be trendsetters. Say, you don't mind if we use this, do you, Matty? I mean, Matthew. It would be awfully good for the town."

I've never met someone in this century that has tried so hard to speak in a transatlantic accent, but Cal is sure fighting hard to bring it back.

"Uh, yeah, go for it." I shoot a look at Avery to see if she caught Cal's antics. Her stifled laugh tells me she did.

"What other things have you been trying, *Matty?*" McKenzie asks, shooting a glare at Avery.

"Yes, what other ideas do you have that might give us an advantage over those blasted Creekers?" Cal adds.

Blasted? Was this guy for real?

"Oh, well, let's see…" Avery taps a gloved finger from her free hand on her lips.

"Road trips," I add. Thankful that I was finally able to contribute something to this conversation. "We've started going on road trips."

"I've even taught him the importance of getting the best gas station candy. And which ones have the worst coffee, isn't that right?" She adds with a giggle.

McKenzie's face puckers. If things were still the same, which the look on her face tells me they are, she hates anything that comes out of a gas station and would never think to eat or drink anything that came from one. Not even if it was a Tim Horton's attached to it.

"And now we can cross tobogganing off our list," Avery finishes with a smile, looking up at me.

"Yeah." Again, one word is all I can get out, especially when she's smiling at me like that.

"Anyway," Avery says, turning back to McKenzie and Cal, who are currently watching us as if we've both grown extra heads. "We should get over to that winner's table. Collect our prize and all that. Right, Matthew?"

"Yup. Trevor will be waiting."

Ha. Five words.

With a nod, we leave the other couple with their fake smiles as we get lost in the crowd.

We receive a few 'congratulations' as we pass through, but make sure not to stop and talk. Only providing a quick 'thank you' as we continue on our mission to the winner's table.

I don't know if Avery can sense that my meter for tolerating crowds is quickly dwindling, but she picks up her speed as we dodge well wishers.

"Matthew! Avery!" Trevor exclaims the closer we get to the winner's table. "Congratulations on winning!" He clasps my shoulder so hard I stumble forward a little. "And just in time. We are about to make the announcement."

"Oh joy," I mutter under my breath.

Avery squeezes my arm reassuringly as she smiles up at me. The vice in my chest lessens a little, but the need to get out of here is still pressing.

"Thank you, everyone, for joining us at our annual Gum Drop Hill Toboggan Race!" Trevor announces into the microphone in his hand. We are excited to announce our winners Matthew Roberts and Avery..." He looks at Avery with a questioning look.

"Geller," she whispers.

"Avery Geller!" He gives the crowd a moment with their applause before continuing. "You won a romantic dinner for two at the Gingy's Grill!" The crowd cheers again.

I nod to Trevor as I accept an envelope from his outstretched hand.

"Gingy's Grill?" Avery whispers.

"I'll explain later." Looking around at the crowd, and seeing the faces of the people that are rushing to congratulate us, I feel the vice returning in my chest. I appreciate the well wishes, but it's a lot when half the town is rushing all at once.

"Hey, do you want to get out of here?" She gives my arm another squeeze while smiling up at me.

I can't express how much it means to me that she understands my desperation to escape this crowd. The only other woman to get how much I really don't like crowds or being bombarded was Emily. That's why I let it last as long as I did. She knew when I'd reached my limit and needed to leave a party or an event. She had no problem taking me by the hand and making up some excuse to leave when my mind would go blank. The only difference is that I didn't have the overwhelmingly strong feelings for Emily that I do for Avery.

"Hey, are you okay?" Avery asks, leading me by the hand through the crowd. A smile is painted on her face, but I can tell it's one just for the crowd surrounding us.

"Yeah. This is just… a lot."

She pulls us off to the side, somewhat shielded by a pine tree that has been decorated with over-the-top tinsel and lights to the point it's almost unrecognizable as a tree.

My attention is drawn back to her when she places her gloved palm on my cheek, guiding me until my gaze meets hers. "What do you need?"

Her voice is low, almost as if she's worried someone will hear us and uncover our little hiding spot.

There's nothing blocking us from the view but the trunk and a few low-laying branches, but it feels like we are in our own little world. I can hear 'O Holy Night' mixed with the chatter of the crowd, but they seem more distant than close.

"This. This is what I need," I whisper back.

I can't stop the smile that spreads across my face as I realize she understands I don't just mean us hiding behind this cedar tree, with its low-hanging branches and twinkling lights. I mean us. Here. Together.

"So, tell me about Gingy's Grill. Please don't tell me they cook steaks with gingerbread seasonings. I love my holiday treats, but not mixed with my meat." Her eyes widen in fear. "They don't grill gingerbread men, do they?"

I can't help but chuckle at the thought. "No, thankfully. Or at least, not that I'm aware of. I think it's more just to keep the theme of the town. I know my mom and dad like going there. She's talked about it non-stop since it opened. It used to be a chain restaurant when I was growing up, but they decided to leave when everything was turning…well, Christmas crazy. That's when Gingy came in and opened the restaurant."

"Wait—that's their actual name?" Avery's eyes widen to the size of snowballs.

"Yup. Well, actually, his name is Sven, I think, but we've always called him Gingy. He's a big lumberjack of a man with shockingly red hair and a matching coloured beard that has somehow never gone white. The man has to be in his sixties, at least by now."

Gingy was a staple in Woodland Springs my whole childhood. At the time, he worked as a head chef at a restaurant a couple towns over, if I remember correctly, but he was always the first to help with church lunches or town events that had food and it was always amazing.

"We have to go there now. I want to see what this Gingy's is all about!" The excitement on her face is remarkable. Looking down at her, I wonder why I was hesitant to show her around. More importantly, I feel a spark of excitement that maybe this town isn't as bad as I remembered it to be. Aside from being obsessed with the holiday and in a feud with Candy Cane Creek that seems to be one sided on our side, maybe it's not all so bad.

"We do have the gift certificate now. I mean, it would be a shame for it to go to waste. But just keep in mind this is a small town, so it won't be like all the fancy restaurants you might get anywhere else."

Avery chuckles. "I don't need fancy, remember? That's not me. I much prefer a town like Gingerbread Grove to the big city, anyway."

"That's good." I feel a sense of relief, even though deep down, I never thought that going to a fancy restaurant for dinner would have appealed to her. Even from the moment I met her in that ridiculous elf costume, I knew that she wasn't like most women I've ever known. There's still something that stops me—makes me hesitate in believing that this is something that could be real or that I need to be concerned with. Looking over her shoulder to see the crowd through the branches, I add, "then we'll go. Just maybe not today."

"Whenever you're ready."

Her words are soft but draw me back to her. I don't know how to thank her for that. For knowing what I need and when I need it. There aren't enough words to express what I'm feeling, so I do the only thing that makes sense to me right now. I bend down and kiss her on her temple before lacing my fingers with hers.

"Do you want to go somewhere? I don't want to stay here, but I'd like to keep hanging out with you, if that's okay?" My heart beats in my chest as I wait for her answer. I want to keep reminding myself that this is fake, but it's getting harder and harder the more time I spend with her.

"That's more than okay." And the smile on her face tells me she means that with her whole heart. "Where do you want to go?"

"I think I know just the place."

Chapter Seventeen

AVERY

"So you wanted to get away from the town, so you brought us to the diner?" I ask, looking up at the building in front of us through the windshield of my car.

"Well, yes, but as you saw, most people are at the hill still, not here. I figured it would be safe. Plus, Nancy knows what table I like, and it's a little hidden."

"Well, aren't you a man of mystery," I laugh, reaching for the door handle. "And here I thought you'd become a recluse since getting back to town."

He lets out a heavy sigh. "Staying at my parents' place isn't productive."

"What do you mean?" I let go of the handle and turn to face him.

"I've been trying to catch up on my own work after the store closes, but it's hard when my dad's hobbling around and my mom is trying to cater to him and insist that my life choices are less than stellar."

"Oh." My heart sinks, thinking of what he must feel like. Going to his childhood home after a long day of running a store that he never wanted to be a part of, only to be pulled away from his actual job.

"Yeah. So, I've been coming to the diner and getting a few hours of work done at night. Nancy's been great about tucking me away in the back corner and keeping me supplied with coffee."

My eyes search his, trying to find what he's not really telling me. I know there's more to it than a hovering mom and injured dad. I start to get more of a glimpse into the sadness that I've always thought followed him around. It's one that I can't even imagine, as my family is so different. My parents have always been encouraging and accepting, even when I told them I was accepting a job as an elf.

"I'm so sorry that you've had to do that. You must be exhausted."

He shrugs, looking down at his hands braced on his legs before peering up at the cafe in front of us, not saying a word.

This only renews my determination to help him see that there are good things around. It doesn't have to be Christmas or the town, but that there are people who love and care for him, regardless of being related to him.

I want nothing more than to reach my hand over and take his. I don't miss the way the tips of his fingers dig into his jeans, his knuckles white as he clings on. I don't know what's stopping me at the moment, whether it's fear of being rejected or not wanting to interrupt whatever's going on in his mind right now, but something does. Maybe it's because I don't have the right to do something so intimate, even if we have already kissed and held hands. But we aren't out in front of anyone. There's no one around to convince. It's not my place. Not as a fake girlfriend, even though the last few days have felt anything *but* fake. Not all the kisses he's given me have been for show, and they certainly didn't feel like they weren't real. At least, they didn't to me.

But then I thought everything I shared with Maxwell was real, too. Maybe I'm not a reliable source.

And our time in the garden crosses my mind. There

wasn't anyone around for that either. So, am I just too much in my head? Am I overthinking things....again?

Taking a deep breath, I know I need to take charge of the situation, or we'll be stuck out here in my car all evening.

"Why don't we go in and you can show me this table?" The corner of my mouth ticks up into a smile. Even though he's not looking at me, I hope he feels the warmth in my words. When he doesn't move or respond, I turn back to my door.

"Wait." Matthew places his hand on my arm, stilling my movements. "I just want to say thank you."

"For what?" I ask, turning to him, and fighting with ever fibre of my body not to look down at his hand on my arm. It's such an innocent thing, and yet it feels like some sort of declaration. A declaration of what? I don't know. But it feels like something.

"For understanding." He takes a deep breath before turning and meeting my gaze. "I don't like big crowds."

"I never would have guessed," I tease.

"Or having a bunch of attention on me," he admits, his cheeks turning an adorable shade of red.

"What? You? No!" I gasp, clutching my chest with my hand dramatically with a smile. "Matthew, there's no need to thank me. I could tell you weren't loving the attention and needed to leave, so we left. It's no big deal."

"But it is a big deal," he pleads.

We sit in the silence of the car for a moment, letting his words hang between us. I'm not sure what to say, because I've never felt the way he does. Crowds don't bother me, and I've done enough training and presentations for work that I'm no longer phased by speaking in front of people. It's now that I realize just how different my life is from Matthew's, but yet we still have the common bond of being hurt by those that were supposed to love us.

"Well…" I start, clearing my throat and pasting on a smile

that I don't quite feel. "The most important part is that you took the chance and got on that toboggan. And we won!"

"Yes, we did." That cute smile of his returns. If I'm not mistaken, I also think there's a hint of a dimple under his dark beard.

He just keeps getting cuter and cuter.

"We should get inside. You know, before someone spots us." He doesn't move. His eyes are trained on me as if he's searching for something; much like I was doing before. "Hey, are you okay?"

"Uh, yeah." He hesitates for another moment before taking his hand off my arm and peeling himself out of my car.

I'm so shaken from his sudden change and quick exit that I sit stunned for a moment. It's not until my door opens and Matthew is standing there with a smile on his face and his hand out that I realize that I have flutters in my stomach and my heart has picked up its pace.

I'm here. With Matthew.

He very easily could have ended our day after the race. He didn't have to ask me to stay and hang around with him. We aren't here to be 'seen' as a couple; he just wanted to spend time with me.

Me.

Without thinking about it too hard, I place my hand in his and let him help me out of the car. He's such a gentleman, closing the car door and waiting for me to lock it before gently guiding me to the diner.

"Matthew! Are you looking for your usual table?" Nancy asks loudly from behind the counter she's wiping as soon as we walk in.

"Hi, Nancy. Yes, please, if it's available."

The server motions to the empty dining space with a chuckle "I think you're okay. Take a seat and I'll be right with you. Avery, it's good to see you again. I'm glad you took my advice to come in tonight."

"Thank you, Nancy."

He leads me through empty tables until we reach the back corner. It's a booth tucked away with high walls that block any view in or out from the main dining area. He helps me shrug off my jacket and hangs in on a hook on the end of the wall before taking off his own and hanging it beside mine.

"You weren't kidding. This is really secluded," I say, scooting into the bench seat of the booth. I don't slide as gracefully across the red imitation leather seat as I'd like, but thankfully, Matthew doesn't seem to notice my less-than-elegant entry into the booth.

While I'm thankful he didn't see my debacle, he seems distracted, and I don't know why. Taking his own—incredibly more graceful—seat across from me in the booth, he doesn't meet my gaze before grabbing his menu, his eyes glossing over the words.

'Well, if it isn't our toboggan winners!" Nancy says, walking up to the table with a pot of coffee in her hand. "Coffee, Matthew?"

"Please." He takes the down turned mug in front of him and flips it around, placing it in front of Nancy.

"And what can I get you, hun?" she asks as she pours Matthew's coffee.

"A peppermint tea, please," I say, shooting Matthew an inquisitive look. "How do you know about the race already?"

"Oh, honey. This is Gingerbread Grove. I had the play-by-play on the app-thing as you two were shooting down the mountain. The video was perfect! Without it, no one would believe Matthew here got onto the back of one!" She laughs, the slight lines around her eyes becoming more apparent.

"Sorry, the app?" I ask, raising my eyebrow at Matthew, but he shrugs and looks just as confused as I am.

"Yes, GingerSnap. Hasn't your mom mentioned anything about it or gotten you on it yet?" She asks Matthew, who replies with wide eyes and a slow-shaking head. "Well, then.

I can't say I was a fan of it when the city council first introduced it, especially with most of the town being us older folks and liking the good ol' fashioned way of face-to-face gossip and news, but I have to say I'm warming up to it! You should download it and get connected since you're back in town."

"Oh, I don't know. I'm just here for the holidays, Nancy..."

"Don't you worry about that. Once a Gingerbreadian, always a Gingerbreadian," she says with a warm smile. "I'll be right back with your tea." She strolls off leaving us alone once again.

Matthew lets out a deep sigh before picking up his menu again.

"Spill it."

"Look, it's nothing. Really. I guess I'm just overwhelmed with everything from today, and now knowing it's recorded on some app for everyone to see. I don't know, it's a lot."

I sit watching him for a moment, knowing there's more to the story he isn't telling me, but I decide it's best not to push him. It's not like our relationship is real. Sure, he asked to spend more time with me today, but what if he just doesn't want to be alone? He's already said being at his parents' place isn't the most comfortable. He probably just asked me to join him because otherwise he'd be alone.

Or maybe he was just being polite. He did say that he did his own work after hours. Maybe I'm distracting him from that? I would hate to be the reason that he was falling behind on his own commitments.

"Hey, now it's my turn to ask. Are you okay?" Matthew grabs my hand, drawing me out of my now overpowering thoughts.

"Yup!" I answer, a little too brightly. Drawing my hand back quickly, I pick up my own menu and start to graze over the items. He grabbed my hand so naturally while I had a near panic attack in the car just thinking about it. *What is wrong with me?*

I have to say, I'm a little surprised that the menu seems relatively—normal. It has your standard diner breakfasts and lunch sandwiches. There's an array of platters and hearty meals for dinners. I flip the laminated menu over and smile. There it is. A whole page dedicated to gingerbread delicacies.

Matthew chuckles from behind his own menu. "You didn't think they would miss the opportunity to have holiday themed food, did you?"

"I was beginning to worry," I tease. "Is this the holiday menu? I would have assumed they would have this type of thing available all year round."

Matthew doesn't say a word as he pushes a smaller laminated menu toward me. It's the official holiday menu with turkey dinner on a plate, turkey dinner sandwiches, and just about every other turkey and cranberry dish you could think of.

"What do you recommend?"

"Well, you can never go wrong with a burger. It's a staple here. Has been even when it was Woodland Springs and it hasn't changed, thank goodness." The last part is muttered under his breath, but I still hear it.

"While that does look amazing, I feel like I would be doing the town an injustice if I didn't have *something* gingerbread while I was here." I flip the menu back over, my eyes widening and stomach rumbling. "B.L.T. with a side of poutine! Yes, please! That's a year-round comfort food."

It has turkey gravy, so I feel like it's a good compromise. At least that's what I'll tell myself.

"Did I hear the B.L.T. with a side of poutine? That's my kind of girl," Nancy says as she walks up, sliding a metal teapot with a paper-wrapped bag in front of me.

"What can I say? I'm easy to please." I sneak a glance at Matthew, who's giving me one of his bright smiles, before I turn back to Nancy. "I think I'm going to do a slice of the gingerbread cheesecake after though. That sounds heavenly."

"It's pretty amazing, if I do say so myself. I have to say, Matthew, I know you've only been back a couple of days, but I'm surprise you haven't brought Avery in here yet." She turns to me and continues. "He's in here most nights working. He says he likes this spot because it's hidden away from most of the other diners, when there are some. Really, I think it's because it's close to the kitchen and he thinks he gets his food faster."

I start laughing with Nancy and am relieved when Matthew joins in.

"I'll neither confirm nor deny that, Nancy."

"Well, you can't blame him for either of those reasons. And for your question, I live in Kamloops and it's the first time I've been able to get away because of work. Plus, I don't want to interrupt him when he's working."

"Well, welcome to Gingerbread Grove. I hope we see you around more. It was nice bumping into you earlier, and I'm glad you both found your way in."

I think back to my run in with her earlier today, so glad that we were able to make it here tonight. She seems like a really welcoming woman, and I feel like she has taken it upon herself to take care of Matthew while he's here.

"Thank you. I'm glad, too." I sneak another glance at Matthew to find him already watching me with a coy smile on his face. I feel my cheeks heating under his gaze and wonder if maybe I'm not alone in having feelings and praying that what's happening between us isn't entirely fake.

"Well, I have Avery's order. What about you, Matthew? Your usual?"

"Uh, yeah. The cheeseburger and fries, please," he responds, not looking away from me.

"A Jolly Ginger Burger coming right up!" Nancy takes our menus and shuffles off, leaving us alone in our corner.

"I love gingerbread, but please tell me there aren't any ginger or holiday spices in that burger."

Matthew laughs. "Thankfully, no. It's just the name they gave it."

"Phew." Reaching for my tea bag, I rip the paper and carefully pull it out before quickly flipping the top of the metal teapot and throwing it in. "I've never understood why they make tea pots all metal. Yes, it holds the heat in longer, but how are you supposed to put the bag in without burning yourself?"

Without a word, Matthew breaks the paper holder on his napkin and unravels it from around his cutlery before bunching it in his hand and using it like a paper hot pad and lifting the lid. The corner of his mouth ticks up in a mischievous way along with his eyebrow.

"Okay, fine, Mr. Smarty-pants," I chuckle, throwing my empty tea bag wrapper at him.

Matthew reaches to the side of the table and grabs a packet of sugar and creamer, pushing aside a cup with plastic tubes filled with liquid.

"What are those?" I ask, narrowing my eyes at them, trying to see.

"Gingerbread honey."

"What now?" I snap my attention to him.

He's unfazed as he adds his sugar and creamer to his coffee before swiftly picking up his spoon and stirring it. "From what I've been able to gather, Candy Cane Creek has candy canes at all their tables for people to mix into their coffees so, of course, we had to have something similar. Someone came up with gingerbread flavoured honey. There's a beekeeper in town here that works with city council to make sure that all the businesses in town with coffee are always fully stocked with it year-round."

"You're joking," I reply blankly.

"I wish," he huffs before taking a sip.

"They really take this feud seriously, huh?"

"The people of Gingerbread Grove do. Apparently, the people of Candy Cane Creek don't pay much attention to it unless they're dragged into it for some reason or another. I don't know, it's a whole thing. I tend to tune out when my mom is going on and on about it."

This makes me even more curious about this feud, but I know I'll have to talk to the townspeople to get more info on this. This town just keeps getting more and more interesting the more I learn about it, and I feel the more I do, the more I'll be able to unravel about this enigma of a man across from me.

Chapter Eighteen

MATTHEW

"So, tell me more about your work." I take another sip of my coffee, hoping that I'll be able to successfully distract her from any more talk about the town. Being home the last few days, and then thrown into being part of their gingerbread party, has been almost too much to handle all at once.

"Busy," she says, wrapping her hands around her teacup. The steam carries the scent of peppermint over to me, making me see just how fitting it is that my little elf drinks tea that would taste like candy canes.

Woah, *my* elf?

"I'm surprised you have the time to—help me out—with it being so close to Christmas and all."

A genuine smile crosses her face. One of the ones I know is reserved exclusively for me. Or, at least I'm the only one in town she's given *this* smile to so far.

"Believe it or not, elves are allowed to clock out," she chuckles. "But it's good. In fact, today was a really good day."

"Oh, yeah? Tell me about it."

And there it is. That smile of hers. The one that reaches her eyes and makes a hint of pink touch her cheeks. It's the one that makes my heart have a weird rhythm and causes the butterflies in my stomach.

"It was just the best. This morning we had our annual toy drive. Every year we work with the biggest hotel in town to collect toys and donations to give out as gifts for the holidays. We have live music, Santa and Mrs. Claus walking around, and everyone who donates is welcome to a big buffet break-fast. We even got the Ice Queen and her sister to come this year to entertain the kids. Normally, we get a good chunk of toys as a final push for our supply for the season, but this morning was next level."

Despite her smile, a slight tear escapes from the corner of her eye. I don't resist. Reaching across the table, I wipe the stray tear, taking an extra moment to caress her cheek.

"I'm sorry, I don't know why I'm getting so emotional."

"Because you care."

"Anyway," she continues, acting as if her display of emotion hadn't happened. I retract my hand, letting it rest on the table in front of me. "People were lined up around the building before we opened the doors. There was a mound of toys, and we could barely keep up with the food and coffee to thank everyone for braving the cold and snow. It was so amazing to see the city come together to help those that would otherwise go without. We even had some prominent businessmen pledge to support multiple families on their own. It was quite incredible."

There was a time when I thought I was different. That I was immune to feeling like I needed to embrace anything to do with the Christmas spirit. But sitting across from Avery now, seeing the joy on her face knowing what she's doing is going to bring so much happiness to so many people, I realize that maybe I got it wrong. Maybe everything I associate with the holiday that's negative is really just also a way to ignore the positive. Nothing about what Avery does has to do with making money or competing to be the best in some made up competition. Instead, she uses it to bless others and make someone's life better.

"You are truly incredible, you know that?"

A blush tinges her cheeks. "I'm just doing my job; I can't take credit for it."

I sit back and watch her for a moment, cradling my coffee mug so I don't do something like taking her hand or brushing the stray strand of hair that has fallen in her face behind her ear. "I'm sure you could. Let me guess, you were highly involved in the organization of the event."

"Well, yes…"

"And you were the first person there and the last person to leave," I continue.

"I mean, there were people already at the hotel cooking when I got there." I narrow my eyes at her. "Okay, yes. I was the first person from C.O.C.O.A. there and the last to leave. But I needed to make sure that everything was just right, and it was ready for everyone else to show up."

"So, you did all of that, put in the full day, and still drove out here to enter into a toboggan race with me?"

Guilt doesn't just creep in when I realize how much she's done today, it floods in. I can't imagine having the day she's had and still sitting across from me like she had the most leisurely day ever.

"Of course, Matthew. I promised I would be here, and I am."

My gaze drifts out the window. The sky is black, lit up only with the constellations and the bright moon. The street-lights have come on, as have all the multicoloured twinkling lights of Christmas. Was the sky just as dark when she left for the hotel this morning? Was she able to go home and have a break before she felt obligated to drive out here to race down a hill with me.

"Hey, are you okay?" Placing her hand on mine, her voice is soft and laced with concern.

"I don't deserve you," I say honestly, looking into her bright blue eyes.

Her mouth opens with a response but is halted when Nancy walks up to our table, holding our plates.

"Here's your food," she says, gently placing the plates in front of us. "Let me know what you think, Avery. I know we can't compete with the big city, but I think we do pretty well."

"I'm sure it's delicious. Oh my, look at that topper!"

We both chuckle at the picks sticking out of her fully stacked sandwich, both adorned with a small plastic gingerbread man. She also wasn't lying about it being delicious. The smell of bacon mixed with the poutine's turkey gravy and cheese makes my mouth water, and rethinking my ordering choice.

"You didn't think we'd leave it out of *everything*, did you? I'm pretty sure Cal would revoke our business license if we didn't include a little gingerbread in everything." Nancy jokes but becomes serious when she sees our stunned faces. "I'm joking—mostly. Let me know if you need anything else.

Nancy walks away, leaving us alone once again. I can't take my eyes off Avery as she stabs her poutine with her fork, making sure to cover the fries with both gravy and cheese before bringing them to her mouth.

"Oh, my goodness, this is good."

"You can't really go wrong with anything from here. It's honestly the only thing I ever missed from home."

Home.

The dreaded word reminds me that I don't live in Gingerbread Grove and neither does she. This is all just a lie until I can go back to Vancouver and end things quietly, going back to a world where I don't know this little elf and the magic she truly brings to the world.

Well doesn't that sound depressing.

We begin to eat our meals in silence, but I can't help but notice the way she makes little happy noises when she takes another bite of her poutine, or the way she does a little dance in her seat when she tries her sandwich.

"Am I doing it again?" she asks, putting her B.L.T. down and wiping the side of her mouth with her napkin.

"Doing what?"

"My food happy dance. I'm sorry, I can't help it. I know it's embarrassing."

My head rears back. "Who would have ever told you it was embarrassing?"

"Maxwell," she says, looking down. "He hated when I did it, but sometimes I honestly don't know that I am. I'm sorry, I'll stop."

"Hey," I say, reaching across the table and lifting her chin with my finger. "You do as many happy dances as you want. Don't listen to him. He was just jealous that he could never find the same joy in life that you do from the little things."

How do I know this? Because I'm jealous I can't find that same joy. Except the difference is I would never ask her to dim her light to make me feel better.

"Do you really mean that?" There's a desperation in her voice that I haven't heard before. It gives me a glimpse into the fact that maybe she's a little more broken than she lets on. She's really good at putting up a front and letting the world know that she's okay. To be the jolly elf that she needs to be.

But I want her to be real with me.

Only me.

"I mean it, Avery. I'm sorry that Maxwell ever made you think that you should be anything other than the authentic you."

The corner of her mouth raises in a weary smile. "Has anyone ever told you how amazing you are Matthew Roberts?"

"Not recently, Avery Geller."

"Then let me be the first to remind you." She takes my hand from her chin and laces our fingers together on the table. "So tell me, as I finish up this amazing dinner and prepare for the cheesecake, what's next on the Gingerbread Grove Yuletide Games."

I sigh, pulling my phone out of my pocket without letting go of her hand. I'm not sure how we're going to finish our meals one-handed, but I'm prepared to try if it means not losing the connection we have.

"According to the schedule on the town's website, which needs updating—badly—tomorrow afternoon is the snowman building competition. They've titled it 'The Frosty Showdown."

"That sounds...serious."

"Oh, it is," I say, placing my phone screen-down on the table. As I was clicking through for the schedule, I noticed some emails from clients and texts from Mitch asking about updates on the project I should be working on. The one I had planned to work on here at the diner, alone, after the toboggan race. But after the high of winning and my kiss with Avery, I wasn't ready for my night with her to end. So what if it means I'll be up all night and need to rely on coffee to open the shop again tomorrow morning? Every minute is worth it.

"How serious are we getting with the snowman? Is it themed? Any rules? This is so exciting!" She's doing her dance again, but this time, there's no hiding her light. She's letting it shine, and I love it.

"No rules that I'm aware of. I don't know, don't you just roll snow and put a face on it?"

She stops her happy dance. "You can't be serious."

"I...am?" It comes out more of a question than a statement.

She stares blankly at me before giving my hand a squeeze. "We can make a regular snowman and jazz it up a bit with accessories. We can try for funny, artistic, a rendering from a favourite Christmas story..."

"All with…snowmen? I don't know how artistic you think I am."

This causes her to chuckle. "You don't have to be *that* artistic. It's all about making it come from the heart."

Great, not sure I can do that, either.

"Hmm…okay, I'll brainstorm tonight."

I pop a fry into my mouth before flipping my phone back over—ignoring the quickly multiplying messages—and pull up the website again.

"Then later this week there's the snowball fight, and on Friday is the finale with a gingerbread competition."

"I have so many questions."

"Shoot," I say, regretfully withdrawing my hand from hers once I realize there's no way I'm going to eat my burger one-handed.

"Snowball fight? Like for real? Last-man-standing type stuff?"

"I have no idea. It doesn't say." I scan the schedule again. "The Snowball Smackdown? They can't be serious."

Avery laughs so hard she snorts. Her hand covers her mouth so all I can see are her widened blue eyes, but her shaking shoulders tells me she's still thoroughly entertained by the ridiculousness of these games.

"The Snowball Smackdown? Is this for real?"

"Oh, I assure you, it is," I huff.

"And the gingerbread house competition?"

I groan, skimming the description. "Extreme Gingerbread: Home Edition. 'Our annual Yuletide Games will conclude with our famous Gingerbread House competition. Contestant couples will display their hard work of edible renderings of what makes Gingerbread Grove such a unique and special place.'"

"We're supposed to replicate something from town? In a few days?"

"Is that…a lot?"

Her fork drops to the table, clanging against the side of the plate as she looks at me in disbelief. "No, that's not nearly enough. We need to plan, prepare, strategize."

"I mean, how hard is it to build a gingerbread house?"

I realize my mistake as soon as I finish uttering the words.

"Matthew!" Nancy says, coming over, most likely to inspect the clatter. "You don't honestly think that, do you?"

"I mean…"

Great, how do I backpedal from this one?

"Oh, there are so many things you could do!" Nancy exclaims, clapping her hands together. "There's the city hall, the gazebo in the square…"

"The diner?" Avery suggests with a wink in my direction.

"Nah, too nondescript," Nancy counters, tapping her lip with the pen in her hand. "I know! How about the town hall? I just can't believe you haven't started yet. Getting the supplies alone has taken some of the couples *weeks*."

Fantastic.

"Oh, it's not his fault, Nancy. We were a late addition. We didn't even know if we were going to make it here in time. We'll sort it out, don't you worry," Avery says, giving me a wink.

Great, she saved me…again.

"I believe you. Well, I'll leave you to your dinner and strategizing," she says with a chuckle as she walks away.

"We don't really need to put that much thought into this, Avery. I mean, winning the games was never part of the plan."

"Maybe not, but now that I've seen the town and how, uh, *competitive* some people can be. I think we really need to put our best foot forward."

"But your job…you're too busy. I couldn't ask you to. Especially so close to Christmas."

"You're not asking. Plus, everything here is after hours,

anyway. I mean, unless you don't want to." She looks down, stabbing a cheese and gravy smothered fry with a fork.

I feel a little like that fry right now. Poked and prodded for information on my life from the townspeople. Smothered by my mother and responsibilities of coming back to run the store.

But looking at Avery now and thinking back at our time tonight, finishing the rest of the events might actually be… fun.

But then there's the issue of the games themselves. The events. The people. The holiday.

Before Avery, this would have made me grab for the closest paper bag and inhaling like the popular Sheldon gif. But instead, I feel oddly…calm.

Against my better judgement, I take a deep breath and reply, "You know what? Let's do it."

Avery glances up from her plate, and the look on her face tells me I said the right thing, even if it might be at the expense of my sanity.

Chapter Nineteen

AVERY

"Do you ever wonder what would happen if an elf were to travel to the real world?"

I hold the wrapped present in my hand, letting it hover mid-air over the box I'm currently packing. Looking up, I see Victoria with a snow globe held up to her face. The floating 'snow' hides her expression, but her distracted tone has me wondering if there's more than just the potential time-travelling hypothetical elves. "Like Buddy?"

She lowers the snow globe and tilts her head, her chocolate coloured eyes narrowing at me. "Buddy was a human raised by elves."

"Good point. So, what are we talking here? Elves that plan an escape, searching for what they think is a better life? Curious ones that want to see what Santa sees? Oh, maybe there are evil elves that banish the high-ranking ones to the real world trying to stop Christmas." I smile, my mind racing with too many hypothetical responses.

"I don't know. I mean, all of the above? Do you think they would feel displaced? Overwhelmed maybe by how different it is from the North Pole?"

"Maybe, but elves *do* have a connection to the real world."

Her eyes narrow even more at my response, as if the words coming out of my mouth were in a foreign language. "Santa. So, even if elves didn't have things like cellphone and the internet—which I wholeheartedly think they would—Santa would be their connection to the 'real world.' Plus, who's to say one has never hitched a ride or rode shotgun in the sleigh? And I think Santa would need an assistant for his biggest night of the year."

"Hmm, you're right. I guess everyone needs a Bernard." Victoria raises the snow globe back up to her face. Now that the snow has settled, the tiny North Pole village is visible, as are her enlarged eyes through the curved glass. "I still think it would be weird."

Lowering the toy into the half-filled box, I contemplate how I'm going to find out what her real question is, as I don't think it has anything to do with elves or the North Pole. Placing my hands on my hips, I watch as she looks at the ceramic scene before her as if it held all the answers. "What's really going on? I don't think you're genuinely asking about elves."

In the three years I've worked with Victoria, I've never seen her like this. She's normally the most chipper, positive elf that could turn even the darkest day into sunshine. So, this why her contemplation of travelling elves and monotone voice is worrisome.

With a heavy sigh, Victoria lowers the globe carefully onto the stack of tissue papers on the desk in front of her. "I just wonder if there's an alternate universe where elves could live among us, and we wouldn't even know."

"Did we somehow stop talking about elves and start talking about aliens?"

"What? No."

"Then I'm struggling to follow your line of thought here."

"Do you remember how Jonathan said he wanted to take me out for a special dinner last night?"

"Yes. We went through about a dozen different dress options because you were worried that the restaurant was 'too fancy' for anything you owned." While I loved helping her out, as Victoria has become more of a friend than a coworker the last few years, it had taken up our whole lunch break earlier this week, just for her to decide on the first dress she had shown me.

"Yes…well…I thought he was going to propose."

My heart stops. My breath stills. This is what Victoria's been wanting for the last three months. Every surprise bouquet of flowers. Every drop in for lunch. Every hint dropped at a future together, it's all been because she thought he was going to finally pop the question after three years together. "And?"

"And nothing," she huffs as she plops down into the chair behind her.

"I mean, it must have been something for him to take you to the fanciest restaurant in town." I pull up a chair next to her and take a seat, really taking her in.

Her deep auburn hair is split into two braids underneath our standard green and red elf hat. Her arms are crossed over our green work t-shirt as she closes in on herself. Her shoulders are slumped. There's a deep frown on her face. I've never seen her so distraught.

"He got a promotion at work."

"That's…great?" I ask cautiously. Normally, that would be something to celebrate, but it seems like there's something other than a missed proposal here.

"He's moving to Calgary, and he wants me to go with him."

"Oh."

"Yeah, oh." She looks down at her folded hands. "What am I going to do, Avery?"

I think back to when I was in this same predicament with Maxwell. I was crushed when I found out that he was moving to Vancouver. My heart sank even more when he asked me to move with him. Everything I know and love is in Kamloops. My family, my job, my friends. While I was willing to make it work for the sake of what I thought was my forever, I'm so glad I didn't in the end.

But if I hadn't gone down that path, I wouldn't have been hurt by him and ultimately, I wouldn't have met Matthew. While I've only known him for a few days, I already know that he's not someone I want to miss out on knowing.

"What does your heart tell you to do?" I ask, mostly because I wish someone would have asked that of me.

Tears fill her eyes as she glances up at me. "It's telling me not to go."

"But Jonathan?" she asks, wiping the tears from her cheeks.

"You'll figure it out." I place my hand on her arm, letting her know I'm here for her. "When does he move?"

"Not until the new year."

"Then you have time," I say with a smile.

Victoria blows out a heavy breath and gives me a weak smile. "Thank you, Avery. Out of everyone here at C.O.C.O.A., I know you understand this situation the best."

"Boy do I ever," I grumble under my breath.

"So now you need to tell me about where you've been sneaking off to the last few days."

I rear back. "Sneaking? I haven't been *sneaking* anywhere."

"Fine, maybe not sneaking. Rushing? Dashing?" Her eyes go wide. "Oh my gosh, you were literally dashing through the snow! Were you in a one horse open sleigh?"

"No," I chuckle, playfully smacking her arm.

But that would be awfully romantic to do with Matthew. Add that to the list of things I'd like to do.

"You can't leave me like this. I know there's something! You've been leaving on time the last couple of days, and you *never* leave on time. Come to think of it, I can't remember any other time you've left before me."

"I'm not that bad," I add.

But am I?

"You're avoiding the question. It must be good." She grasps my hand from her arm and holds it between both of her hands. "Please let me in on it. I need something that will distract me."

"There's nothing really…"

"Please? It will be my Christmas present!"

The wistful smile on her face pulls on my heartstrings. She's such a wonderful person, and the thought of her getting anything other than her happily ever after makes me sad.

"It's nothing, really. I'm just helping a friend."

"Uh huh, and this friend is….?"

Taking my hand back, I get up and walk back to the box I was filling. "You wouldn't know him."

"Ooooh. It's a him." She jumps up and walks to my side. "Wait a minute, what about Maxwell?"

"We, uh, broke up."

"What? When?"

I sigh. "When I was in Vancouver." I gloss over the details, not wanting to relive them myself, but also not wanting to dwell on them, given her own current predicament. What I do spend time on, though, is meeting Matthew. While I don't tell her that we're fake dating for the town, I can't hide my excitement for being in Gingerbread Grove and the games.

"You like him," she says with a grin.

"He's a friend, Vic, nothing more."

"Right…of course. So, tell me more about these games."

She may have dropped it for now, but I know it won't be forever. I will, however, take the reprieve in questions. "Tonight is a snowman building competition."

"Oh, how fun! What do you have planned? Classic Frosty style? Snow sculptures? A mix of the two?"

"I just found out about it last night so I haven't had time to plan too much. I was up late after getting home from the toboggan race. I started to look things up online but then fell asleep to have the most animated dreams about snowmen racing down Gum Drop Hill."

"And yet none of those racing snowmen gave you ideas? Rude," she chuckles.

"Right?" I let out a deep sigh and pick up another wrapped toy to place in the box. "I'm thinking if I just jazz up a standard snowman enough, we can make it to the next round. It's the gingerbread house competition later this week that's going to need all of our attention."

"You're really taking this seriously, aren't you?"

"I just really want to help him. Matthew doesn't realize how special he is, or how much the town loves him. While he may not want to live there, I just want him to feel..." I struggle to find the words.

"Less like an elf stuck in the real world?" Victoria completes for me.

I look up at her and smile. "Yes, exactly that."

"Well," she continues, standing and taking a place next to me, starting to load the next box. "I think you're off to a good start. And who knows? Maybe this will be good for you, too."

"What do you mean?"

"I mean—" she bumps her hip with mine, "maybe Gingerbread Grove is the distraction you, and your heart, needs right now. It may not be the best time with Christmas so close, but this is your favourite time of year."

"Well, yes."

"And it's a town that you've been talking about visiting for a while now."

"I know, but…"

"No, there are no 'buts,'" she says, facing me. "You deserve to be happy, Avery. I can't tell you if Matthew is your Christmas miracle, but I think he's been placed in your life at this moment for a reason. Whether it's to heal your heart, give you ideas for C.O.C.O.A., or just to make you happy, but God placed you there for a reason."

"Maybe." If I'm honest with myself, I've thought about that more than once in the last few days. Maybe there is a reason why things have played out the way they have. It can't be a coincidence that things with Maxwell ended just at the right time for me to be stranded at the airport and then also be able to hitch a ride with Matthew. While lying to everyone about our dating status isn't the most honest thing, I don't regret that it means I get to spend more time with him.

And I may have come up with a few ideas for C.O.C.O.A. to improve the Christmas experience for our families while I've been there. Field trips to Gingerbread Grove and Candy Cane Creek included.

"No, there's no 'maybe.'" She places her hand on my arm, making me turn to face her.

"Maybe I should look on GingerSnap and see if there's anything that's been done in past competitions, or maybe other competitors hinting at what they're doing," I muse, running my finger along a curled piece of ribbon.

"What's GingerSnap?"

"The town's social media app. Our server at the diner said they use it to keep everyone up to date on what's going on."

"That is amazing. Do you have to be a member of the town to join it? Is there a secret passcode to get in? I bet it's something like cookies... no, that's too obvious. Hmmm... cinnamon! Cloves! Nutmeg!" she yells, getting more animated with every suggestion she gives.

"I haven't downloaded it so I don't know, but I bet Matthew could get it for me."

"What are you waiting for? Pull out that phone and download it! I need to see what GingerSnap and Gingerbread Grove are all about!"

Reaching into my back pocket, I shake my head at the

notification staring back at me. "I guess it won't be too hard to find; it looks like I've been invited to join."

She sticks to my side while I follow the prompts to create an account. Each page has an animated gingerbread man with text bubbles to walk you through the sign-up process. From a design standpoint, this is incredibly well made, which is shocking considering how badly the town's website needs to be updated.

"This is the best thing I've seen in, well, forever." Victoria hovers over my shoulder as I click through the screens, each one more incredible than the next. "This town looks like it's right out of a Christmas fairytale."

And I have to agree with her. My feed is filled with pictures of the town getting ready for the holiday, everyone pitching in to decorate the tree and the town square. I recognize some faces that I've been able to meet the last few days, but it's really just a blur of happy faces willing to help out and make the season extra special. Feud or not.

"Is that one you? Oooh, is that Matthew? He is cute!"

The picture in question is, in fact, of me and Matthew. It's a candid shot of us racing down the hill in our toboggan. The more I swipe through, the more I see they've captured more than just the race. There's a shot of us holding hands when we were announced as winners, and of us hugging at the base of the hill.

"Just friends, huh?" Victoria asks smugly as I scroll to the last picture to see us kissing.

I'm not sure how I'm going to talk my way out of this one.

"I mean, friends...kiss?" I can't even say that without wincing.

"Uh huh," she says with a smirk.

"Who's that?" she asks, pointing to the corner of the screen.

Zooming in, I have to laugh when I see the couple in the background. "That's McKenzie and her husband."

"The ex and the mayor? They don't look too happy to see you two kissing," she laughs.

"Nope, not one bit." I don't want to admit the satisfaction I feel with seeing how distraught they are by our happiness, whether from us being together or winning the race, but I want to break out in a happy dance.

"I get it now." She beams up at me. "While I still don't believe you two are just 'friends,' you have to do your best to win this thing. You can't let them win."

I don't know if she means just the games or the overall battle we seem to be fighting. Either way, I know she's right.

A slow smile spreads across my face. "Do you want to help me come up with a game plan?"

Chapter Twenty

MATTHEW

"It's a little dramatic, don't you think?" I ask, my eyes glued to the gazebo in front of me.

Two couples stand huddled together, hands clasped as Cal and McKenzie stand in front of them, wide smiles on their faces. If this was anything other than a Christmas competition, they would almost look like they were enjoying snuffing out the candles inside the lanterns.

"I mean, did you really expect anything different?" Avery whispers back. "I mean, this whole town sorta feeds on dramatics."

"I guess not."

Cal continues to rattle on about the intensity of the games and how, while unfortunate, there needs to be eliminators in order to crown the winners. "In the spirit of Christmas, I would like to think this isn't an extinguishing of light, but rather a way to allow those remaining to burn brighter. By the end of the week, one lantern will remain, burning brighter than ever."

"You've got to be kidding me," I murmur under my breath. Or maybe, I only think I do.

An older couple in front of me that I vaguely recognize

turns around and shushes me, their stern looks letting me know I wasn't as quiet as I thought.

Avery snickers beside me, earning glares of her own.

"Sorry," she says, trying—and failing—to appear serious.

The couple glares a little longer before turning around in time to see the biggest metal candle snuffer I've ever seen appear in Cal's hands.

Like a winterized Vanna White in her light pink ski jacket, white trim, and boots that eat up most of her legs, McKenzie opens the first door, standing to the side and waving her free hand underneath the hanging lantern, making sure everyone knows which couple is the first to be eliminated.

I resist the urge to bite my clenched fist as the need to laugh is overpoweringly strong, but I can't risk being another distraction.

Avery bumps into me slightly, showing she's fighting the urge just as much as I am.

"Trish and Everett," Cal continues, holding up the laughably oversized snuffer, the cover barely fitting through the lantern door. "Please don't see this as an end for your love, just for your journey in this year's Yuletide Games."

With that, he reaches the cover in and extinguishes the light, before moving to the next one, leaving the downhearted looking couple alone on their side of the gazebo.

"Oliver and Sasha," Cal declares as McKenzie rushes over to find her new place, stumbling slightly as she stops abruptly, making sure to steer clear of the snuffer. "The extinguishing of your candle does not dim the light of your love. Please take your light and continue to shine throughout Gingerbread Grove."

Avery's eyes flash open as our gazes meet. She silently mouths, "Is he for real?"

I shrug, biting my lip.

Must. Not. Laugh.

"Hey, do you want to sneak away before the snowman

competition starts?" Avery whispers, her eyes focused on the older couple in front of us, seemingly to make sure we don't draw their attention again.

"It's going to start in a few minutes," I answer, watching in an almost curious horror as members of the town counsel remove the lanterns and carry them in a procession down the gazebo's steps. "You know what? A few minutes away might be a good idea."

"They're only missing the dark cloaks," Avery chuckles, grabbing my hand as she leads me through the crowds.

"Don't give them ideas," I joke.

"Maybe they need to watch some more 'White Christmas' and less 'It's a Wonderful Life.'"

"You're not joking."

Reaching the edge of the crowd, I link our hands more firmly together before turning to her, watching Cal and McKenzie shaking hands and laughing with members of the crowd over Avery's head.

"So, I need your opinion," Avery starts, giving my hand a squeeze.

"If it has to do with lanterns or cookies with ginger, you're out of luck."

"Oh no, I was hoping you would help me bake lantern shaped cookies for our gingerbread house entry." Avery replies dramatically.

"Only as long as we include a book cookie snuffer," I joke back.

Avery laughs and her eyes twinkle in the fading light. "While I do feel like we need to incorporate this into our design if we make it that far, it's not what I wanted to ask you. I was wondering if you could help me get a 3D printer to make some items to put into the baskets for our families. I don't even know if it's possible this close to Christmas…"

"What sort of items?" I shift to block out the scene in front of me.

For the first time since we met—other than the ride from the airport, that is—Avery has asked me for something. All week she's dropped her life for me, and now I feel a sense of pride—and relief—that there's something I can do for her.

"I was thinking of starting simple. Cookie cutters, ornaments, maybe some small decorations. I know there's only a couple of days…"

"Leave it with me," I say with a smile. "Okay?"

"Okay," she says with a smile back at me. Not just any smile. *Her* smile. Her smile for me.

"Contestants, take your positions for The Frosty Showdown!" Trevor's voice echoes through the square as it comes out of the speakers.

"I guess it's our time." The words come out of my mouth, but there's no actual intention behind them. Instead, I stand with my hand linked with hers, gazing into her beautiful blue eyes.

"So, what's his deal? Is he gunning for Cal's job as mayor? Is he his lackey? Like head elf to a power-hungry Santa?"

I don't hold back my laugh this time; every one of her suggestions is more ridiculous than the last. "No, or at least I don't think so. From what he tells me, he's just on the counsel and volunteered to help run things since Cal and McKenzie decided to enter so last minute."

She tilts her head. "Last minute? How last minute?"

"I, uh, don't know."

"Hmm." She puts a finger from her free hand to her lips, tapping as she looks off into the distance.

"Last call for all contestants! Any late entries will be automatically eliminated," Trevor announces.

"We don't want to be eliminated!" Avery exclaims.

"Or, this is our easy out," I reply.

"Matthew! You can't be serious!" She playfully whacks me on my chest. "We have to win this!"

"I don't think a simple snowman is going to win this, anyway."

"Oh, there will not be anything 'simple' about our snowman, I promise you."

My eyebrows draw together. "How…?"

"Leave it with me. Okay?" She repeats my words back to me.

"Okay."

Even though I have a hard time blindly following someone, I know that with Avery, I'm going to be okay.

"Are you sure this is what you planned?" I stand back, observing the mound of snow Avery is packing together.

"Trust me, this is exactly what I want it to be."

My foot hovers above the ground, frozen in indecision of whether continuing would be a good idea or not. We've been packing snow for half an hour, and while everyone else's entry looks more like the classic frozen mascot, we still resemble a snow pile.

"Can you do me a favour and pass me the wooden dowels in the bag over there?" she asks, her hand waving at a blue shopping bag to her right.

Crossing the snow-covered path, I reach down and rifle through the contents. "I don't see any dowels. Just a lot of fabric."

Brightly coloured felt-like fabric that doesn't resemble anything that would go on a snowman.

"Are you sure?" she asks, brushing the snow off of her gloved hands.

I look again, feeling through the fabric. "No, nothing like that in here."

She appears at my side, looking through the bag with me. "I know I put them in here. The same with the pinecones and painted rocks. They're just…gone." Her voice is laced with bewilderment as she looks around the ground, retracing her steps back to where the bag was on the ground.

"I'm sure they're here somewhere," I add reassuringly, although I can't see where they would be.

"I put the bags at the side of the gazebo while they were doing the lantern…I don't even know what to call that. And then I picked it back up right after we came here. I'm sure I put it all in there. I checked it twice."

"Just like a good elf," I add with a smirk.

She stops searching and looks up at me with a sigh and a smile. "Yes, it's what we elves are trained for," she chuckles. "You know what? It's fine. We've got this. We can still make the best snowginger Gingerbread Grove has ever seen."

"A…what?"

"Gingersnow? Snowgingerman?" she whispers, taking a step closer to me and looking around, making sure no one can hear. "I haven't worked out the name yet."

"Okaaaay," I reply, drawing out the word. "And what is that, exactly?"

"A gingerbread man made out of snow, of course."

"Of course," I repeat back, bewildered. For the first time since picking her up outside the airport, I question the situation I've found myself in. She might as well be speaking some secret elf language with the words that she's saying right now. "And how are we doing this?"

"We're just going to have to make do with that we have. You're right, I'm an elf and we elves make the best of any situation." She stands up straighter, turning to me with a mischievous look on her face. "And being my partner makes you an honorary elf."

Holding up my hands in surrender, I take a step back. "Woah, I don't know about that."

"Come on, have faith and a little Christmas cheer." She takes one of my hands, lacing her fingers with mine, and pulls me back over to our snow mound. She lowers her voice as she tucks herself into my side. "It's going to be a gingerbread man jumping out of a present box."

"You said your design wasn't that complicated."

"It's not...not really. I mean, not compared to what I could have come up with if I had more time." She turns back to the mound. "How much time do we have left?"

I look down at my watch. "An hour."

"Oh no," she gasps. "We have to get to work. Why don't you go look for branches that I can use to prop up the arms and I'll finish the present box."

"That's what we've been building!"

"Shhh," she hushes. "We can't let anyone in on this."

"I don't think anyone else would have come up with a ginger..."

"A gingersnowman," Avery completes for me; the corner of her mouth ticked up. "But I also didn't think someone would take my supplies."

"Avery," I huff.

"I know I didn't forget them at home and my bag was left alone." I give her a dubious look. "Shouldn't the big city boy be the one more suspicious of people? I mean, look at the couple with their laughing and jolliness...so suspicious."

"You can't think..."

"What about them?" She nods to another couple. "They're bickering over the scarf placement. Anyone that guilty would be bickering over little things, too."

I narrow my eyes at her. "I can't tell if you're being serious or not."

She rolls her lips into her mouth. "I guess you'll never know."

I laugh. Once again, being with her feels a little...freeing. I don't care how loud my laugh is. I don't care how my head tilts back until it's almost touching my back. I don't care how everyone's looking at us.

For once, I don't care.

"So, how about that branch?" she asks, and I know with the look she's giving me right now, I'd do anything she asks.

"I can't believe you pulled this off," I say, bewildered.

It took all the allotted time for the competition right down to the second, but it's done. The mystery base we had been building turned into a present box with red felt ribbon Bursting out of the box is the top half of a large, snow-white gingerbread man with his arms outstretched. I don't know how Avery made it happen; even with her missing ribbons, mug, and rocks, she made it look like it was coming to life with an icing-lined expression.

"You mean *we* pulled it off," Avery says, bumping her hip with mine.

"I don't know about that."

"My, what do we have here?" McKenzie's voice dips with exaggerated warmth as she comes up behind us. "This is the most…interesting snowman I've ever seen."

"If you can even call it that," Cal adds, coming up beside her. "I say that's more of a snow *sculpture*. It's not even a snowman at all. We'll have to check the rulebook to see if some of the rules weren't bent a bit."

"There were no rules bent, or broken, I assure you," Avery says.

"We'll see about that," Cal mutters.

"Matty! I'm so happy you made it to The Frosty Show-down!" Mom exclaims as she joins our little group. "I just couldn't wait to come down here and see your entry!"

"Mrs. Roberts! You're just in time!" McKenzie walks over to my mom, looping her arm with my mom's. "I think there must have been some misunderstanding. You know how it can be, especially when someone that isn't from town tries to join our traditions."

The glare McKenzie shoots at Avery would make some women cower.

But not Avery.

"No misunderstanding," Avery replies casually.

"Oh, it's okay. You needn't be embarrassed," Cal adds.

"Needn't?" Avery mouths at me.

I shrug.

"There really was no mistake," Avery declares. "I read the contest rules thoroughly on both the town's website and the posts that were made on GingerSnap."

"GingerSnap? But that's only for Gingerbreadians! It's invite only!" McKenzie looks like she's going to snap herself, the way her face is turning red and her eyes are bulging.

"Now, dear, let's be a little more welcoming than that." My mom pats McKenzie's hand that rests on her arm. "And it's okay to admit a mistake, Avery. I'm sure it was easy enough to overlook the requirements, or they're a little more lax where you come from."

"Actually," a man I don't recognize walks up, standing on the other side of Avery. "She's right. The rules themselves don't state that it must be a 'snowman,' but rather a 'snow creation.' So, really, they did nothing wrong."

"Eric, this doesn't concern you," Cal retorts, puffing out his chest. If he had feathers behind him, he would be a peacock.

"Oh, but it does. We wouldn't want anything *unjust* to happen around town, now would we? It wouldn't be very good attention for Gingerbread Grove."

The two men enter into a staring competition, leaving us all slantingly in the middle.

"What's going on?" Avery whispers to me as we all watch in confusion.

"No clue."

"Right. McKenzie and I have important town business to attend to." Cal says, grabbing the lapels of his jacket and popping them up.

I swear this guy doesn't know what decade he belongs in.

"We do?" McKenzie questions.

"We do."

The couple exchanges a silent conversation before she drops Mom's arm and bolts to his side. "Right! We do!"

Without so much as a goodbye, they storm off. Any negativity felt was left in our little circle as they stop and talk to the next townsperson, all smiles and laughs.

"Well, while I do appreciate a good gingerbread creation, I suggest you learn more about the unwritten rules we have here if you think you'll be staying, Avery. No one wants to come in and make a fuss. It'll ruffle feathers."

Yeah, a few peacock feathers.

"I can assure you that's not what I was doing."

"And really, Mom. I also expect better of you. Weren't you just telling me at breakfast this morning that the new town motto was 'to welcome people as warmly as a freshly baked cookie?'"

"Well, yes," she stammers.

"And how the town is built upon the season of giving, so therefore, we must give all the love we have to our neighbours and the people that visit our town?"

"Yes, but…"

"Well, then I think you owe Avery an apology. This is the most incredible snow creation I've ever seen. The impartial judges awarded us first place and I think that should be all the justification you need."

Readjusting the purse on her arm, she looks down and mumbles. "I'm sorry."

"What was that?" I ask, knowing I'm poking the bear and will likely get a lecture tonight on embarrassing her in public, but for once, it doesn't bother me. I know that what I'm doing is the right thing to do.

She straightens with a huff. "I'm sorry, Avery. That was not very Gingerbreadian of me. Your creation is…lovely."

"Thank you, Mrs. Roberts," Avery replies honestly.

"Now, if you'll excuse me, I need to talk to Agnes about the hot cocoa that will be served at the event tomorrow night. I trust there won't be any more bending of the rules now that you have both moved on to the next round."

"Elf's promise." Avery raises her hand in an oath.

"Hmph. I'll see you at home, Matty." With a final look between us, she storms off.

Normally, having the withering look from my mom, along with the promise of her letting me know *exactly* how she feels about the situation, leaves me with a sense of foreboding while also wanting to rub an increasing feeling of pressure in my chest; but Avery grabs my hand and giggles up at me and all I feel is—peace.

"The three of them love their dramatic exits," the man says, reminding me he's still here.

"You're telling me," I reply.

"We haven't met yet. I'm Eric Davies. Owner, well, future owner, of the Gingerbread Inn here in town." He extends his hand, and I shake it with my free one.

"Nice to meet you. I'm Matthew Roberts and this is my girlfriend, Avery Geller."

They say hello before Eric laughs. "Oh, I've heard about you two. The whole town is talking about not only how you two are the forerunners of the Yuletide Games, but also about your return to town, Matthew."

"I'm scared to think of what they're all saying."

"Oh, nothing to be worried about. Well, not with everyone else in town. Not sure about your history there with the mayor and his wife…"

"Ancient history," I reply.

"Well, either way, it's nice to finally be able to meet you. I hope they don't give you too much trouble. They hate to lose, and right now, you two are the only ones that have ever dared to try."

"Is that so?" Avery asks, her gaze drifting to where Cal

and McKenzie laugh with a vendor at their booth. Looking over their shoulders, their smiles dropping slightly before they catch themselves and go back to their conversation.

"Well, I think it's about time they had some competition, don't you think?" Avery asks, that mischievous look back on her face.

Chapter Twenty-One

AVERY

"You really like him, don't you?" Victoria asks, walking up to my desk.

"Good morning to you, too, Victoria. How was your evening?" I look up from my computer screen, her auburn hair braided in two low ponytails under her elf hat.

"Fine. Boring. I stayed at home and watched *Elf*." Taking a seat across the desk from me, she crosses her arms, watching me intently. "How was the competition?"

"Fine," I answer, not ready to talk about what happened last night, because I'm still not entirely sure what happened. "Have you talked to Jonathan?"

"No, and don't change the subject." She leans forward. "Something happened."

"No. Yes. To be honest, I don't know."

"The Snowbread Man didn't work?" she gasps.

"It did; it was wonderful and exactly how we planned it. Well, mostly." I let her in on what happened with my missing items and Cal and McKenzie trying to get us disqualified.

"But we read every rule," she says, shocked.

"I know."

"Twice."

"I know."

"But someone still got up in arms about it?"

"Yup…" I sigh.

"This is the strangest, most interesting town I've ever heard of." She leans forward, resting her elbows on her knees, her curled fists propping up her chin.

"You're telling me," I retort, letting my eyes drag back to the spreadsheet on my screen.

While the town has been more than I ever could have imagined, I have to admit some of the small town politics are making it lose its Christmas glimmer.

"Do you think it's his ex?"

"McKenzie?" I roll my chair back, knowing I need to take a break from looking at the final gift numbers or my eyes will start to blur. "I mean, we definitely aren't in her good books, but I don't know if she would pull this. Wouldn't be very 'small town charm' of her to be stealing mugs and rocks for a snow competition."

"Hmm, you're right. They do seem to be building on the whole Christmas charm thing." Victoria thinks for another moment before her eyes grow as large as lollipops. "What if it's someone from Candy Cane Creek?"

"Why would they care about our competition?"

"*Our* competition?" she jokes.

"You know what I mean."

"Yes, I do," she says with a smile that makes me think she's reading too much into it.

Or maybe she's just too good at reading me.

My phone vibrates on my desk in front of me, the notification showing a new post has been made on GingerSnap.

I pretend not to see it, knowing that Victoria glanced down and saw the app's logo. Her eyes grow as wide as snowballs and she's biting her lip in anticipation, knowing the polite thing to do would be to ignore that she saw my screen.

"So, I'm thinking that today we need to focus on organizing the non-perishable food into the baskets," I say, straightening in my chair, shaking my mouse to wake up my screen. "I have it all listed here by what food allergies the families have, so I think if we send the Reindeer Racers to start working on that, it'll free up the North Pole Ninjas to finish up the last of the gift wrapping."

Victoria is nearly bouncing on the edge of her seat, needing to know what the post was. I doubt she even heard what department I'm assigning to what task for the day.

I stifle a laugh, needing to focus on my screen because if I look at her, I'm going to break out into the laughter I'm so desperately trying to hold in.

"The Sleigh Riders have been doing a great job on delivery logistics. They'll have everything ready to go by delivery in two days."

She's vibrating on her chair.

"The Merry Makers are doing their last practices for the carolling…"

"Please check it!" Victoria bursts.

"Check what? The list? That's what I'm doing. I'm even checking it twice," I add with a smirk.

"Aren't you curious to see what it's about? What if it's an update about the Games? Or Matthew? Or Matthew and you at the games?!" Her voice getting louder and louder with every suggestion.

"What do Matthew and the Games have to do with our delivery schedule? We have eighteen sleighs that we need to start loading…"

"Avery!" Victoria huffs, waving her hands at my phone.

"Oh, that," I respond dramatically. "I guess we could check that." I chuckle, casually reaching for my phone.

With a couple of swipes, I have the app up, and Victoria is hovering over my shoulder like a kid on Christmas morning.

"Is that yours? Avery, you two did such an amazing job!"

The first thing that pops up on my feed is a picture of Matthew and I putting the final touches on our entry. Matthew packing the snow to curve the top of the gingerbread man's head while I'm carefully arranging the ribbon around the box base.

"Yeah, we did, didn't we?" The lazy smile that crosses my lips. It's not just the job we did on our entry—because that exceeded my expectation—but also the way that Matthew and I worked together. Unlike the other couples—the *real* couples —we didn't bicker. There weren't any arguments about how things should go, or how the accessories should be placed. We just…worked. We laughed and talked out any decisions that needed to be made. It felt more like in the beginning of a relationship where we just purely enjoyed being together.

Which is why it hurts so much to remember that we aren't a real couple, and in a week, I likely won't ever see him again.

"Why would someone write that?" Victoria asks, snapping me out of my holiday pity party.

"Huh?"

"The caption. What a horrible thing to say."

Scrolling up past the picture, I focus on the caption underneath it.

InsiderCookie57 The magical event of the annual Gingerbread Grove Frost Snowdown was marred by these outsiders, who not only blatantly broke the rules by creating something other than a snowman, but they also bribed the judges into giving them first place, too. 'Contestant' Avery Geller was seen in cahoots with at least two of the three judges prior to the start of the event, with rumours of possible dealing of illicit cookies in return for votes.

. . .

"CAHOOTS? Illicit cookies? What are they even talking about?" I ponder out loud as I scan the post again. "And posted by someone named InsiderCookie57? Really?"

"There's some *drama* in this little town. If you weren't the one in the middle of it, I would suggest that we grab some popcorn and watch it unfold."

"Hmph," I respond, clicking on InsiderCookie57's profile. "This person's whole page is just post after post, speaking badly about people or events in town."

"That's horrible. Can you see who it is?"

"No, it looks like they've hidden their real name, and their email is just a generic 'gingerbread lover' name."

"Oh, a burner account. How intriguing. But wait, don't you have to be invited to make an account on GingerSnap?" Victoria asks, standing up.

"Yup," I answer as I continue to scroll, hoping the more I tap on things a name will appear.

"So then, someone in town knows who this is. I wonder if there's a way to find out who invited them."

"I'm sure there is, but you would need some sort of special access to the app for that." I huff, putting my phone down on my desk and swivelling my chair to face her. "Who would do this? If it's someone from town, they hide their true feelings really well because everyone I've met so far has been amazing."

"Except McKenzie and Cal," she says, her eyebrows reaching her elf hat.

"Yes, but it would be a horrible political move to be bad mouthing everyone in town, especially when they had such a big hand in changing the town from Woodland Springs to Gingerbread Grove and starting the Yuletide Games."

"True…" She taps her finger to the corner of her mouth,

looking out at the window behind me. "What if it was someone from Candy Cane Creek?"

"I don't know how much I believe in this rivalry. So far I've only heard some of the older ladies from town plotting against them. I haven't heard or seen anything from the Candy Cane Creekers that suggests they have anything to do with what goes on around town."

"That you know of." Her gaze darts back to me. "What if they're so sneaky that no one knows? Like little North Pole ninjas."

I roll my eyes. "Are you sure you're not from Gingerbread Grove?" I laugh.

"Come on, now. Think about it. Things go missing from your bag before the event; there's someone posting bad things about you and Matthew—the couple that's been winning the events."

"But why would they care about who wins this? I don't see what their motive would be."

"You're the one that listens to all those podcasts. Surely you can think of something."

"Are you really comparing this person to a serial killer?"

"Obviously not," she huffs. "I'm just saying that motives are motives. Even the ones that don't make the most sense."

Picking up my phone again, I open the app and scroll through my feed. I don't know what I'm looking for, exactly, other than anything that might stand out.

"I have to go for a meeting with all the Santas," Victoria declares, walking toward my door. She turns with one finger pointing at me. "I expect a full update on anything you find out about this *InsiderCookie* and what they want."

"Yes, ma'am," I say with a mock salute.

"I mean it, Avery. You know I'm living through you right now. I need you to let me know about anything you find. I'm living for this holiday drama. It's better than reality tv."

"I don't know about that..."

"You're right. *Love is Blind* is pretty entertaining. Such a train wreck of a show." She stares off out the window behind me for a moment before giving her head a shake and focusing on me. "Could you imagine that show, but for Christmas?"

"No, I really couldn't." I start to wonder what it's like in Victoria's head, but then realize I don't really want to know.

"Maybe couples get matched up based on holiday traditions. Or preferences. Or cookies!" She hops up and down. "What if people fall in love with their favourite Christmas songs and movies."

While I love the idea of people finding their true loves around the holidays, I don't think doing it as part of a reality tv show is really the way to do it.

"Victoria?"

"Yes?" she responds dreamily.

"Santas."

She snaps to attention. "Right, but don't think this gets you out of filling me in on what you find out."

"Elf's promise."

I breathe a sigh of relief once she's gone. Not that I don't love talking to her, but I don't know what to say. It breaks my heart to think that anyone in Gingerbread Grove—or Candy Cane Creek—would be so hurtful as to create a whole account just to speak poorly of the town and the people in it. I can understand that some may not like that people who aren't actively living in Gingerbread Grove are not only taking part in the games, but at the top of the leaderboard, but Matthew was born there. His family is there. The whole town shops at his father's store. As much as he may not want to accept it, he is one of them, and it's clear from how everyone speaks to or of him.

Well, most people, at least.

Swiping out of GingerSnap, I pull up my texting app, quickly finding Matthew at the top of my list.

Did you see the post on GingerSnap today?

MATTHEW

What makes you think I even have it downloaded?

Because I made you, remember? 😕

That doesn't mean I kept it.

Well, did you?

You'll never know.

gif of Dr. Evil laughing

gif of Judge Judy tapping on her watch

Fine. Yes, I have it and yes, I saw it.

Do you know who it is?

No.

Aren't you curious?

Not really.

gif of Michael Scott shocked face

It shouldn't surprise you I don't care about small town gossip.

But they think I bribed the judges! With cookies! Illicit cookies!

Well, did you?

You can't be serious right now.

gif of angry girl waving a hairbrush

My screen lights up with Matthew's number.

"You can't seriously think I bribed judges with illicit cookies..."

"I mean, did you? What makes the cookies illicit, anyways? I wasn't aware that Gingerbread Grove had a contraband on any type of sweet. Unless it's a candy cane or sugar cookie. Now that you mention it, I haven't seen any of those here since I got back," Matthew muses, a slightly amused tone in his voice.

"I'm being serious, Matthew."

"So am I, Avery. Now that we're talking about it, I want a sugar cookie. Maybe a sugar cookie with a candy cane crushed up on top. Do they have those in Kamloops? You might have to smuggle me one tonight. I'll meet you in the garden. I'll be sure to get rid of any crumbs before the snowball fight."

As much as I had worked myself up about this, I love the humour that's coming through the phone right now. It's the most lighthearted I've heard him since we met.

"If I get you a cookie, will you take this seriously?" I muse, already feeling the stress of the last half an hour starting to leave me.

"That depends. You'll have to tell me how you bribed the judges exactly, and more importantly, why you didn't let me in on it."

"Matthew, I promise you, I didn't bribe anyone," I laugh. "I didn't even know who the judges were before the competition started. I also didn't even bring any cookies with me. But now that I think of it, there were some fake cookies that I had in my bag that I was going to use for our Snowbread Man. Those went missing with everything else."

"It's called a Snowbread Man now?"

"For now. I'm still working on it." I fill him in on what I found while scrolling. The unidentifiable username, all the posts with only negative things to say. "You know computers; is it possible to trace?"

"I mean, sure, if you had access to the backend. They would be able to see who invited them and the IP address."

"So, we need to find someone with that access."

"Or we could just leave it alone. It's a post on a social media app that's just for Gingerbread Grove. It's not that big of a deal."

"Matthew," I sigh.

"Avery," he sighs back, dramatically.

Knowing I'm not going to get any more help; I give it up —for now. "Fine. Do we have a game plan for The Snowball Smackdown tonight?"

"Do we have to call it that?"

And there's the gruffness in his voice again. While light-hearted and joking Matthew was fun, there's something comforting about grumpy Matthew that makes me happy.

"That's its name, isn't it?"

"It's a ridiculous name."

"Either way...I was thinking that our best way to win will be to keep moving and stick together. I did some research last night, and it looks like obstacles will be set up at the base of Gum Drop Hill. We can use those and the trees for cover."

"Research? How did you do research on this?"

"I scrolled through GingerSnap and looked it up online." I roll my eyes.

"Of course."

"So, what do you think?"

"I think..." he says before going silent for a moment. "I think we'll do whatever you think is best. I was just going to throw snowballs and hope for the best."

"Well then, it's a good thing you have me."

"It is a good thing," he replies.

I don't know if he's talking about just for the snowball fight or something else, but my whole body warms as if I'd just had a gingerbread oat latte with eggnog sprinkles.

Chapter Twenty-Two
MATTHEW

"I thought I'd find you here."

Brushing through the last of the cedar hedges, Avery is sitting like an elfish angel on the bench, her face tipped up to the moonlight, her eyes closed.

I don't know if an elfish angel is even a thing, but if there is, she's it.

"I just wanted a little quiet before the chaos begins." A sad smile crosses her face before she opens her eyes and faces me.

"Are you okay?" I sit down on the bench next to her, searching her face for clues.

"Yeah, just a hard day today."

"What happened?" I shift to face her, our legs brushing as I move.

"I had set a quota to bless a certain number of families this year and we didn't meet it." She looks down at her folded hands in her lap, her fingers nervously rubbing together.

"I'm sorry." Placing my hand on her clasped ones, I feel how cold they are, making me wonder how long she's been sitting here. "Are you short by a lot?"

"Twenty. I know it doesn't sound like a lot in the grand scheme of things, but it's a lot to me. That's twenty families that have to go with less than they deserve at the best time of the year. I keep thinking that's twenty families with children that are most likely not going to get presents and may not even get much of a dinner."

I hesitate, making sure that I find the right words to try to comfort her.

I can't imagine being in a position where my job was to help people on that level. Sure, I could argue that making 3D printing software helps people, but I don't have people relying on me in that way. It doesn't make the difference between them being able to eat more than just the bare minimum or lighting up their face with a Christmas present. Those are things that I've just always taken for granted.

I can't imagine the immeasurable stress she's under. But yet, she's here for me, and she's plotted out how to win our events.

She gives and gives, and now I'm sitting here wondering if there's anyone that takes care of her. Who makes sure that *she* has what she needs.

"I think you're an amazing woman who does the most incredible things for everyone else. I know you're disappointed you didn't meet your quota, but just think of all the families you are helping. There must be hundreds of people that will have smiles on their faces because you care. You take the time to make sure that they have a Christmas they'll never forget."

A hint of a blush crosses her cheeks, barely visible in the moonlight. "Thanks." She looks away bashfully before gasping. "Oh! I have something for you."

Again, she's always thinking of everyone else.

I want to laugh when she hands me a clear bag decorated with a curled ribbon. Inside are two sugar cookies shaped like candy canes with the crushed candy on top.

"Did you seriously find these? I was just kidding."

She lets out a laugh that releases some of the tension

building in my chest. "I promise it wasn't that hard. I found them at the cafe I got my coffee at this morning. It's like it was a sign."

"A sign of what, exactly?"

I pull on the ribbon and carefully remove one of the cookies. Breaking it in half, I offer one of the pieces to her. She doesn't take it right away, but after motioning to her a few times, she accepts it.

I take a bite of mine and I'm instantly transported to a time when Christmas was more than just games and competitions. It was when friends and family got together and just spent time with each other. There were presents, but they were simple and homemade. When my mom would laugh in the kitchen, and we would make cookies together. It wasn't about which town could do Christmas the best, or what was 'won' at celebrating. I miss the time when the real meaning of Christmas was celebrated.

"Thank you. I don't know, maybe a sign that you needed some sweetening up?" she jokes, bumping her knee against mine. "No, seriously, maybe that we're on the right path. With the games, with the town…"

"With us?" The words come out of my mouth before I can stop them.

You know when you say something that was supposed to only be an inside thought? One that no one but you is supposed to know? This is one of those times. So instead of me thinking the words and truly starting to believe they are real, I go ahead and spoil it.

The sweet cookie turns to lead in my stomach. My heart rate skyrockets. My palms are sweaty.

I've ruined it. I still don't know what 'it' is when it comes to Avery and me, but I've ruined it. The only thing I can do is look down at the partially eaten broken cookie in my hand, wondering if that is also a sign for us.

"Do you mean that?" Her voice is quiet and unsure.

I wrestle with myself not to look up. I can't stand to think of what expression might be on her beautiful face right now.

"Matthew?" She places her hand lightly on my knee. "Do you really mean that? Do you think *we're* on the right path?"

I don't know how to answer that. I mean, how can I? The only thing we've admitted to each other is that we are fake dating. She is doing this as a favour to me. Come back to town, play in the games, and break up after Christmas. That's it.

But I don't want that to be it. I want more. I want to build more snow creatures with her. I want to try new things—maybe not tobogganing—but explore what I might be missing out on now that I see I'm closing myself off from what could be because of what has been.

"Matthew, answer me. Please."

The pleading in her voice makes me finally look up. I'm not met with any of the emotions I was expecting. Instead, she looks…hopeful.

"Yes, Avery. I think I do."

Then she rewards me with one of her face-splitting smiles. "Good, because I think that, too." She holds my gaze for a moment before leaning in and placing a light kiss to my lips.

I no longer think I want what Avery and I have, I *know* it.

"I CAN'T BELIEVE they make everyone watch the candles getting snuffed out," Avery whispers to me, making sure her voice is low enough for only me to hear this time.

"I think Cal's watched a little too much reality TV if you ask me," I whisper back, not able to take my eyes off the scene in front of us.

We made sure to stand well in the back this time, so that none of the town's seniors would be able to hear us. Even from back here, there's no hiding the crying on one woman's face as their lantern is put out with the oversized snuffer, or how the other two couples watch in a stunned silence as they lose their lights.

"Should we have a game plan for ours if we lose today?" The mischievous grin is back on her face. "We could be over-dramatic. I could wail. Clutch my heart and cry out to the crowd about what a holiday injustice it is."

I try to hold back a laugh, but it comes out as a snort, drawing confused looks from the people in front of us. With a final round of side eyes as I try to compose myself, they turn back around to watch the lanterns being carried down the steps.

"Maybe you should start demanding your illicit cookies back since they broke their end of the deal," I add.

"Hmm, that might only work if the judges are the same today. Plus, I'm sure these hypothetical cookies are long gone. They would want to eat the evidence. Wouldn't want to leave a cookie crumb trail."

"No crumb left behind."

"The GingerSnap sleuths would leave no sprinkle unturned."

We stand there, blocking out the world, staring at each other with silly grins on our faces, but I can't help it. I can't remember the last time I was able to joke around with some-one. Where the banter came so easily.

"Hey! It's time to start heading over," Trevor says, slap-ping a hand down on my shoulder. "The Gingerbread Express is ready to take you guys over."

"The...what?" I ask, finally breaking away from Avery's gaze.

"The Gingerbread Express," he repeats, as if saying the name is going to make me understand any better. When I don't reply, he rolls his eyes and motions with his head behind him.

There I find an extended golf cart decorated like a train. But not just any train. A literal gingerbread train.

Okay, maybe not *literally*. We don't have the Hansel and Gretel of golf carts, but there are wooden boards cut and painted to make it look like a train made out of gingerbread, and the detail is, frankly, pretty impressive.

"That is one of the best things I've ever seen," Avery exclaims beside me, clapping her gloved hands together. "And we get to ride it!?"

"You certainly do! We're using this to bring everyone over to The Snowball Smackdown. Come on, we're moving the contestants first."

The word 'contestant' is like a bucket of snow being dumped on me. I remember that we're about to go into a snowball fight. I haven't been in one since elementary school. I don't want to admit it, but I don't know if I even remember how to make a proper snowball. What if it just falls right apart like a snow puff ball?

Before I can spiral into all the ways this can go horribly wrong, Avery takes me by the hand and leads me into the over-the-top golf cart.

Our ride to the hill is quiet. I clutch onto Avery's hand as we whiz through town. The other couples don't speak. I don't know them, and I'm inwardly grateful they don't want to get to know us. If the side glances and blatant dirty looks are any indication, the rumours on GingerSnap are spreading and people in town are believing them. I don't care what they say about me, but I do care how it impacts Avery. And the way she's squeezing my hand and looking out the side of the cart tells me the icy chill from the other couples hasn't gone unnoticed.

"Hey," I whisper, leaning in.

She slowly turns her head to face me wearing the saddest expression I've ever seen cross her face.

It breaks my heart.

"Hey." She tries to smile, but it's so weak anyone could have missed it if they weren't looking.

I need to do something. She's in this position because of me. If she wasn't here to be my fake—sorta real?—girlfriend, she wouldn't have rumours spread about her over the town's app. She'd be away from whatever small town drama is happening here.

I make sure to keep my voice low, but loud enough to make the other couples think they're overhearing. I just hope Avery picks up on it and plays along. "I was thinking that maybe we can take my dad up on his offer."

Her eyebrows draw together and her nose scrunches. She looks so adorable I almost forget I'm supposed to be working up a distraction.

"Offer?" she asks. I only have to give her a slightly pointed look before her eyes widen and she lowers her voice. "*That* offer? But you were so against it."

We both know there is no offer and I, at least, have no idea what this offer could be, but we will play along.

"It's only fair, don't you think?" I ask, calculating how much longer this ride is going to be.

"Hmm, maybe. Only if you think it's the right thing to do. I trust you."

I know we're both talking about an offer that doesn't exist, but I can't help but want to believe that the last part is true.

"Here's our stop! Gum Drop Hill!" Trevor exclaims, turning around in the driver's seat. "Good luck and happy snowballing!"

We all exit the cart, the other couples chattering excitedly amongst themselves.

"Thank you," Avery whispers once we are out of earshot.

"I don't know if it will do anything but if there's one thing that has stayed the same about this town, it's their love for gossip."

We reach the edge of the temporary course when I see all traces of sadness have evaporated from her.

"I trust you," she echoes. It's all she's able to say before we're thrust to fight for our Yuletide lives.

Forty minutes later, I've got my back up against a wooden cut out of a present, I'm freezing and wet from sitting in the snow, and I'm looking up at a giant cut out of a gingerbread man.

"I think his eyes are following us."

"They're hollow icing eyes. How are they following us?" Avery asks, slightly out of breath from running to this position.

"I don't know, but I swear they are. Do you think it's how everyone seems to know where we are?"

Even though I'm admittedly not the best at this game, I can't figure out how everyone seems to know where we are at any given time. We've narrowly missed being knocked out multiple times, and it's really only because of a miracle that we're still in this.

"I don't know." She pops her head to the side, barely missing a snowball flying past her. "Ugh, they found us *again.*"

"This is getting old," I huff, tilting my head back. "How many teams do you think are left?"

"Seven couples started, four remain," she deadpans, looking over her shoulder before ducking quickly.

"Do you know you're becoming more dramatic the more this Showdown goes on?" I joke.

"This is my house. I have to defend it."

"Did you just quote *Home Alone*?" I raise my eyebrow, wondering what side of Avery this snowball fight is bringing out.

"This is a very serious competition, Matthew."

"I'm beginning to understand that."

"If there was ever a time to be dramatic, it would be now."

I blink, staring at her blankly. "I can't tell if you're serious or not. Also, how do you seem to be one step ahead of them when they always know where we are?"

"Unagi," she says, putting her two fingers to each temple and turning them slightly.

"Fish? I don't get it."

"Ross," she says, dropping her hands and rolling her eyes. When I don't say anything, because I'm thoroughly confused, she continues, "*Friends*."

"Your friend Ross is helping us?"

"You can't be serious. Ross Geller? The show *Friends*?"

"Never seen it."

She gasps. "You get *Home Alone* but you don't get *Friends*? Do you know how excited I was to share a last name with Ross and Monica? How the show utterly defined my sense of humour?"

"All because of a show?" Another snowball flies over our heads. "Maybe we ought to have this discussion at another time. When we aren't being pelted with snowballs."

"Fine," she concedes. "But if you tell me you've never heard of Stars Hollow or the names Lorelai and Rory, I may throw a snowball at you myself."

I have no idea what any of those names are, but I know enough to keep my mouth shut.

Chapter Twenty-Three

AVERY

"**M**el, I'm telling you, it was the most intense snowball fight I've ever been in," I say, talking into my wireless earbuds as I place non-perishable goods in a hamper to be delivered tomorrow.

"And how many snowball fights have you been in, exactly?" she asks. I know she's half distracted with her kids yelling in the background. I smile, picturing my niece and nephew running amok in the living room while Meg attempts to have an adult conversation.

"I'm an elf, Meg. I have at least five a year. But this was intense. There were cutouts that had to have been at least fifteen feet tall and snow mounds that were like boulders."

"I have so many questions, but we don't have a lot of time before my kids start to destroy my living room." She covers the phone so all I can hear is muffled yelling before she comes back. "And what about that app? Anything new on that front?"

"Yes, actually. There was another post late last night. This time, InsiderCookie chose a picture of Cal and McKenzie emerging from the snowball fight—quote, 'like the true champs they are.'"

"Pfft. Sounds biased to me."

"No kidding."

"Anything about you and Matthew?"

"Just a very unflattering picture of both of us being pelted in the face when we were knocked out of the competition."

"So are you both out?" she gasps.

"Thankfully, no. We didn't win the event but we managed to stay in it long enough to avoid elimination."

"No creepy snuffing ceremony of you?" she laughs.

"Not today." I shudder, thinking about the oddly dark portion of the games. For a town that is supposed to be celebrating all things light and seasonal, it was not a curve ball I was expecting from Gingerbread Grove.

"Tell me more about what Matthew said."

"How long were you waiting to be able to change subjects and bring that up?"

She laughs. "How long have we been on the phone? Now, come on, tell me."

"You mean how he alluded to the fact that we may not be all that fake?"

"Yeah, that. Tell me about that."

"He just said we're on the right path. I mean, he didn't *say* we were anything more, but he was acting like maybe it could be?"

"Do you want it to be?"

I still. "I don't know how to answer that. Would I like Matthew and I to be more than just a fake relationship? Yes. He's the most incredible man I've ever met. But he lives in Vancouver and I'm here. I can't do another long-distance relationship."

"Have you actually spoken to him about this?"

"What? No, of course not. Why would I?" I start busying myself again, placing boxes of stuffing and dried mashed potatoes into the hamper.

"Avery, you can't just assume the worst because you don't want to have a serious conversation with him."

"He didn't know who Ross was," I argue.

"Not everyone lived and breathed *Friends*, Avery."

"He didn't get my unagi joke."

"You can't avoid a person because they didn't get your obscure reference."

"I'm pretty sure he's never heard of Stars Hollow, either."

"Avery! Stop deflecting!"

Uh, oh, she used her mom voice on me.

"I'm not deflecting. I just don't want to get hurt again."

"Matthew isn't Maxwell."

"I know that," I huff, fighting the urge to stomp my foot. I don't know why I'm turning into a toddler having a tantrum, but I feel like it.

"Do you?"

"Avery, can you please come to the front desk?" Our speaker system sounds.

"Sorry, Meg, I gotta go." I place the last food item in the hamper and mark it with a red check mark, letting the team know this one's ready to be loaded onto the truck.

"Funny, what good timing you have," she muses.

"Must be a Christmas miracle," I say as I start walking toward the front office.

We say our goodbyes and I click off the call, just as I'm walking through the door to the front office, greeted by Sally, our receptionist, and a grumpy looking delivery man.

"Oh, Avery, thank goodness you're here," Sally says, looking and sounding frustrated. "This gentleman is saying that there's a large order, but I don't have anything recorded."

"And I'm telling you, there's a paper here that says that there is," the man huffs.

Sally wasn't kidding; he is grumpy. And this close to Christmas.

"I'm sure it's just some sort of mistake," I croon. "We have all of our deliveries."

The man huffs and looks down at the paper in his hand. "Are you Avery Geller?"

"Yes..."

"And this is C.O.C.O.A.?"

"Well, yes…"

"Then this is yours. All paid for. Where do you want it?"

He shoves the paper at me, which has an incredibly long list of goods on it. There are twenty fresh turkeys, boxes of stuffing, cans of cranberry sauce, and enough sides and both perishable and non-perishable items for twenty families to have a complete turkey dinner with all the fixings.

Twenty dinners.

To complete the twenty families I thought I would have to turn down this year.

My mouth opens and closes like a fish out of water as my eyes scan the page in my trembling hands.

"Unless you're refusing the delivery…" he says.

"No!" I exclaim, my free hand darting out as if I could grab him and prevent him from leaving. "I'm sorry; I just wasn't expecting this."

"Do you think it's a last minute donor?" Sally asks.

"It must be. But how would they know that's exactly how many we needed?"

"Can you please just sign the order so we can get this unloaded? We have other deliveries to make." The delivery man says gruffly, crossing his arms.

The sewn on name tag reads 'Dan' in bold red lettering, making it stand out against the light blue shirt. The ends of his dark brown hair poke out from behind his backwards cap, curling towards his neck. He's got a neatly kept beard and intense green eyes that say he would rather be anywhere other than here. He would be handsome if it weren't for the scowl on his face. I wonder if anyone's ever told him that. The only thing I know is, it's not going to be me that does it.

Grabbing a pen from Sally's desk, I scribble my signature on the bottom of the page and thrust it back at him. The only thanks I get is a grunt as he turns and heads back out the door.

"Well, he's full of the holiday spirit," Sally muses. "I'm surprised he didn't leave with a 'Bah Humbug.'"

"Just wait. Maybe after he drops everything off."

"Do you have any idea who would do this?" Sally's eyes track Dan as he opens the front door, his dolly stacked high with boxes.

"No, I…" But then I stop. There's one person outside of Victoria and my boss that knew that I had set that goal, let alone that I was twenty families short. Just one person that I'd confided in and told how much it meant to me that I didn't turn any families away this Christmas.

But twenty families is a lot. There's no way that he would have been able to do that, would he?

"You know who it is!" she exclaims, drawing the attention from Dan as he shifts the boxes from the dolly to the floor. He rolls his eyes as he turns and pushes the dolly back through the door.

"I don't know, but I suspect."

"It's him, isn't it?" she squeals. "Your mystery guy from Gingerbread Grove!"

I reel back. "How do you know about that?"

"Oh, please," she waves her hand in front of me. "We all know about him; we just don't have details."

I should ask more questions about how word spread about Matthew around the warehouse, but really, I shouldn't be surprised. I didn't tell Victoria it was a secret, and as she put it, my behaviour with leaving on time was out of character for me.

Dan forcefully opens the door with another dolly filled

with boxes, letting a burst of cold air and snow follow him. I shiver as the blast hits me, and I don't miss the annoyed look on his face, as if it were *my* fault he was out in the blustery weather.

"Are you going back there tonight?" Sally asks, her eyes also tracking Dan's annoyed movements.

"Yes. It's the final event. The gingerbread house competition."

"Oh! What are you going to do? Santa's Workshop! A snow cabin! A barn!"

"A barn?" I turn to her, giving one last look at Dan as he pushes the boxes off his dolly a little harder this time.

"I don't know. Don't all small towns have barns?"

I chuckle. "I'm sure they do, but no, I'm not doing any of those. It has to be a structure from the town."

"And?" She's practically standing on her tiptoes, her hands clasped under her chin.

"The hardware store." The butterflies in my stomach aren't just fluttering, they're crash landing and exploding. They're doing cartwheels and loop-de-loops and flying off the edge of the runway.

"Interesting choice…"

"It's Matthew's family's store. I thought it would be a nice nod to them." I don't want to get into the sorted history between Matthew and his family, especially since it's not my place to say.

What really makes me nervous is that I haven't run the full plan by Matthew. We talked about basics, things to buy, and what needed to be pre-built. He was in charge of picking up the starter package earlier in the week and I gave him a list of supplies that we'll need in order to complete the finishing touches, which we're required to do at the event tonight. It wasn't that I was keeping him in the dark or keeping it a secret, but he's been so busy and tired with running the shop, doing the games, and keeping up with his own business that I didn't want to add yet another thing onto his plate. Not when I'm the one that pushed for us to really try to go as far as we can in these games.

"That's really sweet, and a good way to get into his family's good books," she jokes.

"Yeah…" Looking down at my hands, I start to pick at nothing, avoiding her eyes.

"What?" she asks.

I open my mouth to reply with my standard 'nothing' or 'everything's fine,' but I'm cut off when Dan forces open the door again, sending in another burst of cold and snow.

"This is it," he says, shimmying the boxes off the dolly and stomping toward the door, little piles of snow trailing behind him.

He's almost out the door when Sally stops him. "Merry Christmas, Dan!"

He stares at her blankly for a moment before mumbling something that sounds awfully like 'bah humbug' before letting the door close forcefully behind him.

"Ha! I knew it!" I say, pumping my fist in the air. "He said it."

Sally rolls her eyes. "You don't know what he mumbled there."

"It doesn't matter. What I want to know is, what was that?" I ask.

"What was what?" she shrugs.

"That. You. Dan." I motion my hands between her and the door. "Whatever that was."

"It was nothing. There's no me and Dan."

"Does he deliver here often?"

She bites her lip before looking away. "I'm not answering that. Now, are you going to tell me more about Matthew or are we going to get this food into the fridges until we figure out how to sort them out?"

"Since you're not going to tell me, I guess we're going to sort out these turkeys."

"I'll go get the dolly in the back."

Sally disappears, likely to avoid any more questions from me, which I have plenty of. But I also know what it's like not wanting to answer any.

Thinking of my reason for avoiding questions, I pull out my phone.

> Did you have anything to do with this?

MATTHEW
Do with what?

> You know.

No, I really don't know.

Gif of Jeff Goldblum trying to grasp a thought.

> Don't try to distract me by using a gif. We just got a delivery here with everything we need to bless the twenty families I thought were going to have to go without.

That's great. I'm glad that you will be able to give them what you need.

> Matthew!

Avery!

> I mean it, did you do this?

I'll see you tonight.

Please answer me. I want to make sure that I thank the right person.

A customer just came in. Can't talk. Being on my phone while in the store looks bad. Or so my mom says...

Matthew! Don't leave me hanging!

gif of toddler kicking and crying in the leaves

Chapter Twenty-Four

MATTHEW

"I'm here! I'm here!" Avery rushes toward our table, an oversized box in her hands.

I can barely see her over the cardboard, and I have no clue how she's managing to dodge the tables as swiftly as she is.

"Phew, there were a few close calls there," she says as I take the box from her and place it on our table.

"Traffic was that bad?" I start to open the top flap, but Avery swats it down, her eyes narrowing.

"No peeking. Not until all of it is in here." She starts to pull off her coat and scarf. "And, yes, the highway was jammed up from an accident outside of town. Looks like black ice. Thankfully, everyone was fine."

"That's good. Wait, how do you know that?" I ask, watching as she casually drapes her jacket over the back of her chair.

"I stopped, of course. Thankfully, I had some extra candy canes on me. The kids in the backseat of one of the cars were pretty scared."

"Did you just say the 'double c' word?" Betty Stafford gasps as she walks up to our table. Her white, tightly curled hair wet with snow. "You should be docked marks. Nay, you should be kicked out of the competition!"

"And the town!" Doris Whittaker adds, shaking her cane in Avery's direction.

'Nay?' Who uses that anymore?

"Ladies, please. The treat was given outside of town lines and for a couple of children that were scared. Surely you can overlook this."

"Hmph," Betty says, eyeing our box wearily. "Fine, but only as long as there is not one red and white peppermint flavoured *thing* on your submission *anywhere*."

"Noted," I answer, watching as the two older women walk away.

"What was that?" Avery whispers, now standing at my side.

"That is what happens when you mention anything to do with the town's arch nemesis within the town orders."

"Does *the town that shall not be named* know about the rivalry yet?"

"Not that I'm aware of. Or, if they are, they're being really quiet about it. Rumour is InsiderCookie57 is from there and just playing dirty."

"Didn't I suggest that to you?" she laughs.

"Maybe. I can't keep up with all the gossip."

"Look at you! In the thick of it with the small town life! Next thing you know, you'll be joining town hall meetings and scheming with the rest of them!"

"I will not." I can't hide my eye roll as I move to the other side of the table and pick up the bags of supplies I brought, placing them on the table next to her box.

"Picture it. Sicily, 1922…"

"Is this another TV reference?" I suck in a breath, wondering if I'm going to have to dodge a flying piece of candy for not getting it.

"*Golden Girls,*" she sighs. "We're going to have to get you caught up on all of these shows."

"Is that necessary?" I put on a good front, but if it means I get to spend hours next to Avery while she laughs and provides anecdotes about her favourite shows, I'll do it.

"Necessary? Absolutely. But let's get back to you at the town hall meetings. As much as I love your button-up shirts and sweaters, I'm seeing more flannel and jeans in your future, maybe a backwards cap."

"No way," I protest.

"Fine, it doesn't have to be backwards."

"Shouldn't we get started on this competition?" I start pulling out the candies and chocolates she had asked me to pick up. I'm not sure how they're all going to come together, but I know Avery has a vision.

"Yes. I just have to go get the last box from my car."

"There's *more*?"

"Of course there's more. I wanted to go bigger but I didn't have the time."

"I'll get it for you," I offer, feeling the need to be busy so I don't dwell in my guilt about how all of this has essentially come down to her.

"That would be great. And then I can get started on getting this all set up." She reaches into the pocket of her jacket and pulls out her keys, but another little white circle falls out with it. "What's this?"

I hold out my hand to her and she drops it in my palm. Flipping it over my fingers, I shake my head. "It's a tracking device."

"A what?" she claims, drawing the attention from the people around us.

"A tracking device," I whisper back. "I take it, it's not yours."

"No, it's not mine," she whispers back, staring at the device in my hand. "How did it get in my pocket? Who's tracking me? Do you think it's how all the other couples knew where we were during the snowball fight last night?"

Her questions fly at me as I try to process everything. Someone is taking these games so seriously that they've planted a tracking device on Avery. There's likely one that was placed on me, too. Patting my jacket, I thrust my hands in my pockets and come out with a device exactly like the one that she just found. "What…?"

"Okay, this has to be related to the games now. Why else would we both have the same device planted on us?"

"I don't know, but these games are getting very…odd."

Looking around the room, I'm seeing everyone in a new light. Instead of them being people I started to think of as neighbours or even friends during my week here, I'm seeing people that might have ulterior motives. I thought I had to leave my time not trusting people back in the city, but I guess Gingerbread Grove is just like any other place.

"I'll go get the box. Maybe the sooner we're done, the sooner we can get out of here. "

"Hey," Avery says, placing her hand on my arm. "We'll figure it out."

I nod, accepting her keys and storming out of the room, making sure not to meet anyone's eyes. I don't know what I was thinking, being under the impression that maybe the town had changed, and everyone was happy to see me back here. There's obviously someone, or someones, that aren't. I might be able to buy that it's all someone from Candy Cane Creek if it wasn't for the fact that the posts, the location devices, everything seems to be aimed at Avery and me.

Pushing the doors to open into the parking lot, the crushing pressure is back in my chest for the first time in a long time. I start to rub it, until I notice I'm doing it with the hand that's holding Avery's keys, so it's just a repeated circular motion of stabbing myself with metal mixed with impending doom.

"Hey, Matthew. Are you okay?" Eric asks, coming from between two parked cars.

"Yup, just fine," I reply gruffly. I know it's not his fault. Or, at least, I'm pretty sure it's not his fault. He hasn't been near all the events, and I didn't see him last night at the snowball fight.

"Big day. It's the final event of the games," he says, shoving his hands into the front pocket of his jeans.

"Yup." I look around, seeing if there's anyone here with him. Is this an ambush? Is there someone watching? Waiting so they can make some other kind of move?

"Are you sure you're okay?" he asks, placing his hand on my shoulder.

Before I can think better of it, I brush his hand off and take a step back. "Can I help you, Eric?"

He places his hands up, palms facing me. "Just a concerned friend."

"Is that what we are? Friends?"

I hate how I'm acting right now. I hate that I've resorted to putting up the wall that I always have when I'm at home in the city. I feel like I can't trust anyone and everyone's just out for themselves. I've let myself fall into a false sense of security being here. I let my guard down and now look what has happened.

"I thought we were. Or we were starting to be. I'm sorry if I'm mistaken."

I huff, dropping my shoulders. "No, I'm sorry. There's just been some…developments that have me on edge. That's all."

"Is it the posts?"

"You know about those?"

Eric laughs, dropping his hands. "Everyone who's on the app knows about them. Knows that you're taking over your dad's store for good, too."

"I'm…what?"

"Trish posted all about it. She said she overheard you and

Avery talking about the big deal and how it was going to be finalized soon. Such a smart move, having your company based out of the store, too. Probably saves you a lot of money with the price of office space in the city."

"Uh…"

Well, that got more of out of control than I expected. I just wanted to take some heat off of Avery and now I'm moving back to Gingerbread Grove, taking over my dad's store, and moving my company here.

"You don't look like someone who's excited to do all of that," he observes.

"It's all just…a lot." I scan the parking lot, no longer looking for a secret sleuth but for Avery's car. Or a way to get out of this conversation.

"I get that. The town can be that way. Especially with new people."

"What do you mean?" I snap my head toward him. Now that I think about it, I don't remember him from growing up in Woodland Springs. He looks a few years younger than me, so I chalked it up to my poor memory or teenage selfishness. Now I know that's not the case.

"Not only did I move here, but I moved from Candy Cane Creek."

My eyes bulge wide. "And they let you in?"

"Not at first," he chuckles. "It took a lot of convincing and pleading at the town hall meetings. There were bribes with baked goods. Being voluntold to be on coffee duty for every meeting. I did it all happily, but it still took a year. Or more like it took a year for the senior in town to stop calling me 'Sugar Stick Softie' instead of my real name."

I wince. "Wow, that's bad. Why did you do it? What made you want to be part of this town so bad?"

"I don't know. I loved Candy Cane Creek. I co-managed an inn with my best friend, and I had the girl of my dreams, and I messed it all up. Around that time, Cal reached out and asked if I was interested in running an inn here."

"Cal? Cal reached out to you? No offence, but why would he do that?"

"Cal would stay at The Mistletoe Inn often before the town made the changes. I didn't understand it then, and I can only assume now, but I think it was to get ideas for Gingerbread Grove. See how the Creek was run. Experience the holiday season there."

"Sounds sneaky to me," I muse, finding confirmation that my immediate distrust of the mayor wasn't founded on the fact he's married to McKenzie.

"Something like that. I can't prove anything, but during his last visit, he asked if I liked where I worked and if I had any desire to own an inn myself. Shortly after that, I lost everything keeping me in the town, so I left."

There seems to be more to the story, but I don't press him on it. Not on that aspect, anyway.

"What's happening with the inn? I heard there's a hold up."

He sighs. "Paperwork keeps going missing right before the last steps are about to be approved. No matter how many times I submit or back it up, they say it has never been received by the deadline."

"That's frustrating. Wait, do you submit online? It'll have a time-stamped record…"

"That would be nice, but no. Have you seen the town's website? You can barely find out when your garbage is going to be picked up. It can't handle online submission."

"I did have the pleasure of navigating it," I answer dryly, renewing my curiosity as to why the town has a fully functioning and carefully designed app, but not a website. "What about the people you handed the paperwork to? They must remember."

"They all claim to 'see so many people, they can't remember anything.'"

"Inside job from City Hall?"

"To what gain? Cal was the one who asked me to open it, and it would bring money into the town. Right now, we don't have a functioning inn."

"That's a good point." I scratch my beard while I think, the cold wind picking up and brushing against my face. "What about your old connections in Candy Cane Creek?"

"Jacob and Cassie? I don't think so. They were mad, but they aren't the vengeful type."

"Even with the feud?"

"Believe me, the feud isn't a big deal over there," he laughs.

I look back at the elementary school gym doors, thinking about how much the town has changed since I grew up here. This wasn't 'Gingerbread Grove Elementary,' it was 'Woodland Springs Elementary.' There wasn't a feud with Candy Cane Creek. It was a quaint little town that we all loved to take a drive to visit during the holidays. The people were warm and friendly. They would never speak behind your back.

It seems that it's more than just the name that changed.

And maybe that's a little reflection of the way I've changed since moving to the city. Shutting everyone off. Being suspicious of everyone that's not in my circle.

Before Avery, I wouldn't have minded, or likely even noticed. But now I see that maybe, like the town, not all changes have been for the better. I'm seeing how it can affect people like Eric, who are just looking to find their place.

"I need to get back in there. Do you mind helping me carry something in?"

Chapter Twenty-Five

AVERY

"**W**here is he?" I mutter under my breath, watching the doors like a hawk.

He left to get the final box from my car twenty minutes ago, and there hasn't been a sign from him.

There was a shift in him before he left. Finding the tracking devices in our pockets set something off in him that made him turn back into the man I met the night at the airport. The one that would rather shut down than work through what's going on.

He wouldn't drive off in my car without me, right?

Rather than worrying about it, because he wouldn't do that—or I'm mostly sure he wouldn't—I fidget with the gingerbread pieces I've pulled out of the box and arranged on the table. Rules of the event state that pieces can be pre-designed and cut out, but they can't be assembled until the day of the competition and only when the couple is together.

Which means I'm left poking at the pieces and candy decoration until Matthew gets back.

"Stood up at the candy shack?" McKenzie asks, that fake smile plastered on her face.

"Nope. Matthew just ran to the car to get the rest of our supplies."

"It's been a while. Are you sure he didn't flee? Leave you to deal with the town and pick up the pieces of your failed attempt at the games?"

What is she reading my mind? There's no way I can let her know that, though.

"He'll be back."

"You seem so sure."

"You seem so sure to see the worst in him."

She tilts her head to the side, her smile becoming less fake and more unkind. "You don't know him like I do."

"I don't think you know him at all. Not anymore."

Movement behind McKenzie draws my attention, but I fight to break my eyes away from hers. I want to breathe a sigh of relief when Matthew walks in, my large box in his hands, followed by Eric with the bags I had with it in the trunk.

"Looks like your worries were unfounded. Here he is," I say with a smile just as fake as hers.

"Hmm, for now." She leans in and drops her voice. The painfully overpowering scent of her perfume makes my stomach turn, but I don't let her see it. "Just remember that it's not just me that's watching you, it's the whole town."

"Are you threatening me, McKenzie?"

"Me? Of course not!" Her hand flies to her chest, bright pink nails nearly blending in with her pink sweater. "Just a reminder."

With a final sneer, she walks away, nearly bumping into Matthew.

"Matty," she says sweetly.

"McKenzie," he grunts.

At least he's not falling for her sickly sweet persona. Not to mention the fact that I wasn't the only one that noticed she completely ignored Eric.

"What did she want?" Matthew asks, placing the box on the chair beside me.

"Nothing important," I huff, watching her as she air kisses an older woman, fake smile back on her face. Bringing my gaze to the two men in front of me, I find they are both looking at me quizzically. "What? Do I have icing on my face?" I bring my hand up to the corner of my mouth, wiping, hoping to take off whatever traces are left behind.

"No, or at least, I don't think so," Matthew says. "What, uh, what do we need all of this for?"

"Is this all for one gingerbread house?" Eric asks, handing me the bags he carried in.

"Not a house. A store," I answer, placing the bags on the floor next to me.

"Which store?" Matthew asks.

"Nutmeg & Nails. Your store." I watch his face, waiting for his reaction. I honestly don't know which one I'll get. I was praying he wouldn't be mad. I'm doing it because, while it might not be where he wants to be working right now, it is the reason that we met, and the reason we started fake dating. If we hadn't, we would have just gone our separate ways that night, and I don't want to think about that being the end to our story.

While there is still a very strong possibility that our story will end, I'm glad it wasn't on that night.

"I hope you don't mind, but I went ahead and made the sign up beforehand. Don't worry, I checked it's just the placing together of the pieces and the finishing touches that have to be here today. I made sure to read the rules. Twice." I hesitate before pulling out a rectangular piece from the box on the chair behind me, holding it flat in my hands.

The name 'Nutmeg & Nails' is spelled out in cursive, written in white icing, but beneath it reads 'Roberts & Sons Hardware.'

"That's...wow," he says, not looking up from the cookie sign in my hand.

"Yeah?" I lean forward, placing my hand on his arm. "Is that okay? You're not upset, are you?"

"No, not at all. I just...I don't know what to say."

"What's the name under it?" Eric asks, peering over Matthew's shoulder.

"The original name. Before..." Matthew answers.

"Everything went crazy?" Eric finishes.

"Yeah," he chuckles. "That's one way to put it."

"So, it's okay?" I ask tentatively.

"More than okay," Matthew adds.

I let out a sigh of relief and my hands clutch my chest. "I'm so happy. I wanted to do something special for you and your family. I was really hoping that I didn't cross any boundaries, but once you said our entry had to be a place in the town, I knew that's what we had to do."

We. Because I feel like Matthew is just as much a part of this as I am. I may have planned and prepped, but he's in this with me. We're doing this for him. To prove to him and the town that he's not what they think, and the more that I'm here and find out that people like McKenzie and InsiderCookie57 think they can shove out whoever they deem unfit, it makes me more determined to prove them wrong.

"What do you say we get started, then?" Matthew asks, finally looking up at me.

There's a quiet, reserved feeling to him, making me think that maybe I did the right thing in picking the store. I've been nothing but a nervous ball of tinsel all week getting it ready. But the way he's looking at me, with his mouth ticked up in a coy smile and a shimmer of hope in his eyes, I think I made the right choice. Not just with choosing to do the hardware store for our entry, but also taking the chance on hitching a ride with him from the airport that night and for being with him now.

"I'll leave you to it, then," Eric says, shoving his hands in the pockets of his jacket as he walks off, reminding me that we aren't here alone.

"Right. The competition," Matthew says, looking at the table. "I hope you, uh, have a plan."

"I do!" I begin pulling my iPad out of my bag and tapping it awake.

"How much time did you spend on this, exactly?" he asks, peering over my shoulder.

"Not as much as I wanted to." I tap and swipe until I find the screen I'm looking for. "Ah ha! Here it is! I used Santa's List to make up a rendering."

"I'm sorry, a what?"

I look over my shoulder at him. His eyebrows raised, his hazel eyes wide behind his glasses.

"Right. Elf lingo," I laugh. "It's the organization program we use at work. We make lists for the families and have the option to check everything twice…"

"Do you have a naughty or nice list, too?" he chuckles.

"Yes, but we don't call it that."

"Wait, really?"

"It's more for the employees. Technically, we have to call it 'performance reviews,' but everyone in management knows what it really is."

"And how do gingerbread houses fit into this?"

"Well…" I start, turning the iPad to face him. "When we had the program built, we wanted a creative space. Here, we are able to work with actual dimensions of candies, cookies, and everything we might need to make the houses themselves not just beautiful, but also structurally sound."

"That's…incredible." He takes the iPad from my hands and explores what I've created. "And you did all of this? The detail you have—are you sure we can recreate this?"

"I am! I used our gingerbread cutter to get the proportions right."

"Gingerbread cutter? Just how many gingerbread houses do you all make?"

"Oh, loads!" I exclaim. "We do it as a team building exercise before the start of the season, and then we try to make kits for each of the families. We try our best to match it to their favourite candies or whatever theme they want."

"You really try to make it special for the families, don't you?"

"I mean, we try," I shrug. "It means a lot to me—to all of us—that the families have the best Christmas they can. If there's anything we can do to make it better for them, we want to do that."

"You're amazing, you know that?"

"I mean, I'm just doing what anyone would…"

"No, you really aren't." He grabs my hands and waits until my eyes meet his. Everything about him in this moment tells me he means everything he's saying. "Most people wouldn't do what you're doing, Avery. And if they wanted to do something, they wouldn't go to the lengths you are. You are truly incredible."

"Thank you, Matthew." I can't take my eyes off his grin as he looks at me like he means every word he just said. Which, knowing Matthew even the fraction of the amount that I do, I know he means it. I don't know how to respond to it, really. I love my job and I love helping people. There's not much more to it than that. I've been blessed to have found a place that I love being and I get to work with amazing people to help others. I couldn't ask for a better job.

Which is why I'm thinking that it was meant to be that I found out about Maxwell and we broke up. It physically hurt to think of me leaving C.O.C.O.A. to move to the city, even when it meant that I was going to be with the man I thought I loved. But now I see that God had another plan for me, and I'm where I'm supposed to be.

"So," he starts, clearing his throat and looking at the table.

"Why don't you show me how we're going to assemble this. I don't think I've touched one since I was a kid."

"Don't worry, it's simple." I take the iPad back from him and point out the different pieces. "We're just going to make it like a rectangular box. Since the store itself is on the main street and boxed in with other stores on each side, I've designed a sort of Christmas mural on the walls."

"I hope you aren't expecting me to draw that. I can code a program to do that, I can't draw it myself. "

I laugh. "Don't worry. I've got that covered. Years of decorating these babies and sugar cookies, I can do that. What I need you to do is assemble." Reaching into a bag, I grab a baking sheet and a bag of sugar, handing it to him and I rifle through the rest of the bag.

"Isn't the sugar usually made into icing? Did you bring a mixer?"

"No, silly. I have icing sugar for the decorations. You're going to be melting sugar to hold the pieces together."

"I'm going to...what?"

"Ah ha!" I exclaim, reaching into the bottom of the bag and pulling out what I was looking for. "You're going to melt the sugar on the baking sheet using this."

"You brought a torch?"

"Not just any torch. A kitchen torch. If you use the melted sugar to hold the pieces together, it'll act like cement. Much sturdier than royal icing. You'll be trying to hold the walls up all day."

He stares at me blankly, still holding the baking sheet and sugar.

"Isn't melted sugar supposed to be extremely hot? How do you do that without burning yourself?"

"Oh! I have something for that!" Picking up another bag, I reach in and grab a pair of gloves. "These will protect you. The sugar melts fast so you shouldn't have to use it for too long."

I show him how to use everything and after picking it up quickly, he's off on his own piecing everything together. That leaves me to finish the decoration.

"What are those?" he asks, looking over as he's holding two pieces of cookie together.

"Bricks."

"Bricks…" he repeats flatly.

"Right, you just saw the structural drawing, not the finished product." I grab the iPad once more, tapping away.

"How detailed is this app?"

"Oh, very! Here." I turn the tablet to show him a completed rendering. Cookie bricks make up all the sides. A small awning hangs over top and above is the sign.

"What are the windows made out of?" he asks, not looking up from the screen.

"Melted sugar. I made them this morning."

"How do you have time? Between this, your job, the snowball fight…do you not sleep?"

"I run on a coffee IV," I say flatly. When I realize he doesn't get the joke, or the reference to Lorelei Gilmore, I laugh. "I'm kidding. I don't use an IV. I drink it in copious amounts like normal people."

"Not hot cocoa? I thought elves couldn't have coffee." The corner of his mouth fights to tick up in a smile, but he clamps it down.

"Common misconception. Elves love, and require, coffee just as much as everyone else. More so in December."

"Well, my little elf, we'd better make sure you have enough caffeine." He takes his gloves off and puts down the torch. "I saw a coffee station when I first came in. Let me get you some fuel."

I watch in awe as he walks away.

Did he just call me *his* little elf?

Chapter Twenty-Six

AVERY

His elf...
       Unless it was for show, there's no way he meant to say that. But there's no one around. No one paying attention to us, anyway. The other couples are busy concentrating on their creations. There are some townspeople wandering around observing, but no one within hearing distance of us.

Unless...he meant it.

"Ninety more minutes," a voice declares over the speaker in a very dramatic announcer tone.

"Jingle Balls!" I say under my breath, putting my iPad back in my bag.

Thankfully, Matthew constructed the base structure very quickly, and the sugar is holding the cookies together as it should.

Picking up a bag of icing, I squeeze some white onto a cookie brick and lay it across the foundation. Or where the foundation would be if this were a real store. If I hurry, I can get the bricks on quickly; it'll give me enough time to decorate the murals and the windows, after I install them.

Time ticks by, and all my focus is on what I'm doing. I may need Santa's magic in order to get all of this done on time if we have a hope of adding all the details to make sure that we win.

"One elf coffee here for you," Matthew says, placing a cup in front of me. Or I assume that's what it is, as all my concentration is on making the brick straight. "Thank you."

"What do you need me to do now?"

"Hmm…" I sit back after placing the last piece and pick up my coffee, taking a sip. I let the warmth of the drink mixed with the spices of nutmeg and cinnamon calm me. But looking around the table, my heart rate picks up and stomach drops looking at what there is left to do. "I have to finish these bricks and do the mural on the sides. I need to install the windows and decorate them. Then there's the cobblestone street, and the paved sidewalk…"

"Avery," he says, taking the cup away from me. "Maybe the coffee was a little too much with how stressed you are. I think you've had enough for today."

"You can't take that away from me. It's my emotional support drink. I won't be able to get through the rest of the competition without it."

"Avery," he sighs.

"I mean it, Matthew. I stop drinking coffee and I stop functioning. There won't be any more decorating. We'll lose the competition. We'll be out. Our lanterns will get snuffed. Snuffed!" My mind is racing thinking about the domino effect of losing this competition. Will that be an indicator of how tomorrow will go delivering the baskets to the families? Will it be a failure? Will I fail Christmas?

"Avery," he says, a little calmer, gaining my attention, placing his hands on my shoulders. "I know this is the last thing I'm ever supposed to say in this moment, but I can't think of anything else. I need to you to try and stay calm."

My attention snaps to him. "You can't take away my coffee and tell me to be calm, Matthew."

He doesn't break eye contact with me as he slowly hands

me back my coffee cup. "What would you like me to do? I can't draw fancy murals, but I can be a bricklayer."

I take a sip, letting the warm liquid start to calm some of my nerves.

"You aren't in this alone, Avery. I'm in this just as much as you are. I appreciate all the planning and prep that you've done for this. Believe me, I wouldn't have even thought of going nearly as far as this, but you need to let me help. I *want* to help." Matthew pleads with me, placing his hand on my arm.

I take a deep breath, enjoying the smell of the roasted coffee mixed with the spices and milk. I close my eyes and feel myself start to calm. There's a jazz version of 'Santa Claus is Coming to Town' over the speakers. The gentle hum of the surrounding conversations is like a relaxing tune.

With one last deep breath, I open my eyes. "You're right, I'm sorry. I'm just so used to having to be in charge that it's hard for me to accept help when it's given."

His hand slides up my arm as he pulls me in for a hug. I move my coffee out of the way at the last minute, nearly avoiding a messy disaster, as I wrap my arms around him.

Being in his arms is like coming home. Like a silent strength I didn't know I needed.

I don't know what I'm going to do if he wakes up tomorrow and realizes with the games being over, he doesn't need me around anymore.

"I'm here for you, Avery. I want to help. Let me help."

Resting my head on his chest and feeling his warmth around me, I let myself sag into him. "Thank you, Matthew. I would love it if you could finish the bricks."

He gives me a kiss on the top of the head before pulling back. "So, do you want me to keep going with this all the way around?"

"Yes, please. I'll start working on the window art and we can install it when you're done with the front."

Taking our seats next to each other at the table, we work in peace as we concentrate on our tasks. I can't help but glance over every few seconds to see how the bricks are coming along, but find that I am always pleasantly surprised, and instantly calmed, to see Matthew working meticulously to line the bricks up in a straight row.

"You're doing it again," he chuckles.

"Doing what?" I force myself to look down at the Santa I'm painting on the window.

"Don't think I can't see you looking over. I may not have built a gingerbread house in decades, but I think I can make things straight." His voice is soft and lighthearted, which makes me breathe a sigh of relief.

"I'm sorry."

"You don't have to be sorry. I know it's part of who you are." He places his current brick and looks over. 'Wow, Avery. That's incredible. I can't believe you did that."

The window art in front of me isn't what I would have done if I had more time, but I'm happy with the results. One window is Santa in his sleigh, the reindeer pulling him toward the moon in the starry sky. The second is of children laughing and throwing snowballs at each other.

"Thank you. I always loved to draw, so this is how I stay creative."

"It shows."

I'm lost in the kindness of his words and the light in his eyes as my gaze locks with his. I don't know how he has this effect on me. How he's able to both give me breath and take it away at the same time. His quiet support and encouraging words are unlike anything I've ever felt before.

"One hour!" The voice announces again.

"Oh no, we need to pick up the pace!" The rising tension returns to my stomach when I think of how much we have left to do.

"Here, I'm just finishing the last brick on the front. Why

don't we install the windows and then you can move on to your next step while I do the bricks on the back?"

"What about the sides?" I start to panic.

You're going to do the murals. It won't need the bricks as much. And like you said, in real life they're covered by other stores, anyway."

"You're right," I breathe.

And that's exactly what we do. The windows go in without breaking or smudging. Maybe I did get a little bit of Santa's magic after all.

Once they're installed and glued in place with the royal icing, we get back to work on our next task. Since Matthew has finished placing the bricks on the front, he begins on the back while I start placing the larger cookie tiles as the sidewalk in the front.

We work in silence, wordlessly passing each other the items we need as if we've worked together a hundred times before. For the rest of our allotted time, we work in sync as we complete our tasks, creating a cookie and candy replica of his family's store. By the time the final seconds are counted down, we're covered in icing and cookie dust; we're standing in front of the table with bright smiles on our faces.

"We did it," I say, amazed.

"We did it," Matthew repeats quietly.

I look over and find him looking at me, not our creation. He's giving me a look of such hope and adoration that I want to think that there really is a 'we.' It can't be a coincidence that we work so well together. That the way we just—fit— works. There doesn't feel anything 'fake' about us.

"Avery, I was thinking…" Matthew starts.

"Oh, my goodness, look at this!" a man says, snapping pictures of us and the gingerbread store.

"I'm sorry, you are?" Matthew says, holding me close to his side.

"Of course, you probably don't remember me. I'm Sam

Barrett from the Gingerbread Gazette. We went to school together, but it's been a long time." He shifts his camera to his left hand and holds his right out to Matthew.

"Yes, sorry. I do remember you. It's been a while."

"Nice to meet you officially, Avery. You've been the talk of the town for a bit, but I haven't had the pleasure." He shifts his hand to me, and I take it.

"Nice to meet you, too."

I try not to think about how I might be 'the talk of the town,' but between everyone seeing me as the reason Matthew is back in town and the posts on GingerSnap, I can see what that may be.

"Do you mind if I get a picture of you both behind the table?" he asks, pulling his hand back and holding his camera up.

"Not at all," I say cheerily.

We move to the other side of the table, and I find myself tucked right back to his side. His arm slides around my waist and pulls me close, like it's the most natural thing in the world. I can't help but look up at him as I wrap my arm around him, thinking that even if this is only for the shortest amount of time, I'm the luckiest girl in the world.

"Thank you so much," Sam says, lowering his camera after taking a few shots. "I have to get around and take pictures of everyone, but I'm truly amazed at your entry. If you don't win, I'll be shocked." With a nod, he takes off, leaving us standing alone once more.

"Do you really think we will win?" I ask, not dropping my arm from around him.

"I don't know; I haven't seen many of the other entries, but I know that you deserve to. You deserve everything, Avery."

"I can't stop thinking about what you said the other day. How you think that we're on the right path."

"Yeah, I did say that," he says with a coy smile as he reaches up and brushes a stray lock of hair behind my ear.

"And I was hoping maybe you'd elaborate. You know, for what that means after all of this is over. This may not be the right time or place, but I hope we have that conversation."

"I'd really like to have that conversation, too." He gives my side a squeeze. "I'm, uh, not really one to talk about feelings and all that, but I really like you, Avery."

"I really like you, too, Matthew. And I know you don't want to admit it, or tell me how you managed to pull it off, but I know you're behind those twenty extra turkeys and gifts showing up. I don't know how you did it but thank you."

Pink colours his cheeks under his beard. "Maybe you can just thank Santa for that."

"The judges are coming!" Eric announces, rushing to our table. "I've been looking around and so far, you guys have everyone beat by a long shot. The judges are still a couple of tables away, but everyone's talking about how you guys are a shoo-in."

"I doubt that," I say. "I'm sure there are lots of great entries."

"Sure, but none by a real elf," Matthew whispers in my ear, making me giggle. Having him so close to me, calling me an elf. Making me think about when he called me his elf…

"Here they come! They're at the next table!" Eric exclaims.

The next few moments can only be described as one of those many moments where you feel as if time slows down. Your brain can predict what is about to happen, but your body is frozen and unable to stop it.

A person in a black sweater with their hood up and face covered walks behind Eric, bumping into him and making him lose his balance. His arms fly out in front of him and his legs buckle, no longer able to do anything but try to instinctively get his footing while losing his balance. Matthew and I reach out our hands, hoping to grab him, but he's too far away. The table between us is too wide.

All I can do is stand and watch as Eric crashes into the table, using our gingerbread entry to break his fall.

The figure keeps moving and is lost in the crowd as everyone rushes over. Matthew and I rush to help Eric up, making sure he's alright before surveying the damage.

"I'm so sorry," he pleads. "I don't know what happened. All of a sudden I was being bumped and I lost my balance."

"I'm okay; it's not your fault," I say, fighting back tears.

It's not so much the loss of the gingerbread store, although that makes me sad, but it's that we instantly went from possibly being the forerunner for winning the final competition to being disqualified. Looking at the broken pieces of the store, the crushed candy roof and the shattered windows, there's no hope to be able to restore anything, even if we were able to be granted more time.

"Maybe we can ask the judges for consideration," Eric says as we slowly help him up. It's clear that he's favouring his left side as he straightens with a wince. "I'll explain it's my fault."

"It's really not necessary," Matthew says sadly, looking down at the broken table.

"I...ugh," Eric says, lifting his hand behind his head and wincing.

"Are you sure you're okay?" I ask, checking him over once again. I don't see anything bleeding, but he's definitely in pain.

"Don't worry about me. Worry about your gingerbread store."

"Oh goodness, what a mess," McKenzie says, standing on the other side of Matthew. "Such a shame. I guess we'll never know how you and your little store would have scored."

"You'd better stop now, or someone will think you're actually upset," I say sarcastically under my breath.

"Now that's not a very elf-like response, Allison," she says.

I put on a fake smile, no longer caring if she believes me or not. "I'm off the clock, Madison."

"Hmm..." She flicks her hair over her shoulder and walks off.

"How does she always know where to be?" I ask, watching her as she fades back into the crowd.

My mind thinks back to the location devices we found in our pockets earlier that day, but she couldn't be involved in that. She wasn't near us last night, not until the snowball fight started, and even then, she didn't get close enough to slip something into both of our pockets. She certainly wasn't the one that knocked into Eric just now. The height and build didn't match the flash of black sweater I saw before it happened.

"Next we have Matthew Roberts and Avery Geller," June Williamson says, looking up from her clipboard. "Oh dear, what happened here?"

I look past Eric and lock eyes with Matthew. I'm feeling all sorts of emotions. I'm sad and angry about what happened to our entry. I'm upset for Eric being hurt because of someone's carelessness—or ill will—toward us. But at the end of the day, I'm just grateful that I'm able to go through this all with Matthew, because the way he's looking at me right now tells me that no matter what happens with the Yuletide Games, I've already won.

Chapter Twenty-Seven

MATTHEW

"So, what are you going to do now?" Mitch asks, his voice loud and clear through the speakers in my dad's car.

"What do you mean?" I ask, taking my left turn, giving a small wave to Dave Miller, the town's pharmacist.

"Well, you're out of the games; it's Christmas Eve so I'm assuming the store is closing early today. What's your plan? Are you coming back on the next flight?"

As tempting as that sounds, I have to admit that I hadn't actually thought about it. As much as I'd like to get out from under my parents' roof and back under my own, being with Avery has been such a wonderful distraction that I find I haven't thought about Vancouver in days.

"I don't know," I admit.

"What do you mean you don't know? It's all done. You did what your parents asked you to. You said yourself your dad is getting better."

I did say that. I caught him trying to shovel snow yesterday after getting home from the gingerbread competition. I agreed to keep it from Mom in exchange for him paying Johnny Mathers, his part-time seasonal employee, to work the morning and close up so I can surprise Avery.

"Matthew? Did you cut out? Don't tell me they tried to build candy cell towers instead of regular ones."

"No, I'm here. But I wouldn't try to put it past Cal."

"It's that bad, huh?"

"That bad," I agree.

I pull onto the highway, looking in the rearview mirror to double check I still have the box I picked up before leaving town.

"Are you finally going to tell me why we had to rush to reach out to every business contact we have to donate to a company I've never heard of before? It's a good thing I know you so well, because 'trust me' only gets you so far."

I suck in a breath. "It's the company Avery works for."

"I should have known," Mitch groans.

"I wasn't lying when I said it's good for the community."

"But you just happened to leave out the part where it's good for your fake girlfriend as well?"

"Probably not-fake girlfriend."

"What?" I cringe at the volume of Mitch's voice.

"It's complicated. I need to talk to Avery before I say anything else."

He lets out a heavy breath. "What happened to swearing off long-distance relationships?"

"And what happened to telling me I need to get out there and not hide away?" I retort. I can feel my anger rising, but I know it shouldn't be aimed at Mitch. He was there for me after finding out about McKenzie's engagement to Cal. Through my time with Emily. I know he's just trying to look out for me, and while I appreciate that, he doesn't understand how it is with Avery. She's unlike any woman I've ever met.

"I'm sorry," I continue. "But I need to talk to her before I can answer any questions.

"And our company? What about everything we've worked for?"

"Nothing's changing there. I still love our company."

"I hope you remember that when you're talking with her."

"Look, I've got to go. I'm at my exit." I may have lied a little, as I'm still about fifteen minutes away, but I no longer have anything to add to this conversation. "Merry Christmas, Mitch."

He sighs. "Merry Christmas, Matthew. And make sure you find time to watch *Miracle on 34th Street* tonight after all the Gingerbreadian hoopla."

"What makes you think I watch that?" I straighten in my seat, gripping onto the steering wheel.

"Really think I don't know? You're not as stealthy as you think you are." He laughs as he hangs up.

After fighting my way through traffic, I finally pull up to the C.O.C.O.A warehouse. Elves in their full costumes rush from truck to truck, their arms filled with boxes and bags. To me, it's chaos. But knowing Avery, it's an organized chaos.

"Does anyone know where Blitzen is?" the elf in question shouts in the middle of the parking lot.

"Here!" A shorter male elf responds, rushing through the crowd. "Sorry, the hot cocoa machine broke before we could finish filling the thermoses."

They speak in hushed tones as he reaches her, and I find I can't turn away. Seeing her at work is like seeing a completely different side of her. She's confident as well as kind. She always has a smile on her face, and everyone eagerly approaches her.

It truly makes me in awe of her.

"Matthew?" I finally catch her eye. "What are you doing here?"

"I wanted to surprise you." I close the distance between us, holding out a paper cup in my hand.

"And you brought me coffee?" She takes a sip. "A Gingerbread oat latte with eggnog sprinkles? From Brew Haven?"

"I have to say, it's not as bad as I thought. A little sweet for

229

me, but still good..." I take a sip from the remaining cup in my hand.

"You got yourself one?" Her eyes track my movements as I take another sip.

"I figured I'd need a little fuel, too. I was hoping you'd let me tag along today. Maybe be an honorary elf?"

"Nothing would make me happier." The glint in her eyes and the smile on her face tell me I made the right decision to leave Gingerbread Grove and be with her today. I'm risking a lot not being available on the last day of the year for my company and getting my dad to have Johnny work, but the look on her face makes it worth it.

"Miss Avery?" A young boy in a fleece elf one piece pyjama set asks shyly as he walks up.

"Yes, Oliver?" Turning to him, she bends slightly to meet his eye level, but doesn't have to bend far. The red-headed boy is tall, reaching to her nose.

"I know I'm here to help get the sleighs ready, but I was hoping I could ride in one, too. I'd really like to be an elf in training. I want to be a real elf when I grow up, just like you!"

I watch as Avery is taken aback for a moment, her eyes glistening with tears.

"My mom said I had to ask you if it was okay," he continues.

"Of course. I think you would be the *best* elf in training."

"Thankyouthankyouthankyou!" he exclaims in one breath, throwing his arms around her.

She closes her eyes and hugs him back, her face relaxing into another smile. I'd be lying if I said that I wasn't overcome with emotion witnessing that as well. It's just another reason that I'm in awe of her. Not only does she run herself ragged doing things for others, but she's an inspiration, too. I'm just happy that others are seeing it, too.

"Mom! Mom! She said yes!" he yells as he runs to a woman waiting with open arms.

"That's really special."

"He's a special boy," she says, following him with her gaze.

"So, since you're accepting elves-in-training, what would you like me to do?"

"Let me check Santa's List." She pulls on a strap that crosses her body until her iPad is in her hands.

"Are you wearing your iPad like a bag?"

"What? No. That'd be silly. What could you possibly keep in a tablet like a purse? No, it's just clipped to me."

She says that with a straight face, as if wearing a tablet *clipped* to you is the most normal thing in the world.

She taps intensely, the space between her eyebrows creasing. "Check. Check. Double check," she mutters to herself.

I peek over the screen to see her checking off a digital checklist. There are two columns so that the same tasks can be checked twice.

Like a literal Santa list.

"I think that's it." Looking up from her screen, she surveys the parking lot to find the chaos has quieted and most of the elves are either tapping on their own iPads that are clipped to them, or simply taking in a few moments of the calm before the second round of activity starts. "I think it's time we get the sleighs on the road. Would you mind standing with me while I give the send off?"

"Of course." I take her hand, and we walk to the centre of the parking lot, all the elves fall in a circle around us.

"Thank you, everyone, for all of your hard work this year. This has been our biggest year yet, thanks to all of you, and our donors." She sends me a side glance and squeezes my hand, but I just wink in return.

I haven't actually admitted to my part in making sure she reached her personal goal, and I don't plan to.

"Now that all the sleighs are loaded up and everyone is ready to make their journeys today, I just wanted to express my gratitude for all of our hard work. I pray that the families have a wonderful and joyous Christmas, that all deliveries are made without delays, and that you all return here safe in a few hours. Remember that we will be having our annual Christmas wrap up party when you get back, so don't rush off once the sleighs are all unloaded."

"Oh! And there's one more thing," I say, remembering the box in my car. "Sorry, just one second."

Handing my cup off to a confused Avery, I jog over to my dad's car and grab the box. Making my way through the crowd one by one, I encourage them to take a neatly packed bag, one for every family and every elf that's here tonight. By the time I reach Avery, I have just one special bag left, made just for her.

"I hope you don't mind; I had all of these made up. There's one for everyone. This one, though, is just for you."

She takes the bag from my hand and opens it, pulling out a 3D printed ornament of the gingerbread store. The same one she designed for us that was destroyed last night before we could be judged.

"How did you?"

"I may have taken a picture of your rendering yesterday while you were drawing the murals and texted it off to a friend of mine. You had asked for ornaments and things for the families, so I had him send over as many as they would print and have shipped here for first thing in the morning. I hope you don't mind."

"That's just the most wonderful Christmas surprise I can think of. Other than you showing up here to spend the day with me, of course. Which reminds me! Stay right here!" She runs off toward a truck, and I lose her for a moment as everyone disperses on their way.

All the trucks are the same sized cubes, the boxes painted bright red with a large waving Santa taking up most of the side. They all have different sayings from 'Merry Christmas' to ''Tis the Season' written on them.

Returning with green fabric in her hand, I try to hide my groan as she reaches up and places what I know is an elf hat on my head.

"There! You can't be an elf-in-training without a hat!"

"Only for you," I chuckle. "But no pictures. I draw the line at that."

"Yes, sir," she chuckles, giving me a salute. "Now, let's get this show on the road! It's the happiest day of the year and I can't wait to get it started!"

"THIS IS IT! OUR FIRST STOP!" Avery puts the truck in park and unbuckles her seatbelt.

We've parked in the loading zone of an older apartment building from a side of town I've never seen before. I haven't spent a lot of time in Kamloops, even while growing up, but it's not in the main area. Areas of the bricks are broken and in need of repair. The sidewalk is cracked, and the walk leading to the front door is uneven. Snow is piled up on either side of the walkways; a single string of lights hangs around the front door. Looking up, I see some of the windows themselves have a string of lights or some window stickers, but it's not the over-the-top decorating that is back home in Gingerbread Grove or even Vancouver.

"Come on, Elfy!" Avery yells from the other side of my window.

"Elfy?" I think to myself, as she's already rounded the back of the truck.

Climbing down, I follow her to see she's climbed into the back of the box, pulling out bins and baskets with the name 'Thompson' written on them.

"Here we go! If you could carry those two boxes there, I

can manage this bag and the remaining box." She shuffles two boxes toward me before jumping down from the box.

"Can you not do that with snow on the ground? You're going to slip."

"Have you seen these boots? These are elf boots. They've got Christmas magic in them."

"Are you feeling okay?"

"Never better! It's Christmas Eve and we're about to make the first stop of the night." She looks behind us to see a sedan pull up, parking behind us. "Oh good, the rest of the crew is here."

"The...what?"

A man dressed in a Santa outfit gets out of the driver's seat while two elves pile out of the car with him.

"Good timing! We're ready to go in," Avery says, grabbing her boxes and putting them on the ground. "Matthew, grab yours so I can close this up."

Taking my box, I watch in awe as she closes and locks the rolling door before picking her stack back up. If I didn't know better, I would think that she wasn't fully human and had some sort of magical elf in her.

After being buzzed in, we make our way up the creaky steps until we reach the third floor. Children's laughter and sounds of Christmas carols echo through the door, their excitement evident as they await their delivery.

Avery knocks on the door, and it's immediately opened by a little girl, no more than three years old, dressed in a velvet red dress, her blonde hair up in pigtails. She reminds me of that little girl from *The Grinch*, all blue eyed and full of wonder.

"I knew it! Mom! It's Santa and his elves!"

A woman in a black dress appears behind her, her matching blonde hair falling around her shoulders, her blue eyes watering. "It is, Darcy. Let's let them in."

They move to the side, and we file in, all of us taking up

most of their living room. An artificial tree with twinkling mismatched lights and handmade ornaments stands in the corner. There are small snow globes adorning the coffee tables, and pictures drawn by Darcy hang on the walls. It's a mix of nostalgia from my Christmases growing up with hand-made items and sentimental decorations, but on a much smaller scale. I finally understand what Avery means when she talks about wanting to bring Christmas to the ones that wouldn't normally experience it like most people do. It's one thing to hear her talk about it, but a completely different to experience it.

Avery and I place the boxes on the coffee table as Santa bends down and welcomes Darcy into a hug.

"Merry Christmas, Darcy. I hear you've been an awfully good girl this year."

"I have! I tried real hard!"

"I know you did. Which is why I brought you something extra special. Elf Avery, would you mind passing me my sack, please?"

Avery hops into motion, reaching into a bag and pulling out a big red sack, handing it to Santa.

"I heard this is what you asked for most of all, and I had to make sure I had one specially made for you."

The little girl's eyes light up as he pulls out a wrapped rectangular box, the green curled ribbon on the top contrasting with the bright red wrapping paper.

Darcy stands in front of him, staring at the box, afraid to move.

"Come on, Darcy," her mom encourages sweetly.

Holding out her little hands, she takes the box from him, but just stares at it for another moment before carefully peeling off the wrapping paper from the side. She takes her time, not rushing as she removes the ribbon and the rest of the wrapping paper, eyes wide to reveal the boxed doll underneath.

"Is this…?"

"The horseback riding doll you wanted? You bet it is," Santa finishes, cheerily. "And look, I have another box here with your name on it."

Darcy gasps while she places the box carefully on the floor, picking up the wrapping paper and handing it to her mom. "Here, Mommy. We can save this and use again."

I sniff back the rising emotion as she carefully opens the next box, making sure not to rip the paper as she goes.

I've never had to worry about not ripping the paper. My brother and I would make it snow wrapping paper on Christmas morning, tearing through the presents without really taking in what we got until the excitement of unwrapping was over. We had presents under the tree starting mid-December. We had to use every ounce of willpower not to shake or snoop, under direct orders from our mom that it would go right back to the store if we tried.

Seeing Darcy and her family experiencing Christmas in such a different fashion than I do makes me see that I was going about Christmas all wrong. It's not something that should be shunned because I didn't like what my town was doing. I should have been looking at other ways to celebrate that would benefit others.

It's never been more evident as I watch Avery with her hands clasped under her chin, knowing this is her Christmas. Watching Darcy open her presents while the other elves sing 'Silent Night' in the background is all she wants to see today, and the memory of it tomorrow morning is worth more than anything that can be placed under a tree.

Chapter Twenty-Eight

AVERY

Being able to get off my feet and sip on a cup of hot apple cider is the best feeling in the world right now.

My feet throb, my back aches, and my shoulders are stiff, but my heart is full. All of the deliveries went off without a hitch, and all the families have been blessed with their Christmases. Seeing all the joyful faces made every ache and pain worth it.

Now, we're all back at the warehouse having our own little Christmas party before we disperse back to our families for our own 'elfernation' or 'elf hibernation' until mid-January. But for now, 'Jingle Bells' plays over a speaker, and everyone chats and gushes about their day as we all unwind from our hectic holiday season.

"Here, you need to eat something," Matthew says, sliding a slice of pizza onto the table in front of me. He takes a seat next to me, careful not to knock my feet that rest on an empty chair, as he takes a bite of his own slice.

"Did you know 'Jingle Bells' was the first Christmas song ever played in space?"

He holds his slice of pizza over his plate, letting it hover as he's about to take a bite. "I, uh, didn't know that."

"Yup, the Gemini 6A flight in 1965. It's in the Guinness World Records and everything."

"And how do you know this, exactly?" He places his slice back on his plate, leaning back and crossing his arms over his chest. He ditched his elf hat as soon as we made our last delivery, not even making it back to the truck before he tore it off and shoved it in his pocket, but I didn't miss the way his eyes lit—and even teared—up when a child opened a present, or how his smiles came more freely the more the day went on.

But now he seems to have lost a little of his wonder.

I hope it's just from exhaustion and not from already forgetting what the magic of Christmas truly is.

"Unagi, remember," I joke. I'm too tired to raise my fingers to my temple, but it doesn't stop me from laughing at my own joke.

"I still don't get it."

"We still need to watch *Friends*."

"That we do."

Our eyes link and the joyful feeling in my chest increases. If the only thing I do for Christmases going forward is deliver baskets and boxes to families and end the day with Matthew, it would be more than I could ever ask for.

"Tell me, do you think we could, uh, start watching that after Christmas? Maybe you even move on to that Moon Hollow show?"

"Stars Hollow?" I laugh. "I will never turn down an opportunity to watch *Gilmore Girls*. Ever."

"And maybe, we could get dinners together, too." He looks down as he takes my hand, linking his fingers with mine.

"I think we could arrange that." My pulse skitters as I answer.

I'm hopeful as to where this conversation is going. I hope it means that come tomorrow, our relationship isn't over. That we don't have to pretend that we have feelings for each other, because we both have very *real* feelings.

His thumb brushes over the back of my hand. *Back and forth. Back and forth.* The steady thrum of his movement acts like a metronome for my beating heart.

"I guess there's just the matter of where we live…"

I suck in a breath, taking back my hand from his and lowering my feet to the ground. "We don't have to talk about this now…"

"But I want to. I don't want it to be this—thing between us. There has to be a way that we both continue to do what we love while being together; I believe there's a way. I have to."

The sincerity in his voice makes me a little less focused on running from this conversation.

"When are you heading back?" I pick at the crust of my pizza, the smell of it mixes with the apple cider I drank turning my stomach.

"I haven't set a date yet." He uncrosses his arms and leans forward. "I promised my mom I'd stay through Christmas, but I haven't agreed to anything beyond that.

"And your company?"

"Closed until the new year after today."

My eyes lock with his. "So, you don't have to go back for a week and a half?"

"Nope."

"And I have about three weeks off…"

"Yup."

We both let our words hang between us for a moment. "We could get through a lot of *Friends* and *Gilmore Girls* in that time. Maybe even some *Golden Girls*. Really make sure you get my references."

"How do you remember these, anyways?"

"I mean, I'm not one to blow my own vertubenflugen…"

"You're…what?"

"Rose?" When he still has a confused look on my face, I continue. "*Golden Girls.*"

"I feel like I'm going to need to take notes when watching these."

"Would it make you feel better if I quoted *Star Wars*? Marvel? I'll do *Die Hard*, but it's still not a Christmas movie."

"Not really. I can't say it would."

"With great power, comes great responsibility…"

"Please stop." He takes his glasses off and rubs his eyes, earning a chuckle from me.

"I can do this all day…"

"Avery," he sighs.

I bite my lip, stifling a laugh. "Fine, even though it pains me."

"I think you'll live," he huffs, placing his glasses back on.

We settle into a comfortable silence, listening while Frank Sinatra croons about having a merry little Christmas. I watch as everyone starts to say their goodbyes, ready to brave the snow that's picking up so they can be with their loved ones. They've earned it. They deserve to be able to go home to their families after spreading so much joy to others.

"Let me help you clean up so you can get out of here," he says, looking across the room.

"It's okay, there's not much to do."

"Avery, please let me help you," he pleads. "I'm being a little selfish, too. I know you must be exhausted and have plans with your family, but I'm hoping you can come back to Gingerbread Grove with me for a little bit. Now that we are officially not fake, I would like you to experience Christmas Eve in the Grove."

"'In the Grove,' hmm? You sound like a true Gingerbreadian," I joke.

"You know what I mean." He glances at me, his cheeks reddening.

"Turns out that I actually don't have plans with my family

until tomorrow morning. They usually let me go home and rest after the deliveries."

"If you're too tired…" he starts, but I cut him off by placing my hand on his.

"I'd love nothing more than to see what 'the Grove' has planned for Christmas Eve."

"It'll mean we see our lanterns being snuffed out."

I laugh. "I think I can handle that."

"They'll carry it down the gazebo steps."

"As the ceremony dictates…"

"We'll be placed alongside all the other failed Yuletide Games contestants and have to watch as McKenzie and Cal take their awards."

"It's fine. There's no crying in baseball."

"Baseball? You mean the snowball fight."

I sigh. "Add *A League of Their Own* to the watch list. I'm going to need to start making an actual list."

He stands, holding out a hand to me. I place my hand in his, letting him help me up. "I don't think you'd be able to keep up with all the movies you need me to watch."

"No, probably not. We'd need more than a week and a half."

"More than three weeks," he adds.

He takes a step closer to me, our breaths mixing as we look into each other's eyes.

"Do you think a lifetime would do?" he whispers.

I suck in a breath. "I don't know. There's a lot of TV shows and movies to catch up on."

"It might be…inconceivable." He winks and walks away, leaving me stunned.

"Did you just quote *The Princess Bride*?" When he doesn't turn around, I chase after him. "You did! You know more than you're letting on!"

❄

"THIS IS A LOT LESS...HEARTBREAKING than I thought it'd be," I whisper as we stand up on the gazebo, watching as our lantern candle gets extinguished by the unusually long snuffer.

"What do you think would happen if Cal and McKenzie had been knocked out? Would he use that thing on his own lantern?" Matthew whispers back.

"I think he'd have to. I mean, who else would want to be seen holding that thing?"

"Do you mind?" Cal asks loudly, giving us both a very pointed look. "This is a very solemn moment. It deserves respect."

"Sorry, of course," I say, biting my lip and nodding my head.

"You're absolutely right," Matthew adds, and I have no idea how he does it with a straight face.

"Matthew and Avery. The games have spoken. You've been eliminated from the Yuletide Games."

"The *Games* have spoken?" I whisper.

Matthew chuckles but turns it into a cough when Cal looks our way. He reaches up and covers his mouth with a fist. "Sorry, I must have sucked in some of that candle smoke."

Cal gives us one final look before moving on to the next couple, going through the same motions, except they look a lot more forlorn that we do. Maybe we should have played up the sadness a bit more.

But now that I know that Matthew has real feelings for me, just like I do for him, I no longer care about the games. Everything I want for Christmas has come true, and nothing to do with these games could have made it any better.

Looking up at Matthew and seeing how lighthearted he seems right now; I think about how much of a contrast that is from when we first arrived in Gingerbread Grove. In less than a week, I can feel that some of the hurt from the town has been healed. Maybe he's even been able to get past a little of the hurt he's experienced from his parents. I'm not so disillusioned to think that it'll all be forgiven in such a short period of time, but I'd like to think this was a start.

"Remember, just because you didn't win the games, doesn't mean that you don't win at love," Cal states, standing beside me and addressing the crowd, sounding like an actor from the 1940s.

I press my nails into my palm, thankful I can still feel the pressure through my gloved hands. It's the perfect distraction to stop myself from laughing.

He continues with his speech, but my attention is drawn to the crowd as they all look down at their phones in waves, murmuring to each other while looking up at us.

"What do you think is going on?" I whisper.

"No idea," Matthew whispers back, looking just as stunned as I am.

"Now, now, everyone. I'm sure whatever it is that has captured all of your attentions can wait just a moment. We're just about ready to crown the winners of the Yuletide Games."

"He's acting like it's some big surprise," I whisper.

Matthew opens his mouth to retort, but a shout from the crowd stops him.

"You're not really dating?"

"What is she, an actress?" Someone else yells.

"Is this a joke? Like a yuletide prank?" shouts another voice.

Matthew and I look at each other when we realize the questions are being aimed at *us*.

"Matthew, how could you?"

"We accepted you as a Gingerbreadian, Avery!"

"We even let you on GingerSnap!"

The app! It has to have something to do with that.

Pulling out my phone, I see a notification for a new post on GingerSnap.

"What is it?" Matthew stands over my shoulder, watching my screen.

"InsiderCookie57," I groan. "There's another post."

My eyes scan the words, but I can barely read them. After the first line, there isn't much else I need to know to find out what everyone's gossiping about.

'MATTHEW AND AVERY'S RELATIONSHIP CONFIRMED AS FAKE.'

Chapter Twenty-Nine

GINGERSNAP: THE OFFICIAL APP OF GINGERBREAD GROVE

InsiderCookie57 MATTHEW AND AVERY'S RELATIONSHIP CONFIRMED AS FAKE.

Gingerbread Grove's supposed 'it' couple has been outed as fake. Official sources confirm that they have not been romantically linked for months, like they had claimed to be, but rather only met the day prior to coming to Gingerbread Grove. Sources confirm that they were both meant to be flying from Vancouver to Kamloops on December seventeenth, but due to a cancelled flight, rented a car and drove up together. Tickets and receipts have been confirmed with these dates. It's also been confirmed that Avery was dating a Maxwell Gladwin of Vancouver until she met Matthew. Dates of the breakup and fake relationship are vague.

It's on this fated road trip that the ruse to date had been hashed in order to show that the games are nothing but a joke. A ruse. Matthew's hatred for the holiday extended so much that they were going to extinguish the games and have them crumble, much like their gingerbread entry into the games.

Had it not been for the quick thinking of Mr. Eric Davies to ruin their creation before they swept the games (minus the snowball fight, which had been valiantly won by Mayor Cal Smith and his wife McKenzie) and pull off their grand finale of making a mockery of the games. Thankfully the trophy has likely been awarded to the rightful winners by the time this post is seen by the good people of Gingerbread Grove.

Let this be a lesson to all of us that even those that grew up with us can't always be trusted. Be vigilant. Be aware. Be Gingerbreadians.

Chapter Thirty

MATTHEW

"Did you ever think you'd be run out of Gingerbread Grove by an angry mob?" Avery asks, resting the straw from her fountain pop on her lip.

"Nope, can't say I have." I take a bite of a fry, looking out the front windshield of Avery's car. After being swarmed with angry townspeople after finding out that we weren't entirely truthful, I grabbed Avery's hand and made a dash for her car. She'd thrown me the keys as she jumped into the passenger's seat, trusting me to guide us out of town before we could get stopped by a human barricade demanding answers.

This isn't how I pictured having Christmas Eve dinner, in the parking lot of a fast food restaurant just outside of town, but here we are.

"Good thing they didn't have pitchforks."

"Is there a Christmas equivalent? If there was, I bet they'd have it." I pick at another fry from the cardboard container.

"If they really wanted, they could wrap them in red and white duct tape."

"Too close to a candy cane. They'd never go for it."

"Green and red then." She takes a sip of her pop before

placing it in the cup holder and turning in the passenger seat to face me. "We need to find out who InsiderCookie57 is. Is there any way you can use your computer superpowers for this?"

"Superpowers?" I scoff.

"Yeah, you know," she moves her fingers in a typing motion. "Get on the ol' internets and do some sleuthing behind the scenes. I can do front end social media stuff, but I don't know anything about how to do it back there."

"Not without breaking laws, no. I don't think that this is serious enough to risk me going to jail, do you?" I shoot her a glance from the corner of my eye. When she doesn't answer right away, I turn to her. "Avery, you can't really be contemplating this."

"What? No…I mean, no. Of course not."

I breathe a little sigh of relief, but I know that her answer is not entirely true.

"Wait! What about Trevor? Do you think he would help? I mean, if you think you can trust him. Do we know *who* we can trust in Gingerbread Grove?"

"Avery," I sigh, putting my empty fry container back in the paper bag.

"I mean, we don't know who InsiderCookie57 is. It could be anyone. And to think that everyone had been so nice. Well, mostly everyone."

"Avery," I say a little louder.

"We know it's not your parents. My top runners are still McKenzie and Cal, but they wouldn't be doing it so openly. Not with him being the mayor…"

"Avery!"

She stops mid-thought and looks at me, eyes wide and mouth slack in surprise. "Yes?"

"Say we find out who InsiderCookie57 is; what then? Technically, everything they posted is true, except for McKenzie and Cal being the top couple or whatever. But we *were* fake dating. That is how we met. Technically, they didn't post anything that wasn't true about us."

"Well, no… But what about all the sabotage? The location devices? The crushing of the gingerbread store?"

"All unfortunate, but in the end, so what? We don't live or work in Gingerbread Grove. I've managed to avoid the people, and the town, for almost ten years. I can do it again."

Avery sinks into her seat.

"It's Christmas Eve, Avery. Do you really want to spend it worrying about someone that has nothing better to do than run us out of a town we don't belong to?"

Thinking I don't belong and saying it out loud are two very different things. I haven't felt like I belonged to Gingerbread Grove since high school, and usually I'm okay with it. But saying it out loud and admitting it to Avery, that causes a pang in my heart I wasn't prepared for.

"No, I can't say I thought I'd be spending my Christmas Eve in the parking lot of a fast food restaurant. But at least I'm with you."

She gives me a shy smile that takes away a little of the sting from my admission.

"That's all that matters to me, too. What do you say about going back to Kamloops for tonight? I'm sure I can find a last minute hotel room."

"What about your mom? You promised you would spend Christmas with her."

"I'll go back and see her tomorrow. I'm not ready to face that interrogation tonight. I'm sure she's already losing her Christmas-cool over whatever gossip the town is spreading."

"That's true." She straightens suddenly, nearly knocking over the bag of food beside her on the arm rest. "That means we can watch *Miracle on 34th Street*?" she asks hopefully.

"We can watch *Miracle on 34th Street*," I repeat, unable to look away from the hopeful joy in her eyes.

I want to be embarrassed that I told her that, and she

remembers, but I don't have it in me to be. Even after everything that's happened, the only thing I want to do is watch a Christmas movie with the woman next to me.

FINDING a hotel in Kamloops on Christmas Eve is harder than I thought.

It didn't help that we didn't get into town until late at night. So instead of booking a motel that looked like it was out of a horror movie, I agree to stay on Avery's couch. Which ends up being a blessing, because now she's curled up beside me, covered in a throw blanket, surrounded by gas station snacks while the end credits for the movie flash in their black and white screens.

I've got my arm around her and she's asleep on my chest, and I think this is the most at peace I've ever felt.

The movie ends and it moves onto another one. It's a feel-good romance movie that always plays this time of year. Usually, I would change the channel before the title can be played, but the remote is next to my foot on the coffee table and there's no way I'm risking waking Avery. Even if it means I have to sit through a city guy and a small town girl falling in love over silly holiday traditions.

How fitting.

Shifting slightly, I pull my phone out of my jeans pocket, sighing at the screen full of messages I've been avoiding all night.

MOM

> You were fake dating Avery this whole time? Why?

> You brought her around to meet me. I thought I was finally getting to see you settle down!

How could you do this to me?

Answer me!

DAD

Answer your mother, please. She's pacing
the room like a lost reindeer.

Clicking off that family group chat, I pull up one from
Mitch.

MITCH

I thought you were going to finish the
proposal for the new client today.

Don't worry, I finished it, but you could have
at least told me you weren't going to be able
to do it.

And now you're MIA?

I drop my head, letting it sit on the back of the couch. With
everything that happened today with the deliveries and the
drama in town, I completely forgot that I said I would finish
that by the time we closed the office for the holidays.

MITCH

Why am I getting texts about you being
chased out of Gingerbread Grove?
Something about a Gingersnap? I guess I'll
let it slide about the proposal since it sounds
like you had a lot on your hands today.

Can you please answer me and let me know
they didn't feed you to the Cookie Monster or
some equally weird Christmas version?

Chuckling, I type out a response.

> Sorry about the proposal. It has been a long, and very odd, day.

> No monsters. Just someone hiding behind an app that has it in for us for some reason.

Want me to look into it?

> No, there's no point. I'll be back in Vancouver soon.

I place my phone screen down on the arm rest beside me and close my eyes. I try to focus on Avery wrapped up next to me, the sounds of the dialogue between the couple on the TV filling the silence. They're arguing over some bakery that's up for sale in the small town. He wants to buy it to turn it into a big chain, she wants to keep it 'true to its roots.'

I scoff. Like a conversation like this would ever happen in real life.

If only our problems were as easily fixed as those on the screen right now. If things just magically worked out, and we didn't need to worry about family, Christmas-crazed towns, or anonymous social media posters.

The snow outside the window starts to pick up, as does the wind. There is only a sheet of white visible on the other side of the glass, but everything in here is the picture-perfect of calm. Avery's tree stands in the corner with its white lights and strategically placed ornaments with wrapped presents around the base. Garland and twinkling lights sit on the mantle above the electric fireplace, giving the living room a warm and cozy feel.

Just another thing that represents our life right now. Crazy and wild on the outside but in here, where it's just us, this is where the peace is.

I'm quickly beginning to understand that Avery is my peace. That with her, I'm finding how to find my calm and shut out the craziness of the world.

Holding her closer to me, I know that this is all I need.

Chapter Thirty-One

AVERY

"I've never seen you this glum on Christmas before," Meg says, taking a seat beside me on our parents' couch.

It's Christmas morning and we've opened all our presents and eaten our traditional breakfast of pancakes and waffles. Now the adults are relaxing by the fire with our coffees while Meg's kids are playing with their new toys.

"Is this still to do with the Gingerbread Grove business?" Mom asks, sitting in her chair as she places a plate of cookies on the coffee table in front of her.

"I still don't get why someone would go to such lengths to make sure you don't win a game," Meg's husband, James, says, taking a sip of his coffee.

"They take the Yuletide Games very seriously," I add.

"A little too seriously," Dad comments. "But you also had no right entering to begin with. Who pretends to date someone, anyway?"

"Regardless, it's such a shame that it all had to end like that," Mom says. "But he's right, honey. You shouldn't have lied about that."

"Mom, Dad, I told you. I did it to help him out. You

should have seen how sad he was about going back to his hometown."

"It shouldn't have mattered anyway. You weren't *fake* dating by the end of it." Meg sends me a wink from behind her coffee mug, knowing the trouble she just started for me.

"What?" Dad exclaims the same time Mom clasps her hands and says, "Really?"

"Thanks, Meg," I mutter.

"Welcome, Sis," she chuckles.

"So, when do we get to meet him?" Mom asks.

"Does he know anything about these games shenanigans?" Dad adds.

"Look what you did, Meg," James sighs.

"Isn't it glorious?" she replies.

"Oh, look. A phone call." I place my mug on the coffee table and stand. "I'm going to take this outside."

"I don't hear a phone ringing." Meg smirks at me.

"It's on silent. I'll be right back."

I don't wait for any more questions. I make my way to the door, only stopping to grab my jacket and put on my boots.

I shiver as I take a seat on the porch swing, thinking about how different my life turned out to be compared to what I dreamed of when I was a kid swinging on this very seat.

Back then, I assumed by thirty I would be married with kids, starting our own Christmas traditions. Instead, I'm now dating my fake boyfriend after being ejected from Christmas-style *Survivor*.

At least I have my dream job.

Digging for my phone in my jacket pocket, I look, confused as I also pull out a business card for 'The Sugar House Candy Shoppe' in Woodland Springs is stuck on to my phone.

Not Gingerbread Grove. Woodland Springs.

"What is this?" I ask no one. Not only do I not remember putting this in my pocket, but I couldn't even place where the store would be in town. I know I haven't been there during the times that I visited.

I take a picture and send it to Matthew.

> Did you give me this? Is this where you got the candy for the competition?

I don't have to wait long for him to respond, and I wonder if he's avoiding his family, just like I am.

MATTHEW

> No, I got them at the grocery store. I don't even know where that is.

How curious.

Pulling up my search engine, I type in the name, and it takes me to an outdated website for an old-fashioned candy shop in an old house just outside of town.

I forward the link to Matthew.

> I think I remember this from when I was a kid. I haven't heard or seen anything about it since I've been back.

> Think you can get away for a bit and meet me there?

> Are you asking me to sneak out of my parents' house on Christmas Day?

> You're such a bad influence.

> *gif of Joey's shocked face*

> Don't act like you don't want to know what's going on, too.

> I'll have you home in time for turkey dinner.

> What a gentleman.

"I TAKE IT BACK. I don't think I want to spend my Christmas Day here."

Looking up at the dark house in front of me, it looks more like something out of a scary fairy tale than a house that belongs in a cute town like Gingerbread Grove.

"I doubt the witch that ran the store still lives here."

"What?" I gasp, looking up at Matthew.

"I'm kidding," he chuckles.

I playfully swat at his arm. "Now is not the time to break out that sense of humour of yours."

"I think it's the perfect time," he adds with a smirk.

With a huff, I look back up at the house in front of us. "What was it you found out about this again?"

"My mom said that the owners retired when the town started to change over. They saw it as a good opportunity to bow out and move away. She said she'd forgotten all about it until I asked her."

"What happened to it then?"

"She said she thinks the city bought it. Something about it being a heritage site."

"Hmm." The house is two levels and looks to be from the early nineteenth century. There are large windows on both floors and a covered porch that spans the whole width of the building. What makes it look really eerie are all the trees that seem to snarl around it, the only thing about the property that seems to be unkept.

"I called Trevor on my way here," Matthew says.

I snap my attention to him. "Really? Are you sure we can trust him?"

"Can we afford not to try? He hasn't done anything to make me think that he's been involved in what's happened. Plus, we need to start somewhere."

"I thought you were against us looking into all of this."

"What can I say? It's either this or my mom pestering me for more information about what happened." He shrugs. "I took the option that got me out of the house."

"Is that the only thing?" I joke, thinking that maybe he'd admit to some of his curiosity, too.

"I wanted to see you."

His answer takes my breath away. I wasn't expecting it, but his honest response makes me realize that finding out what happened during the games isn't the big picture. He is. And I'll take any chance I can get to spend time with him while we're both in the same part of the province.

But I *really* want to know what's going on with the games, too.

"Since we're here, what do you say about going in and taking a look?" I ask, taking a hold of his hand.

"Avery Geller, are you suggesting we break and enter? What's with you trying to get me sent to jail these last two days?"

I laugh. "I mean, we won't have to *break* and enter. If the door or window just so *happens* to be left open, we could just be doing our neighbourly duty in closing it up for whoever owns this place…"

"I never knew you were this much of a rebel. Who knew elves were so mischievous?"

"I prefer adventurous."

Leading him up the stairs, I try not to act like my stomach drops when the old wood creaks, or how the corners look like they have eyes watching us.

For a house that's been abandoned, the walk from the street to the house is nicely shovelled except for a small dusting of snow. The windows don't look frosted over, and the stairs are cleaned.

"Are you sure no one lives here?" I ask, reaching the door and trying to peer into the window.

"Not according to what my mom says, and she makes it

her business to know what's going on around town." He reaches for the door, grasping the doorknob with his hand. "Here goes nothing."

With a turn of his wrist, the door opens.

"I can't say I was expecting it to be that easy." I stare in wonder at the open door.

"Christmas miracle?" He asks with a smile.

I roll my eyes. "Or small town."

The inside is only lit by the early afternoon sunlight streaming through the oversized windows. Large glass counters line three of the walls with shelves that go from floor to ceiling behind them. Although they're all empty, I can imagine them filled with all sorts of candies and treats.

"I'll start on the right if you want to do the left," Matthew says, stalking over to the wall closest to him.

"And what are we looking for, exactly?" I ask as I drift over to my side, letting my eyes roam over the glass cases that hold so much history.

"Anything that will give us a clue as to how that card ended up in your jacket pocket."

We work in silence as we look through the shelves and cases. It doesn't take long, as there isn't anything more than cobwebs and the odd piece of paper that had been left behind.

"How do you think you open this thing?" I ask when we get to the antique register.

He takes a look around the large metal machine, finding the crank and turning it until the drawer pops open. We both jump with a start as a bell rings and echoes through the room.

"You're not going to be sneaking around and fooling anyone by doing things like that," a voice sounds at the door, making us both jump again.

"Trevor, that's not funny." I clutch at my chest, making sure my heart isn't about to jump right out of it.

Trevor stands in the doorway with Eric behind him, the bitter cold wind bursting past them.

"Did you find anything?" Eric asks, closing the door and shutting out the Christmas storm picking up outside.

I eye Eric wearily, even though I hate that it's my gut reaction. He's been nothing but kind and helpful to us, and I'm letting a post by InsiderCookie change my opinion of him.

"I ran into Eric on my way out of City Hall. I hope you don't mind," Trevor says.

"I hope you don't mind I tagged along," Eric says, taking off his gloves and stuffing them in his jacket pockets. "I'm curious and I wanted to help if I can."

Matthew nods. "We haven't found anything yet." Matthew reaches into the register. "Except this."

I gasp has he pulls out a card that looks exactly like the one I found in my pocket this morning.

"At least we know where the person got it from," Trevor adds.

"Did you find anything at City Hall?" I ask, moving closer to Matthew. His warmth is a comfort as I begin to feel very closed in. There are counters and people between us and the door. I don't know why that makes me feel uneasy, but it does. If Matthew trusts these people, it should be good enough for me.

"I did. Once the owners of the candy store put it up for sale, it was bought by a holding company."

"Do you know who owns it?" Matthew asks.

"No, I couldn't find anything other than a numbered company."

"That's odd." I move to look out the window, but my foot gets caught on something. I lose my balance, falling right into Matthew's arms.

"I heard you two weren't fake dating anymore, but you didn't need to prove it to us," Eric jokes.

"Ha. Ha. I tripped on something." I bend down, pulling out the string of a bag. "How did this get here?"

Matthew bends down next to me, peering in. "Is this it?"

"What?" Trevor asks.

"What's what?" Eric questions, leaning over the counter, looking down at where we are knelt.

I pull out all of my missing items from The Frosty Showdown. "How did these get here?" I ask.

"I put them there."

Chapter Thirty-Two

MATTHEW

The dark-haired woman standing in front of me looks familiar, but I can't place her. She's looking around the room at us, wide eyed and pale faced, as if she's afraid to step more than a foot into the room.

"Fiona?" Trevor asks, shocked. "Why would you do something like that?"

"I had no choice," she says in a quiet voice, looking down at her folded hands in front of her.

"What do you mean?" Avery asks, still plastered to my side.

"I wasn't even supposed to be in the games at all. My boyfriend, Lance, and I broke up the week before the games. We had told the organizers that we were going to pull out, but Cal insisted that we stay in to make the number of couples even after you both joined."

"Why would he care about that?" I ask.

"At the time, I didn't know. I was so heartbroken that I just went along with it all, hoping that maybe if we did the games together things would change, and we would get back together. But after the toboggan race, Cal pulled us aside and gave us a proposition."

I look at Avery, who's looking just as confused as I do.

"He said that he had to make sure that he and McKenzie won and that the reputation of the town was riding on it. If we didn't help him, then all the changes we made to have Woodland Springs turn into Gingerbread Grove would be for nothing."

"So you took my accessories for the snowbread man?"

"The…what?" she asks confused.

"The snow sculpture," I clarify.

"I'll get a name that sticks one of these days," Avery mutters.

"Yes, I took them when you went off to speak with Matthew. I felt bad, so I only took the ones that I didn't think you would absolutely need." She looks back down for a moment before confessing. "I was really happy you won. I loved your sculpture."

"Thank you," Avery says hesitantly. "Did you do the location devices, too?"

Fiona sighs. "Yes. We were behind you in the golf cart that took us to Gum Drop Hill. We slipped them in your pockets while you were talking about taking your dad's offer. Which, I hope is true, by the way."

I don't know why she's invested in me moving back to Gingerbread Grove. Whatever her reasoning, I put my arm around Avery and hold her closer to me.

"And the gingerbread competition?" Eric cuts her a glare.

"That was Lance. We were already eliminated at that point, so I wasn't there. I didn't know he was planning on doing that until after it had happened."

"That one hurt. Physically and emotionally." Eric clutches at is chest.

"So, who's InsiderCookie57?" Avery asks, wrapping her arm around my waist.

"Me," Fiona admits "I really didn't want to be, but once the town started getting excited about you two doing so well.

Cal wanted to add a little 'fuel to the fire' as he said. So, he got me an account.

"And you spread those lies about me breaking the ginger-store on purpose?" Eric raises his voice, his eyebrows nearly reaching his hairline.

"How come 'gingerstore' sounds so good but I can't make 'snowgingerman' work?" Avery mutters.

"Focus, Avery. Gingerbreadian reputations are at stake here." Eric snaps his attention to Avery before turning back to Fiona. "Continue."

"McKenzie was the one that told me that you two were fake dating and that I needed to make the post with the picture of your—gingerstore—being ruined. I don't know how she got that information…I'm so sorry. I really didn't mean to hurt anyone."

"Then why tell us now?" I ask, but my attention drifts to Trevor, who's started walking toward the other side of the room.

"I feel bad. I went along with it because Lance said the games were making him think of the old times together and that he wanted to restore our dream of opening an inn together."

"Wait, opening an inn?" Eric asks.

"Yes. Lance was working with Cal to buy the old inn in town. We were going to restore it and make it fit with the theme of the town. But after we were eliminated and there was no way that Matthew and Avery were going to win the competition, he broke up with me for good."

"That explains why all of your paperwork kept going missing," I say to Eric.

"What do you mean?" Fiona asks.

"I've been working with Cal for months on getting the inn up and running. I bought it last year but every time I try to get the permits and licenses, they always 'go missing.'"

"Um, guys?" Matthew asks, staring down at a cabinet behind the counter.

We all rush over to see shelves fully stocked with candy canes. There are different colours and flavours, each shelf bursting with the peppermint treats.

"I thought these were banned," Avery says, peering over the cabinet door.

"They are. When Cal turned everything into gingerbread, he passed a by-law that no stores were allowed to sell these. It was something about a 'good faith rule.'" Trevor says.

"So who owns this place and why do they have a secret candy cane stash?"

"I do," a man says from the doorway, standing next to Cal and McKenzie.

"Lance?" Fiona asks, stunned.

He doesn't even look her way. He has his eyes trained on mine. "I bought this place, hoping that I could start up a gingerbread empire. I'd start with the candy store and the inn, then work my way through stores in town. With you and your brother out of town, I had my eyes on the hardware store next."

"You were going to push my dad out of his store?" My hearts stops with my next thought. "You didn't actually push him, did you?"

"No," Lance chuckles. "The old man did it himself. I was just going to hop onto the opportunity of him being off work to try and encourage him into early retirement. I had everything lined up getting the store and the inn open with the hardware store next, but then you came back to Gingerbread Grove and ruined it all."

"I can't believe you lied to me, Cal. After talking me into coming here. Why did you do that?" Eric asks.

"It wasn't hard to overhear your problems in Candy Cane Creek when I visited, I was looking for a way to stir up the drama between the towns. I needed Gingerbread Grove to be

265

the tourist destination during the holiday season. Lance expressed interest after you bought the inn. I thought that once your paperwork kept getting 'misplaced' you'd give up and be looking to sell it to someone else. I didn't count on you being so…determined."

"Rude," Eric huffs.

"And what do you get out of all of this, Cal? Why are you so invested in winning the games and having Lance run the town with you?" Avery asks.

"Before you came to town, I made a bet with William Claus, the mayor of Candy Cane Creek. If I won, he had to make his annual Christmas in July speech wearing a ginger-bread man costume."

Avery snickers beside me before Cal's gaze shoots daggers at her. She clears her throat and mutters, 'Sorry."

"And if you lose?" I ask.

Cal huffs, crossing his arms over his chest, running his tongue along his teeth. "I would have had to decorate city hall like a candy cane house for the whole month of July."

Everyone but the annoyed trio at the door burst out in laughter.

"But it doesn't matter, because McKenzie and I won," Cal shouts over the laughter.

"But you didn't." Trevor takes a step forward. "Not really. Sabotaging another couple gets you disqualified."

"You don't have any proof. All you have is the testimony of a heartbroken woman who admitted she did it."

"Actually, there are more witnesses," Sam says, stepping into the store with his camera in his hand. "Plus, I was recording the whole conversation from just outside the door."

"Why are there so many people here?" I ask Avery. "Aren't people usually with their families on Christmas?"

"You underestimate the power of being nosey in a small town," Eric replies, appearing at my other side.

"I didn't consent to being recorded," Cal insists.

"B.C. is a one-party consent state. Doesn't matter." Sam grins widely.

"Well, I never…" Cal stammers.

"But, seriously. What's with the candy cane stash?" Trevor asks, reaching down and pulling out an oversized plastic candy canes. "For someone that it supposed to hate candy cane's you sure have a lot of them."

"Those aren't mine," he insists.

"Liar," Lance says under his breath.

"What?" Cal and McKenzie gasp at the same time, turning to him.

McKenzie has been oddly quiet during this whole exchange, only standing next to her husband as the whole thing unfolds. Another curious development.

"I'm tired of lying for you, Cal. It's obvious I'm not going to be getting the inn, or the candy store, running at this point, so I might as well take you down with me." He turns to Sam, raising his voice to make sure it's on record, wherever the device is. Cal has been shredding all the documents that Eric has submitted, making sure that he never reaches his deadlines for the inn. He promised me all the approvals in exchange for making sure that he and McKenzie won the Yuletide Games."

"Lies! They're lies, I tell you!" Cal exclaims to the hidden device.

"He also made sure the city sold this property to me for under value."

"Lance!" McKenzie shouts, as Cal rubs his face with his hands.

"What? Might as well get it all out there. If I'm going down, you're going down with me. Speaking of, McKenzie is the one that came up with all the ways to get you two booted from the games."

"You weren't even supposed to be here," she throws my way.

"I didn't ask to be here," I reply. "I didn't ask for any of this."

"Then you show up with...her." McKenzie waves a hand at Avery with a disgusted look on her face. "You ruined everything."

"Watch it, McKenzie. Don't speak bad about Avery. She didn't do anything."

"Now you talk back?" McKenzie says. "Where was that when we were together? Why did you never stand up for me?"

"You never let me!" I yell, letting years of pent up anger and resentment over what happened out. "You never needed me to defend you or stand up for you. You didn't need me for anything other than helping you with your homework. So no, McKenzie, I never did. I also never had feelings for you like I do for Avery. I love Avery!"

And now I'm having a panic attack.

My chest constricts. I can't breathe. My pulse is pounding in my ears.

Did I really just say that?

I'm looking straight ahead, trying to take a breath. I know everyone's eyes are on me. Avery's eyes are on me, but I can't look that way. I can't meet her gaze. If I do, it will all be real. I'll have to admit in a way that I was hoping to do while we were alone, not while everyone is watching us.

"Do you mean that?" she whispers to me.

I suck in a breath. "Yes."

I still can't look at her. My eyes are locked forward as she wraps her arm around mine, linking our fingers as she leans in and whispers.

"I love you, too."

"Now that everything's worked out and these two love each other, I think we should get going," Cal says, turning to the door, but is stopped by Sam.

"Not so fast. Don't think you're going to be able to just walk away from this," he says.

"Come on, now. It's just some silly games. No harm, no foul."

"Except that I'm the owner of an inn that I can't get approval for," Eric says, walking from behind the counter and toward Cal.

"And you had me running around for games that you fixed against my friends," Trevor takes a step toward him as well, holding the oversized candy cane in his hands.

"Hey now," Cal says, taking a step backward with his hands up in front of him, nearly knocking over McKenzie. "We can work this out."

"Sam, what do you say we call the police and let them hear the recording?" Eric says, taking another step. "I'm sure there are laws about favouritism and doing deals for buddies."

"There were definite ethics laws that were broken," Trevor agrees, taking another step.

"I..." Cal opens his mouth to retort, but then runs, barrelling through Sam.

"Get him!" Eric yells, running after him.

Through the open door, I see Trevor hot on his heels, narrowly missing him. At the last second, he wields the candy cane like a shepherd's hook, grabbing Cal around his midsection and pulling him back. Losing his footing, Cal slips on the snow and slams to the ground, still with the hook around his waist.

Or should I say, the warble, thanks to Avery.

"Cal!" McKenzie yells, rushing through the door and down the steps to her husband.

Avery looks up at me, a tug of a smile on her face. "Well, that just happened."

269

Chapter Thirty-Three

AVERY

There's something wonderful about the stillness that comes with a snowfall.

Sitting by the well in the garden, hidden from the town, I smile up at the night sky, thinking about how much can change in just a few days. After Cal tried to escape on Christmas Day, the police came to the candy store and took him and McKenzie down to the station to ask about possible ethics violations within his inner political circle. He stepped down as mayor of Gingerbread Grove on Boxing Day, and the days after were a flurry of gossip and assumptions both about Matthew and me and of Cal.

We both laid low after it happened, going back to our families for Christmas dinner (Matthew kept his promise), and only speaking by text and phone call. Matthew let me know that many people from town dropped by the store or his parents' home to see what information they could gather. He wouldn't comment on anything, but his mom was more than happy to 'hold court' as he put it and talk about how her son and his girlfriend uncovered an underground plot to overtake the hardworking business owners of Gingerbread Grove.

For me, it only added to my hesitation of coming back to town. I didn't know what the response would be, given the role that Matthew and I played in the downfall of Cal and McKenzie. I didn't know if it would be a warm welcome, with the gossip being split between sympathy for us and wanting justice for 'dishonourable gossip and rumours' against Cal.

But here I am, on New Year's Eve, waiting in the middle of the town square. At least I'm surrounded by the hedges that block this secret garden from view.

I managed to make it from my car to here without being seen, thankful the bench and garden is enclosed and hidden from view. It also means I'm able to take a moment to enjoy the beauty that I know Gingerbread Grove can be, if run by the right person. I think of how in awe of the town I was when I first arrived two weeks ago. I couldn't stop looking at the buildings that have the facades that make them look as if they were actually made out of cookies, but also wooden and plastic candy accents that adorn the brick walls. Awnings are made to look like icing. Windows are decorated with painted holiday scenes and well wishes for the season.

I hope the town gets back to focusing on the warm welcomes that come with that.

"You look deep in thought," Matthew says, appearing through the hedges.

He passes me a paper cup, the spices from the hot apple cider wafting over me.

"How did you get this so late? I didn't think anything would be open at this time." I accept the cup happily, embracing the warmth as I hold it in my hands.

"'I have my sources." He takes a seat beside me, sipping from his own cup.

"Do you ever wonder how the hedges keep their shape?" I ask, taking a sip of my cider. I continue when Matthew glances at me from the corner of his eye. "How many people walk through here and you can never tell. There's no discolouration. There aren't any permanent gaps."

His gaze drifts to the space he just walked through. "I've never thought about it."

"Magic," I joke, bumping my shoulder with his.

He scoffs. "Careful. You'll start another rumour."

We sit in silence for a few moments, letting the snow drift down on us, enjoying the peace.

"Are we going to talk about it?" Matthew asks, once again looking at me.

"Which 'it' are we talking about? How you won't admit how much like Ross you can be or how much of a tragedy it is you don't like marshmallows." I smile thinking about the time we've spent the last few nights watching *Friends* together, while talking on the phone.

"I wasn't going to talk about either of those, actually."

"You just need to promise never to comment on the whole 'we were on a break' thing. It might jeopardize our relationship."

"Who was on a break from what?" He looks at me, eyebrow raised.

"Don't worry, we haven't gotten there yet."

"No...the whole 'I love you' thing."

"Ah, *that* thing." I repeat, resting the lid of my cup against my lip, breathing in the sweet and spicy scent of my drink.

"Are you going to make this harder than it has to be?" He drops his head, resting it on the tree trunk behind the bench.

"Hi, I'm Avery. I try to make jokes when I'm uncomfortable."

"Joey?" he asks, lifting his head.

"Chandler." I shift in my seat, lowering the cup to rest on my lap, cradling it in my hands. "Did you mean it?"

"I did." He turns to face me, taking the cup out of my hands and placing it on the ground along with his. Now with free hands, he holds mine and forces me to look into his eyes.

272

"I mean it, Avery. I love you. I didn't mean to tell you the way that I did. I shouldn't have done it that way, and I'm sorry. But I do love you."

I bite my lip, hoping this isn't some sleep-deprived induced dream.

"You're going to make this harder, aren't you?" He sighs.

"I'm sorry; I just need a minute to make sure I didn't mishear you." I hold his hands harder, letting out a deep breath. "I love you, too, Matthew."

"Are we crazy? I mean, we only met two weeks ago."

"Maybe Gingerbread Grove does have magic," I joke. "So, what do we do now? You're still in Vancouver. I'm in Kamloops."

"Maybe you need to call on some of that Christmas magic to figure it out."

His thumb brushes softly along the back of my hand. Even through the fabric of my gloves, my hand feels alive at his touch.

"Christmas is over. Do you think there's such a thing as New Year's magic?"

"No, I can't say I've heard of that."

"What if…" I take a deep breath, looking down at our joined hands. "What if we tried long-distance for a while? Until we see how things go? But with rules."

"What sort of rules?"

I straighten, looking into his hazel eyes, sparkling with hope from behind his glasses. "We have some point of contact every day. Even if it's just a gif saying we're alive."

"Learn to speak in gifs. Got it."

"Rule two, let's try not to go more than two weeks without seeing each other in person. Merritt might have to become our new favourite place."

"Or Yale."

"Or Hope. They've got a great coffee shop."

"You and your coffee." He shakes his head.

"Never underestimate the power of coffee." There are two things that I wholeheartedly believe in. Love will always win, and there's nothing that a good cup of coffee can't do.

"I think we can make this happen."

"Wait, you sold your truck…"

"I'll figure it out." Lines pull at the corner of his mouth. "There are these things called rental cars. Or even….dealerships."

"Matthew…" I huff.

"Avery…" he huffs back in a joking tone. "Rule three?"

"No matter what, we figure it out together."

"Agreed." His foot taps nervously against the grass underneath. "I have one I'd like to add."

"What's that?"

"You let me add to our TV and movie watch list."

"What are we talking? Marvel? *Star Wars*? DC?"

"Hockey," he says, making me rear my head back.

"Hockey? But you don't like sports."

"No, I don't like *playing* sports. I like watching this one."

"Huh, I never would have guessed that."

"I'll have to bring you down for a game some time. Nothing beats seeing it live."

"I'd like that." I have that goofy smile on my face. It's the type of smile that if we were in a Disney movie, there would be sparkles in our eyes and soft music playing behind us.

That gets me thinking what sort of Disney princess I'd be. On second thought, I don't think I'd want to see what I would be. A clumsy girl mixed with an elf that speaks in pop culture references.

"You know, it is New Year's Eve…" Matthew turns his wrist, looking at his watch. "And it's close to midnight," he says, leaning in closer to me.

"You don't say…" I lean in as well, leaving only a breath between us.

"They say that if you kiss someone at midnight, it brings you good luck and strengthens your relationship."

"You don't say…"

"I mean, we wouldn't want to start off the new year on the wrong foot."

"We wouldn't want that."

He breaks our gaze for a moment, just to take a look at his watch. "Ten seconds."

"We'd better hurry." I say, leaning in just a little more.

"Wouldn't want to miss it."

"Five seconds," he breathes.

"What are you waiting for?"

He hesitates for another moment before leaning in and closing the distance, pressing his lips to mine.

A clock strikes twelve from the church in town, reminding me that there's a greater reason for me being here. It wasn't an accident that our flight was cancelled that night, or that I ended up sharing the ride with Matthew.

I've never been so thankful for a flight being canceled or a snowstorm that resulted in a shortage of rental cars.

I certainly never thought that what I had considered to be the worst day of my life, ended up being one of the most significant.

But sitting here, kissing Matthew at the stroke of midnight at the start of a new year, I see that's how it was all supposed to be.

Epilogue

AVERY

A few months later

"Matthew, have you seen the latest shipment of ornaments?" I ask, rifling through a stack of boxes.

"I think it's in the corner." His voice shouts from the next room.

"Which corner?" I mutter under my breath, looking across the room at an equally large stack of boxes. Right now, the glass counters are still empty and the walls are bare, except for one photo. Shortly after we took possession, Sam gifted us a framed copy of us and our gingerbread store before it was ruined. I smile as I glance at it, thinking of how much has happened since that day.

Placing my hands on my waist, I turn toward the boxes in front of me, huffing.

"Find it?" Matthew asks, wrapping his arms around my waist from behind me.

I lean back into him, taking a deep breath, feeling my stress start to lessen. "No."

"It's in here somewhere." He kisses the side of my head

before unfolding himself from around me and walking to the other stack of boxes.

It's been a month since the sale of the candy store put the property into our names, making us the official owners of what was The Sugar House Candy Shoppe. After it was discovered that Cal and Lance were doing some unethical business, the police got involved, which resulted in Lance being forced to sell all of his properties. Matthew and I saw this as the perfect opportunity to start our new lives together.

So now, I run the Gingerbread Grove office for C.O.C.O.A., expanding the number of families we can help outside of the Kamloops area and arranging day trips for our families to experience the Grove on bus tours. I've also been active with the city on revitalizing the tourism to the town, working more to promote a welcoming atmosphere, instead of one centred on rivalries and competitive games.

There are, however, certain people in town that will not leave Candy Cane Creek alone and have staged a sort of…off-season battle. I'm still in the middle of discovering what that all means, but posts on GingerSnap show that it's thankfully nothing more than more knitted gingerbread men cast about the other town and retaliation in the form of plastic candy canes being stuck all over the middle of our town square.

It's a work in progress.

As for Matthew, he's moved his business into the back of the store, running his portion of the company from there. Mitch still works out of Vancouver, and there's a little bit of tension between them because of it, but for now, it works. And the best part? We live in the apartment above. It's covered in just as many unpacked boxes and mismatched furniture shoved into rooms, but it's ours.

"Is this the one you're looking for? He asks, holding out a red box."

"Hmmm, maybe." I take it from him, not recognizing the

decoration on the top. "Wait, no. I didn't order anything that looks like this."

"Why don't you open it and find out?" He's staring at me intently, which makes me narrow my eyes at him.

"Is something going to jump out at me?"

"What? No. Why would you ask that?" His eyes open wide in shock.

"Is it alive?"

"No."

"Are you sure? I mean, I don't see air holes, but…"

"Avery, just open the box," he sighs.

Giving him one last once over to make sure none of his normal tells lets me know there's anything that will make me drop and run, I pop the lid off the top to reveal a small velvet box inside.

"I definitely didn't order this."

"Are you sure?" He takes the box from me, sliding the smaller one out and dropping to one knee.

"Did you drop something?" I get down on a knee, too, feeling around the ground for anything that might have fallen.

"Avery…"

"Yeah?" I ask, looking around, trying to see anything that might have been dropped on the wooden floor.

"Avery, look at me…" The tone in his voice has me snapping my attention up to him.

He has opened the box to reveal a round diamond with emerald and ruby stone accents to make it look like holly wrapping around it.

I gasp, bringing my hand to my mouth.

"Avery, will you marry me?"

Tears fill my eyes when I take in the picture in front of me. It's not just Matthew asking me to marry him; he's asking me to build a life with him. Share our hopes and dreams. Work towards a shared goal and future where we watch TV shows and movies together. He laughs at my corny jokes and pretends like speaking in quotes is hilarious.

Where we can spend every Christmas together for the rest of our lives.

When I give him a wholehearted 'yes' and fling my arms around him, knocking him to the floor, I'm not just saying yes to the dress and the party. I'm saying yes to us. Forever.

And that makes me the happiest elf on the planet.

Acknowledgments

I don't even know where to begin with this. There are so many people to thank!

First and foremost, thank you to my family. You've put up with me tied to my laptop for a long time, listening to me say 'just let me finish this one thing.'

Thank you to my husband and kids for encouraging me and inspiring a lot of the shenanigans that happen in this book. You're just as invested, and excited, for this book as I am, which keeps me going.

Thank you to my mom and sister for watching the kids so I could get writing time in between all the activities and drop off/pick ups. Thank you supporting me along the way.

To Monique, I couldn't do this without you. Literally. I don't even know how to thank you enough. From making my gorgeous covers to taking me down when I overthink things, you really are my bestie. Thank you for everything.

To Colleen, thank you so much for being my go-to and putting up with all my crazy.

Jane, thank you for being my beta reader and allowing me to send things to you as I write, because I can never get my act together enough to do it all at once.

Thank you so much to all of my readers. I appreciate every book read, review left, post liked, and newsletter opened. All of is means so much to me. I really can't thank you all enough.

About the Author

Kimberly Ann lives in BC, Canada with her husband, two children and adorable German Shepherd. She's a stay-at-home mom who also homeschools her two children as they explore and learn the world together. Kimberly loves to read, drink coffee, and explore the world around her.

Kimberly writes sweet small town romance filled with emotion, hope, and love

Also by Kimberly Hanson

Please see Kimberly's website for her up-to-date releases.

https://kimberlyhanson.ca/books